SOCIAL EXCLUSION, COMPOUND TRAUMA AND RECOVERY

of related interest

Working with Young Homeless People
Phil Robinson
ISBN 978 1 84310 611 1
eISBN 978 1 84642 815 9

Service User Involvement
Reaching the Hard to Reach in Supported Housing
Helen Brafield and Terry Eckersley
ISBN 978 1 84310 343 1
eISBN 978 1 84642 745 9

A Practical Guide to Therapeutic Work with Asylum-Seekers and Refugees
Angelina Jalonen and Paul Cilia La Corte
ISBN 978 1 78592 073 8
eISBN 978 1 78450 334 5

The Theory and Practice of Democratic Therapeutic Community Treatment
Steve Pearce and Rex Haigh
ISBN 978 1 78592 205 3
eISBN 978 1 78450 483 0

The Reality of Recovery in Personality Disorder
Heather Castillo
ISBN 978 1 84905 605 2
eISBN 978 1 78450 071 9

Comparative Psychology for Clinical Psychologists and Therapists
What Animal Behavior Can Tell Us about Human Psychology
Daniel C. Marston and Terry L. Maple
ISBN 978 1 84905 743 1
eISBN 978 1 78450 161 7

SOCIAL EXCLUSION, COMPOUND TRAUMA AND RECOVERY

Applying Psychology, Psychotherapy and PIE to Homelessness and Complex Neeeds

Edited by **PETER COCKERSELL**

Jessica Kingsley *Publishers*
London and Philadelphia

Lists on pp.18–19 are reprinted with kind permission of the author, Maguire.
Figure 1.1 is reprinted with kind permission of St Mungo's.
Table 14.1 is reprinted with kind permission of the authors, Hendry and Dorney-Smith.
Figure 14.1 is reprinted with kind permission of CDC.
The epigraph on p.248 was originally published in *Borderline Welfare: Feeling and Fear of Feeling in Modern Welfare* by Andrew Cooper and Julian Lousada (published by Karnac Books in 2005), and is reprinted with kind permission of Karnac Books.

First published in 2018
by Jessica Kingsley Publishers
73 Collier Street
London N1 9BE, UK
and
400 Market Street, Suite 400
Philadelphia, PA 19106, USA

www.jkp.com

Copyright © Jessica Kingsley Publishers 2018

All rights reserved. No part of this publication may be reproduced in any material form (including photocopying, storing in any medium by electronic means or transmitting) without the written permission of the copyright owner except in accordance with the provisions of the law or under terms of a licence issued in the UK by the Copyright Licensing Agency Ltd. www.cla.co.uk or in overseas territories by the relevant reproduction rights organisation, for details see www.ifrro.org. Applications for the copyright owner's written permission to reproduce any part of this publication should be addressed to the publisher.

Warning: The doing of an unauthorised act in relation to a copyright work may result in both a civil claim for damages and criminal prosecution.

Library of Congress Cataloging in Publication Data
Names: Cockersell, Peter, editor.
Title: Social exclusion, compound trauma and recovery : applying psychology, psychotherapy and PIE to homelessness and complex needs / edited by Peter Cockersell.
Description: London ; Philadelphia : Jessica Kingsley Publishers, 2018. | Includes bibliographical references and index.
Identifiers: LCCN 2017040231 | ISBN 9781785922848 (alk. paper)
Subjects: LCSH: Social work with the homeless--Great Britain. | Social work with people with social disabilities--Great Britain. | Homeless persons--Mental health services--Great Britain. | Homeless persons--Services for--Great Britain. | Post-traumatic stress disorder--Great Britain. | Marginality, Social--Great Britain.
Classification: LCC HV4545.A4 S63 2018 | DDC 362.5/92860941--dc23 LC record available at https://lccn.loc.gov/2017040231

British Library Cataloguing in Publication Data
A CIP catalogue record for this book is available from the British Library

ISBN 978 1 78592 284 8
eISBN 978 1 78450 588 2

Printed and bound in Great Britain

Contents

Preface. 7

1 Understanding the Problem

1. Social Exclusion, Complex Needs and Homelessness 13
Dr Peter Cockersell

2. Compound Trauma and Complex Needs 26
Dr Peter Cockersell

3. The Process of Social Exclusion 37
Dr Peter Cockersell

2 Solutions: Principles of Practice

4. A Psychological Perspective on Recovery. 61
Dr Peter Cockersell

5. Applying Psychology as a Response to the Impact of Social Exclusion: PIE and Psychotherapy in Homelessness Services. 80
Dr Peter Cockersell

3 Solutions: Practice and Experience

6. Pre-treatment Therapy Approach for Single Homeless People: The Co-Construction of Recovery/Discovery . . . 109
John Conolly

7. Psychotherapy with Homeless Women 134
Nicola Saunders

8. PIE-oneering Psychological Integration in
   Homeless Hostels. 149
   Dr Emma Williamson

9. PIE: What the People Say 160
   Dr Catriona Reid

10. Streetlight: Homeless Psychotherapy in
    Britain's Happiest Town 175
    Dr Sally Read

11. I Held the Ticket in My Hand 192
    Terry Hutton

4 Conclusion: Contextualising the Problem in the Culture and System of Care

12. The Problem and Potential of Complexity 209
    Dr Peter Cockersell

13. The Treatment of Multi-morbidity 227
    Dr Peter Cockersell

14. The Dependency Paradox 242
    Dr Emma Williamson

   Authors' Biographies 254
   Subject Index 257
   Author Index 261

Preface

The question this book is directed towards is 'How do we understand and effectively work with people who have experienced/are experiencing social exclusion and/or compound trauma?'

These people are found disproportionately among homeless people, rough sleepers, people in psychiatric institutions or services, people in the criminal justice system, people with drug and alcohol dependencies, asylum seekers, refugees, and ethnic, religious and sexual minorities. There are a lot of them.

There are also a lot of services involved with them. Yet, despite this, they continue to be there, and they continue to need the services, and in fact their numbers continue to rise, with many of those in the system staying in the system, and new people coming into it all the time.

I once asked a young rough sleeper what 'home' meant to him; he said, 'Home means my mother's blood sprayed across the walls.' The idea that somebody coming from a place like that could be given somewhere to live and then have a 'home' is simply absurd. 'Home' has to be a place of psychological and emotional safety to be somewhere we want to be: it cannot be a place of oppression, fear or terror.

It has been my privilege to work with homeless people and rough sleepers – people of enormous courage and resourcefulness who have often faced the most horrendous difficulties and experiences – for some 25 years now. I have worked as a volunteer, in resettlement, supported housing, and as a 'frontline', middle and senior manager; I have also worked for nearly 20 years as a clinician, providing formal psychotherapy to homeless people, rough sleepers and people experiencing high levels of mental distress including diagnosed and undiagnosed drug and alcohol dependencies, psychoses and 'personality disorders'.

The more I have worked in these fields, the more it has become obvious to me just how important it is to work with the *experience* of trauma and exclusion and what that experience means to the individual affected. How someone sees the world, and the relationship between that and their real experience of the world, is critical to understanding what is going on for them, and to working with them to help them make changes in their lives. Without recognising this interactivity between someone's past and ongoing experience of the world and how they think, behave and live now – which means at the very least acknowledging the hostile interventions of the external world as well as the reactive perspectives of the individual – it is very difficult to help them change anything else in their lives. It is also important to recognise the legitimacy of their aspirations: just like the rest of us, they aspire to have somewhere to live, something meaningful to do, someone to love and be loved by. In the case of socially excluded people who have experienced compound trauma such as chronic rough sleepers, they sometimes never had these, and sometimes have had them often violently ripped away. What these ordinary people with very difficult life experiences need in order to achieve these ordinary but life-critical aspirations are emotional and psychological support *and* access to opportunities to participate in society, including stable housing. This book is about the emotional and psychological support side of the deal.

The book is written mainly by clinicians working with homeless people and rough sleepers in a variety of settings including hostels, drop-ins, primary care and women-specific services; the authors combine a huge wealth of experience and understanding from their training, their clinical work and from years of learning from the socially excluded people they work with. It is the latter part that illuminates the theory and practice in this book. It is a book full of practice-based evidence: this is not about academic theory applied in rarefied research methodology situations, it is real-life practice-based evidence built on practice-honed theory.

There is also a chapter written by a non-clinician, who had moved on from homelessness. He gives a vivid account of the experience of homelessness. It is deliberately not about histories of compound trauma, though it could have been; rather, it illustrates the degree to which homelessness and rough sleeping themselves are traumatic. One of the reasons that most people experiencing rough sleeping and chronic homelessness also experience compound trauma is simply because of this:

homelessness and rough sleeping are themselves episodes of exposure to traumatic emotional and psychological experiences, very often as well as physical trauma of various kinds.

The main body of the book is about psychologically informed interventions and the value they bring to enabling people experiencing social exclusion and compound trauma to embark on their recovery journeys. The vivid experience of the homeless and ex-homeless authors gives a real perspective on where the psychologically informed interventions properly sit: they are a part of the person's experience, and a part of their recovery journey – an absolutely critical part, but still just a part. The majority of the work with the socially excluded is not clinical in nature, and is provided by the often tremendously skilful, compassionate and caring staff in outreach teams, hostels, shelters and day centres. Psychologically informed interventions and psychotherapy are an important, and often critical, part of the mix in enabling socially excluded people and people affected by compound trauma to embark successfully on sustainable recovery journeys, but they are an adjunct to the services provided by the (largely) voluntary sector agencies who support the people that statutory agencies let fall through the net. This book is about understanding the psychological processes behind compound trauma and its relationship to social exclusion, and about the practical application of psychologically informed interventions to help break that relationship; it is not arguing that there is a purely clinical solution to social exclusion.

What the book is intended to do is give readers ideas, to stimulate thinking about, and support and encourage taking action on, psychological and emotional support for homeless people and rough sleepers. It offers a theoretical perspective in the hope of stimulating thought and discussion about *why* we need to offer psychological and emotional support and how that works in enabling and supporting recovery. It offers a practical perspective in the hope of stimulating and supporting those who are developing or implementing psychological, psychotherapy or psychosocial services for people affected by social exclusion and/or compound trauma. And it offers an experiential perspective from both clinicians and clients/patients in the hope of stimulating thought and discussion about the experience of social exclusion and the experience of working with people who have been or are socially excluded and/or who have experiences of compound trauma.

From my experience, many of the policy-makers, commissioners and senior managers responsible for services to people who are socially excluded and/or have experienced compound trauma have a tendency to over-simplify what is happening and to look to systems-based solutions that work as management models but are actually not founded in any understanding of either the real nature of the problems people encounter, or the real likelihood of their resolution. This makes sense from their internal world perspective full of management studies and theories, and is supported and colluded with by their peers who also have a vested interest in the same models. If only it were that simple, then the problems of social exclusion and the psychological and emotional impacts of trauma would have been resolved by now. Doing the same thing gets the same results: the manufacturing production-based models of management theory fail in the field of health and social care because they are inappropriate. At the end of this book, we offer alternative perspectives; throughout the book, we offer theoretical, practical and experiential accounts of why we need alternative perspectives to work effectively with the people we are charged with helping.

In the last few years, I have moved from working mainly with people who are homeless and rough sleepers to mainly working with people who are experiencing high levels of mental distress. The ideas in this book are just as relevant in this field of work as in homelessness services, maybe even more so: they are directly relevant to any work with people who have been or are socially excluded and/or have experienced compound trauma – this might include ethnic or religious or sexual minorities, refugees and asylum seekers, adults who have been abused as children, children who have been abused, and people in the psychiatric system or the criminal justice system. I think that the ideas and practices in this book, if implemented by services working with any of the severely disadvantaged groups or individuals in our society, would enable higher levels of recovery and better outcomes, both for the clients/patients of the services and for the services themselves.

Finally, I'd like to propose this as a 'thinking and doing' book – please, dear readers, think about the ideas put forward here, and see what it feels like to apply them to your own situation and practice.

Best wishes
Peter Cockersell

1
UNDERSTANDING THE PROBLEM

1

SOCIAL EXCLUSION, COMPLEX NEEDS AND HOMELESSNESS

DR PETER COCKERSELL

Introduction

This book is intended to be about the application of psychological principles and understandings to work with socially excluded people with histories of compound trauma and presentations of complex needs. The second half of the book (Parts 3 and 4) is about the application; the first half (Parts 1 and 2) is about the principles and understanding. Of course, all parts contain both theory and application: practice without theory is dangerous, theory without practice is sterile and dangerous.

In Parts 1 and 2 I will try to draw out a few themes of relevant psychological theory, relating it throughout to what really happens in the real world of compound trauma and social exclusion; these themes then find echoes in the practical experience described by the authors of the chapters in Parts 3 and 4 of the book, writing about the work they do, the people they do it with, and the interactions they have with them.

The hope is that the whole book, combining practice-based evidence with a grounding in well-researched but cutting-edge theory, will serve as an evidence-based guide that will inspire and encourage other homelessness service providers, staff, commissioners and clinicians to develop their own psychologically informed services and their own psychotherapy practices with this population of people. They deserve something that really respects where they are coming from.

We will begin with an overview of the association between trauma, complex needs, social exclusion and homelessness and rough sleeping.

Social exclusion and homelessness

Social exclusion is defined by the Oxford Dictionary as 'Exclusion from the prevailing social system and its rights and privileges, typically as a result of poverty or the fact of belonging to a minority social group' (Oxford Dictionary, 2017). An excellent report on social exclusion in Britain commissioned by the Social Exclusion Unit, part of the Cabinet Office, summarised a long and thorough look at definitions of social exclusion as follows:

> Social exclusion is a complex and multi-dimensional process. It involves the lack or denial of resources, rights, goods and services, and the inability to participate in the normal relationships and activities, available to the majority of people in a society, whether in economic, social, cultural or political arenas. It affects both the quality of life of individuals and the equity and cohesion of society as a whole. (Levitas et al., 2007, p.25)

Homeless people, and particularly rough sleepers – people who sleep out on the streets at night –have long been among the most visibly socially excluded. Homelessness is a powerful indicator of social exclusion because it involves the lack of a very fundamental resource in our society, a home; and that lack or loss leads to other losses, such as warmth, shelter, stability, and makes accessing many other important resources, from social status through to healthcare, education or work, very difficult. It also implies another set of lacks or losses – relationships, family, loved ones: home is more than just shelter or an address; it is the base within and around which our relationships develop and from which we go out to explore and engage with the rest of the world. Rough sleeping is an even more pronounced version of this lack or loss: David Miliband talked of it in terms of 'deep exclusion' (Levitas et al., 2007, p.26).

Rough sleepers and homeless people are often described as the most visible form of social exclusion (Guardian, 2016; Crisis, 2017a), but I think it's useful to think of them as visible yet invisible: one client, who slept rough less than half a mile from the Houses of Parliament, told me, 'I sit beside the black binliners on the pavement and nobody notices me; the only difference between me and the binliners is that somebody comes to collect them each day' (personal communication). Or 'the homeless are what you step over when you come out of the opera', as Sir George Young, then Housing Minister, infamously remarked (Young, 2017). I will come back to this idea of invisibility as well as visibility later.

Homeless people are, of course, not homogenous: there are as many different histories of becoming homeless as there are homeless people. However, I have suggested elsewhere (Cockersell, 2011, 2017) that there are two broad categories of homeless people:

- those who are *chronically homeless*, who may have experienced very long-term or repeated episodes of homelessness, often including lengthy periods of rough sleeping, throughout their lives
- those who are homeless following a discrete set of events, whom I have called the *transient homeless* as they usually pass through the homelessness system relatively speedily, and who may or may not have spent periods of sleeping rough, but not long term.

I have to add two caveats to this. First, many chronically homeless people do move out of homelessness and the homelessness system in the end (though by no means all – sadly many die homeless or in the homelessness system), so could be described as 'eventually transient'. I once worked with a man who had spent an astonishing 28 years rough sleeping in London, and who managed to 'come in': he was eventually offered housing directly into a flat as he had for years refused to go into a homelessness hostel or shelter, and he accepted this. I met him by chance a couple of years after I'd finished my work with him, which was mainly to help with the practical aspects – furniture, managing redecoration, bills, utilities, etc. – of settling him into his new flat, and he was still in his flat, now had a regular job in a street market which he enjoyed, and he described himself as happy. Second, people who are transiently homeless develop some of the characteristics, such as poorer physical and mental health, increased levels of drug and/or alcohol dependency, of those who are chronically homeless if they spend a long time rough sleeping (Homeless Link, 2014).

Transient homeless people can become chronically homeless if timely interventions are not available.

Transient homeless people may become homeless for many reasons, but they become homeless because of a single event, or a limited number of discrete events – typically either economic or relational. Transient homelessness is sometimes called economic homelessness because it rises at times of 'austerity' and when there are increases in poverty and social deprivation: rough sleeping in England has doubled in the years between 2010, when the Coalition Government began their austerity drive, and 2016, and statutory homelessness applications have risen by 11 per cent in the same period (Crisis, 2017b). But transient homelessness is not just economic: another main reason is relationship breakdown. Many people become homeless as a result of leaving their families or partners, for example because of divorce or bereavement, or fleeing domestic abuse (adults) or escaping from abusive home situations (young people), or because they have no resources to access housing, for example on discharge from prison or other institutions, such as hospital, or because of their status, as (increasingly) with some classes of refugee or immigrant.

When I began working in homelessness in London in the 1990s, I volunteered with and then became an employee of St Mungo's, a large London-based homelessness agency. The year I started, its annual review was headlined 'Homelessness is not a housing issue.' In fact, for the transient homeless, homelessness often is principally a housing issue. It is very difficult to rebuild your life without somewhere to live, regardless of whether you became homeless because of relationship breakdown, because of financial pressures, because of adverse domestic situations, or because of leaving an institution. This is the logic behind the North American 'housing first' movement, which is now gaining considerable support and traction in Western Europe (see Feantsa, 2016). It can equally be argued that for the chronically homeless housing is also a necessary and primary step: for the man I mentioned earlier who had spent 28 years living on the streets, housing was a significant step in his recovery, and, without it, it is very unlikely that he would have been in the (literally) happy position he was when I re-met him years later.

However, this does not mean that the author of the 1993 St Mungo's review was completely wrong: it would have been more accurate, though, to have used the headline 'Homelessness is not *just* a housing issue'. For many homeless people, and almost by definition for the chronically homeless, housing is not the only – or even necessarily the most important – issue. In their peer-researched report on how ex-homeless people had made the journey out of homelessness and the homeless system, Groundswell found that housing was hardly mentioned (Groundswell, 2010). From my own experience, I worked with a man who had been rehoused 88 times in his life; he kept a record of how many times he had been housed, and how many times he had lost or left his accommodation. For him, homelessness was not primarily a housing issue: it was a product of his sense of relatedness and stability, or rather his sense of unrelatedness and instability, a sense that arose from specific experiences and relationships in his childhood compounded by later experiences and relationships as he grew up. He had what has been neatly termed an 'unhoused mind' (Adlam and Scanlon, 2006).

Homelessness and trauma

There is a large body of evidence now of the association between trauma and homelessness, and particularly of the association between 'compound trauma', often referred to as 'complex trauma' (see Chapter 2 for the argument as to why compound trauma is a better name), and homelessness. As mentioned in the Preface, when I asked about what having a home would mean to him, a young man I was working with replied that 'Home is my mother's blood spraying across the wall' (personal communication). 'Home' is not always a happy concept: home can be the place where you are not safe, where you are attacked, where the horror is; home can be and feel unbearable. Home can be the site of, and, for a very long time or even forever, associated with trauma.

Compound trauma describes a situation in which a person experiences a sequence of traumatic events usually beginning in infancy or childhood with what are known as 'adverse childhood events'. Indeed, trauma sometimes predates even infancy: for example, I worked with a homeless man whose father had tried to murder his mother while he was still in her womb (the man was convicted of attempted murder, but returned to see the woman and child he had tried to kill when my client was about ten years old, even though she was in another – also abusive, but less life-threatening – relationship by then).

The prevalence of compound trauma in the histories of long-term, chronically homeless people has been highlighted in many studies.

A very good study on trauma and homelessness in Glasgow, both its prevalence and some of the effective responses, was published by the Glasgow Homeless Network (GHN, 2003). However, perhaps the most influential study published in England demonstrating the link between compound trauma and homelessness was Dr Nick Maguire's literature review, which detailed a large amount of academic and clinical evidence from across the developed world illustrating the wide prevalence of compound trauma in the histories of chronically homeless people (Maguire et al., 2009). *Meeting the Psychological and Emotional Needs of People Who Are Homeless* (Maguire et al., 2010), published online by the now-disbanded National Mental Health Development Unit (NMHDU), which was part of the Department of Health, built on this and laid down some ideas on potential ways to work with this understanding of the trauma-related underpinnings of chronic homelessness; unfortunately, the 2009 publication is no longer available. I think it is worth quoting at length some of its key findings here: interested readers can refer to the original source for further information.

Links between complex trauma and homelessness:

1. It is clear from the vast majority of the literature that there is strong and consistent evidence supporting an association between homelessness and complex trauma. Some papers investigated homelessness as a risk factor for trauma (e.g. Goodman et al., 1991), whereas others noted that trauma precedes homelessness (e.g. Taylor and Sharpe, 2008). Other studies quantified this relationship (e.g. North and Smith (1992) found that for almost three quarters of cases, PTSD preceded the onset of homelessness.

2. There is a complex relationship between traumatic experience, mental health issues, behavioural factors and homeless status. Although a number of models have been proposed, few have been empirically evaluated (e.g. Martijn and Sharpe, 2006).

3. Evidence from research with young homeless people supports the complexity of the relationship between multiple traumas, homelessness, and mental health outcomes. Young people are more likely than adults to have experienced earlier trauma, abuse, or neglect and been accommodated in care; but are also more likely to experience similar traumas in later life (Taylor et al., 2006).

Complex trauma in relation to other factors in homelessness:

1. Early traumatic experiences are associated with such factors as low levels of social support, low levels of family support, and 'deviant' peer associations.

2. There is an association between traumatic experience and maladaptive behaviours such as: drug and alcohol abuse; conduct disorders; sexual risk taking (and other sex-related behaviours). Other behavioural factors include sexual victimization, increased use of health and social services, and reduced participation in the labour force.

Mental health and homelessness:

1. There are higher rates of mental health problems, both Axis I (anxiety disorders, depression, dementia and psychosis disorders) and Axis II (personality disorders) than non-clinical populations. Evidence indicates that rates are comparable with psychiatric populations.

(Maguire *et al.*, 2009, pp.4–5)

Dr Maguire used formal academic and clinical research papers for his literature review, i.e. published research that met the standards that are seen as best practice in medical research. Research methodologies vary from discipline to discipline, and what is seen as 'gold standard' in one field is not necessarily seen as best practice in another field of study (see Cartwright, 2007). Most homelessness and other social agencies' research does not use the same methodologies as clinical research does. I published further evidence, some taken from my work at St Mungo's (where I was by this time Director of Health and Recovery), and some from other homelessness agencies and researchers, in an article on psychotherapy with homeless people (Cockersell, 2011).

I found a very high prevalence of experiences of trauma in childhood – adverse childhood events – in data gathered from homeless and rough sleeper clients through the work of the psychotherapy team that I set up in St Mungo's in 2007:

- forty-seven per cent experience of neglect/emotional abuse
- thirty-four per cent early loss of parents through abandonment, separation or divorce

- thirty-one per cent early loss of parents through death (including murder and suicide)
- twenty-seven per cent sexual abuse
- high levels of parental alcoholism, drug use and domestic violence.

(Internal data, St Mungo's, 2011)

Compound trauma refers to adverse childhood events then compounded by adolescent and adult traumas (see Chapter 2). Among homeless women, St Mungo's *Shattered Lives* (2013) research showed high levels of adult trauma. It also confirmed the 'High levels of parental alcoholism, drug use, and domestic violence' referred to by the clients of the psychotherapy service:

- 48 per cent had a substance dependency (p.14)
- 27 per cent had physical health, mental health and substance dependency problems
- Almost 50 per cent had experienced violence or abuse from family/a partner (p.4)
- Over 33 per cent had been involved in prostitution (p.4)
- 79 per cent of those who were mothers had had their children taken into care (p.4).

(St Mungo's, 2013)

In my study referred to above, which used some academic studies but also evidence collected from large-scale surveys of homeless people by homelessness organisations, I also found strong prevalence of mental health problems – the prevalence recorded in various studies of homeless people is listed first and in studies of the general population in brackets:

- schizophrenia 16–30 per cent (1–4%)
- personality disorder 50–70 per cent (5–13%)
- anxiety disorders and depression 50–80 per cent (11%)
- attempted suicide 42 per cent (1.3%).

(Cockersell, 2011)

Under the leadership of Helen Keats, who was at the time Rough Sleeping Advisor to the DCLG (Department of Communities and Local Government) and had been involved in both the NMHDU and Dr Maguire's research, ideas for effective practice with homeless people who had histories of compound trauma were collated into a proposed way of working called Psychologically Informed Environments, or PIEs. *Psychologically Informed Services for Homeless People*, which became known as 'the PIE guidance', was published in 2012 (Keats *et al.*, 2012). See Chapters 4 and 5 of this book for a more detailed look at the theory and practice in PIEs.

Further research since has continued to evidence high levels of association between compound trauma and homelessness, for example Homeless Link's 'health audit' based on in-depth interviews with over 2500 homeless people and rough sleepers (Homeless Link, 2014), or Lankelly Chase's *Hard Edges* report into what they termed 'severe and multiple disadvantage' (Lankelly Chase, 2015).

Homeless Link found a prevalence of diagnosed and undiagnosed mental health issues at 80 per cent across their sample (p.3), with evidence that those in poorer housing status (rough sleeping or squats) had worse mental health and higher levels of drug and alcohol use than those in more stable accommodation with homelessness agencies (p.17).

Lankelly Chase's report defined severe and multiple disadvantage as being in homelessness, prison or drug/alcohol treatment services in a specific year; being in one was called SMD1, being in two in the same year SMD2 and being in all three was labelled SMD3. Their study found that there were 58,000 people in the SMD3 category in England; in other words 58,000 people had been in homelessness services, prison and drug/alcohol services within that year (p.13). Of these 58,000, 85 per cent had had what Lankelly Chase called 'traumatic experiences in childhood' (p.28); this is a quote they give from one of the people in the survey on the causes of their belonging to the SMD3 category:

> a part of it is down to drinking, your family life, how you're treated in your family. Like me, personally, my mum give me my drink at nine; both my parents were alcoholic. I went through crime and everything because I didn't want to be at home... (Lankelly Chase, 2015)

This report suggests that there is a significant number of people affected by compound trauma who are using society's most expensive emergency social containment services – prison, homelessness and drug/alcohol treatment services. They are very probably also using some mental health services, but no correlatable data was available from NHS mental health services; many more are probably not using NHS mental health services, but dealing with undiagnosed mental health problems through antisocial behaviour and drug and/or alcohol use. Of the 58,000 people in the SMD3 category, Lankelly Chase found that almost 60 per cent were in regular contact with their children, a finding which again echoes the data presented earlier from St Mungo's psychotherapy clients: it is predictable from what we know that a significant number of these children will also pass through prisons, drug/alcohol treatment services and homelessness agencies.

Complex needs

The term 'complex needs' is widely used in homelessness and health services to describe a certain cohort of clients/patients, as in the expression 'Michael has complex needs', or 'this service works with complex needs' or is a 'complex needs service', or even 'this service can't work with Michael, his needs are too complex'. The medical dictionary defines complex needs as: 'A general UK term for a patient with multifactorial needs, both medical (e.g. diagnostic, therapeutic, rehabilitative) and social (e.g. housing, nutritional, interpersonal)' (Segen's Medical Dictionary, 2012).

We can see from this definition that the 58,000 people in the SMD3 category of Lankelly Chase's report all have complex needs: drug/alcohol dependency, criminal activities and a lack of housing. Many of them no doubt also have diagnosed and undiagnosed mental health problems, as we have seen from all the homelessness data. Another 96,000 people in the Lankelly Chase report fall into the SMD2 category (p.13), and many of those will also fall into the complex needs group – they will have drug/alcohol dependencies and housing needs or criminal activities, or they will have criminal activities and mental health problems and housing problems. Similarly, there are high levels of complex needs in homelessness clients (see Figure 1.1).

The clients involved in this survey are, of course, all also homeless, so at least have housing need as well as the combinations of physical health, mental health and substance dependency issues in the Venn diagram. Homeless Link's health audit demonstrates the same prevalence of complex needs. We will look in more detail at what 'complex needs' really means, and other ways we might have of thinking about them, in the final part of this book, in Chapters 12–14.

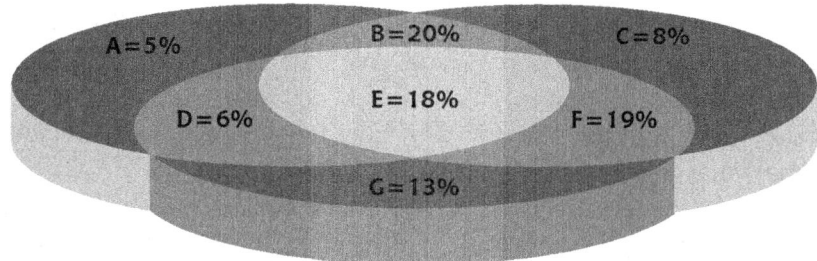

A - Mental health
B - Mental health and physical health
C - Physical health
D - Mental health and substance use
E - Mental health, physical health and substance use
F - Physical health and substance use
G - Substance use

No substance use, physical health or mental health needs: 11%

Figure 1.1
Source: St Mungo's (2014)

As we saw at the beginning of this chapter, homeless people, and particularly rough sleepers, are the most visible examples of social exclusion. They experience 'the lack or denial of resources, rights, goods and services, and the inability to participate in the normal relationships and activities, available to the majority of people in a society, whether in economic, social, cultural or political arenas' (Levitas *et al.*, 2007, p.25). They do not have access to housing: that is what homelessness means. They do not access healthcare well (Brighter Futures, 2011; Homeless Link, 2014). They can't use restaurants because they are poor and because they are dirty, or smelly, or just 'street people'. They can't work because they haven't got anywhere to get ready to go to work, and most places won't give jobs to people with no address and who don't look the part. They may not have education, or even literacy. They may get moved on by the police, or hosed down by the local authority or office block owners, or they may get beaten up just for being there and looking homeless. There are myriad ways of experiencing exclusion. They are visible, yet invisible: we see them, yet we walk past them, do not look in their faces or eyes; we are aware they are there, but we studiously ignore their presence. This social invisibility is just a marker of their level of exclusion – what David Milliband, then the Minister responsible for homelessness, called 'deep exclusion' (Levitas *et al.*, 2007, p.26).

Homelessness, complex needs and social exclusion

The evidence, as we have seen, strongly suggests that we have a population in homelessness – and probably in populations such as offenders, refugees, gypsies and travellers – with a very high prevalence of complex needs, and a very high prevalence of compound trauma, and who experience a very high level of social exclusion.

This raises the interesting question of what the association means. How does it come about? What, if anything, can we do about it, either for those who have yet to follow the path of compound trauma/complex needs/social exclusion or for those who are a long way down it? The rest of this book is intended to illuminate some perspectives in theory and interventions in practice (because theory and practice should never be divorced) that might at least begin to answer these questions.

References

Adlam, J. and Scanlon, C. (2006) 'Housing "unhoused minds": inter-personality disorder in the organisation?' *Housing, Care and Support 9*, 3, 9–14.

Brighter Futures (2011) *Rough Treatment for Rough Sleepers*. Accessed February 2017 at www.brighter-futures.org.uk

Cartwright, N. (2007) *Are RCTs the Gold Standard?* Accessed February 2017 at www.lse.ac.uk/CPNSS/research/concludedResearchProjects/ContingencyDissent InScience/DP/Cartwright.pdf

Cockersell, P. (2011) 'Homelessness and mental health: adding clinical mental health interventions to existing social ones can greatly enhance positive outcomes.' *Journal of Public Mental Health 10*, 2, 88–98.

Cockersell, P. (2017) 'Social Exclusion and Anti-Discriminatory Practice: The Case of Older Homeless People' in P. Lane and R. Tribe (eds) *Anti-Discriminatory Practice in Mental Health for Older People*. London: Jessica Kingsley Publishers.

Crisis (2017a) *It's No Life at All*. Accessed February 2017 at www.crisis.org.uk/data/files/publications/714_ITS_NO_LIFE_AT_ALL_violence%20asb_FINAL_sp.pdf

Crisis (2017b) *About Homelessness: Definitions and Numbers*. Accessed February 2017 at www.crisis.org.uk/pages/homeless-def-numbers.html

Feantsa (2016) *Housing First Europe Hub*. Accessed February 2017 at www.feantsa.org/en/network/2016/11/14/housing-first-europe-hub

GHN (2003) *Disempowerment and Disconnection: Trauma and Homelessness*. Accessed February 2017 at http://ghn.org.uk/sites/default/files/GHN_Trauma_and_Homelessness_Report.pdf

Groundswell (2010) *The Escape Plan*. Accessed October 2017 at http://groundswell.org.uk/what-we-do/peer-research/the-escape-plan

Guardian (2016) 'Britain's rough sleepers are only the tip of the homelessness iceberg.' Accessed February 2017 at www.theguardian.com/society/2016/mar/09/britain-rough-sleepers-homelessness-housing-crisis

Homeless Link (2014) *The Unhealthy State of Homelessness*. Accessed February 2017 at www.homeless.org.uk/sites/default/files/site-attachments/The%20unhealthy%20state%20of%20homelessness%20FINAL.pdf

Keats, H., Cockersell, P., Johnson, R. and Maguire, N. (2012) *Psychologically Informed Services for Homeless People*. Accessed October 2017 at www.rjaconsultancy.org.uk/6454%20clg%20pie%20operational%20document%20aw-1.pdf

Lankelly Chase (2015) *Hard Edges: Mapping Severe and Multiple Disadvantage in England*. Accessed February 2017 at http://lankellychase.org.uk/multiple-disadvantage/publications/hard-edges

Levitas, R., Pantazis, C., Fahmy, E., Gordon, D., Lloyd, E. and Patsios, D. (2007) *The Multi-Dimensional Analysis of Social Exclusion*. Accessed December 2014 at http://dera.ioe.ac.uk/6853/1/multidimensional.pdf

Maguire, N.J., Johnson, R., Vostanis, P., Keats, H. and Remington, R.E. (2009) *Homelessness and Complex Trauma: A Review of the Literature.*

Maguire, N.J., Johnson, R., Vostanis, P., and Keats, H. (2010) *Meeting the Psychological and Emotional Needs of Homeless People*. Accessed October 2017 at https://eprints.soton.ac.uk/187695

Martijn, C. and Sharpe, L. (2006) 'Pathways to Youth Homelessness.' *Social Science and Medicine*, 62, 1, 1–12.

North, C.S., and Smith, E.M. (1992) 'Posttraumatic stress disorder among homeless men and women.' *Hospital Community Psychiatry*, 43, 10, 1010–6.

Oxford Dictionary (2017) accessed December 2017 at https://en.oxforddictionaries.com/definition/social_exclusion

Segen's Medical Dictionary (2012) *Complex Needs*. Accessed February 2017 at http://medical-dictionary.thefreedictionary.com/complex+needs

St Mungo's (2013) *Rebuilding Shattered Lives*. Accessed October 2017 at http://rebuildingshatteredlives.org

St Mungo's (2014) Client Needs Survey. Internal document.

Taylor, H., Stuttaford, M., Broad, B., and Vostanis, P. (2006) 'Why a 'roof' is not enough: The characteristics of young homeless people referred to a designated Mental Health Service.' *Journal of Mental Health*, 15, 4, 491–501.

Taylor, K.M. and Sharpe, L. (2008) 'Trauma and post-traumatic stress disorder among homeless adults in Sydney.' *Australian and New Zealand Journal of Psychiatry*, 42, 3, 206–213.

Young (2017) 'Sir George Young appointed as new Chief Whip.' Accessed February 2017 at www.newstatesman.com/politics/2012/10/sir-george-young-appointed-new-chief-whip

2

COMPOUND TRAUMA AND COMPLEX NEEDS

DR PETER COCKERSELL

In this chapter I look at some of the psychological and psychosocial processes behind the situation that I outlined in Chapter 1, where you have a population – in this case the chronically homeless – characterised by high prevalence of compound trauma, complex needs and social exclusion. I am going to look at complex needs and how they are defined and redefined in interaction with the complex care systems of NHS healthcare, local authority housing and third sector homelessness agencies in Chapter 12. Here I want to focus on a) compound trauma and b) complex needs, or poly- or multi-morbidity.

'Complex trauma' or 'compound trauma'?

What is 'trauma'? A trauma is defined as a 'deeply distressing or disturbing experience' or a 'physical injury (medical)' such as a 'rupture' or a 'wound'; it derives from the Greek word *trauma*, which means 'wound' (OUP, 2017).

I think that the medical definition of trauma is useful because of the dual aspects of the words 'rupture' and 'wound': 'rupture' can be seen as the separation of one part from its relationship with another, and 'wound' as the breaking and penetration of a boundary. Trauma, whether physical or psychological, very often has both of these connotations, but each is perhaps worthy of consideration separately.

However, before we do that, I would like to think about the 'compound' in compound trauma. As I said in the previous chapter, it seems to me that 'compound trauma' is a far more appropriate name than 'complex trauma'. The phenomenon that we are talking about here is cumulative:

- Someone is exposed to trauma, usually in early infancy or childhood.
- S/he is not able or supported to process or recover from that trauma.
- S/he is exposed to another trauma.
- S/he is not able or supported to process or recover from that trauma, and its impact is added to or held alongside the impact of the previous trauma.
- S/he is exposed to another trauma.
- S/he is not able or supported to process or recover from that trauma, and its impact is added to or held alongside the impact of the previous traumas.

And so on – you get the idea. This is a process of compounding: it compounds the trauma, it compounds the impact of the trauma, and it compounds the damage the trauma does to the person's developmental and relational growth. It is, quite literally and directly, compound trauma.

Of course, there is also a complexity here, or at least a complexity of effect. What, in essence, you have is the overlaying of one trauma incident, impact and response by another trauma incident, impact and response, and then another; the earlier impacts and responses will very probably get mixed up with the later impacts and responses, and the end result is likely to be a confusion of impacts and responses. The aetiology of any one traumatic event and its impact is likely to be hard, or more likely still impossible, to discern, and therefore the chain of cause and effect (and for treatments based on medical models, the chain of diagnosis and treatment) also seems not to be directly or simply discernible. To the clinician it becomes complex indeed: there are too many causes and too many effects, and precious little linearity between any pair of them, and so formulation or diagnosis apparently become problematic, or at the very least very complex. However, it does not seem to me to be good clinical practice or useful for understanding the phenomenon we are dealing with to use the clinician's experience of complexity to define the patient/client's situation. For the patient/client it is very simple and very clear: too many traumatic experiences have made it very difficult for them to manage their own experience of themselves. Their experience has simply been too much, and, by definition almost, they have probably never had any or enough help in managing their overloaded experience of themselves.

Words and labels have an impact on the real world. In focusing on this apparent complexity by using the label 'complex trauma', the real dynamic gets disguised and we do our patients/clients and ourselves as clinicians/professionals a disservice. We are saying that this kind of trauma is really hard to understand: we risk both feeling overwhelmed ourselves and thinking that what is happening for them is something we cannot understand or make sense of, so that ultimately we also cannot process their experience and enable recovery. They pick up on our feelings and see that we too think their experience is too much, that it is overwhelming and unmanageable, and we risk confirming their own world view and, worse still, thereby further compound their trauma.

However, if we use the term 'compound trauma' we are using words which are actually more descriptive of the phenomenon we are trying to understand and work with. Compound trauma means that the person has experienced several or many traumatic experiences without the time, support or capacity to process each of them or to recover. It is trauma compounded. I think that if we think about this phenomenon in this way, then we can get to work on the fundamental aspect of it, on what really does lie behind it: we can begin to make the formulation, or the diagnosis and treatment. It becomes simple, not complex. We are working with the experience of trauma – lots of trauma, but still 'just' trauma. And if we understand the effects of trauma, and have some understanding and skills in working to enable people to recover from these effects, then we can work effectively with people with the sorts of experiences we are considering here.

Put simply, bad, difficult or painful experiences and damaging, negative relationships cause trauma; good, stimulating and positive experiences and respectful, creative relationships heal trauma. From this perspective, working with people who have experienced compound trauma is not complex.

However, in practice it is complex: because all people are complex and working in depth with anyone is a complex business; because it means working with people who have had damaging experiences and damaging relationships, and so are likely to experience the caregiver as threatening, attacking and/or downright dangerous; because trauma is, of its nature, the experience of difficult feelings that people (both clinicians and patients/clients) tend to defend against feeling or acknowledging; because it is difficult, and traumatising, to recognise the levels of abuse and neglect that exist in our society, and that our clients/patients have experienced, and often continue to experience even from the agencies established to help them; and because it is traumatising to experience trauma even vicariously. As Sister Ellen, who used to run The Passage day centre for homeless people and rough sleepers in Victoria, London, said, 'We exclude people because we cannot bear their suffering' (personal communication). When we say that compound trauma is difficult to understand we are perhaps really referring to the emotional difficulty we have in thinking about it and processing it, rather than a difficulty arising from some supposed complexity.

What is complex, and requires understanding, skill and sensitivity, is the actual one-to-one and group dynamics that staff involved in homelessness service provision, and some clinicians, work with day in, day out. I am not going to go into the complex detail of the capacity for effective working with homeless people who have experienced compound trauma here. Key elements are understanding attachment and other motivational systems, understanding the concept of the inner world and inner working models, managing transferences, understanding countertransferences, being aware of projections and projective identification, using mentalisation and ego-integration techniques, understanding the physiology of trauma and so on. There is a wealth of practice-based evidence, technique, skill and knowledge in the chapters on practice (Chapters 4–8), where the other contributors to this book describe their insights and experiences; as well as a discussion of some of the principles of practice in the chapter on recovery (Chapter 4) and on applied psychology as a response to social exclusion (Chapter 3).

There are also many excellent sources of information on the impact of trauma on development, and on the dynamics of working with people impacted by trauma within various support, care and health systems (see Schore, 1994; McCluskey and Hooper, 2000; Solomon and Siegel, 2003, Van der Kolk, 2005; Baradon, 2010).

What I will explore next is the idea of 'complex needs' and 'poly-' or 'multi-morbidity', which I think has some parallels with the argument about so-called 'complex', as opposed to compound, trauma.

'Complex needs', 'poly-morbidity', or 'one thing leads to another'?

Compound trauma, as we have seen, begins with 'adverse childhood events' – and adverse childhood events very often begin with *very* early childhood trauma: infantile or perinatal trauma (Van der Kolk, 2005; Lanius, Vermetten and Pain, 2010; Roos *et al.*, 2013; Liotti, 2016). What we are first considering, then, is the impact of trauma on babies.

When we looked at the histories of homeless people in Chapter 1 we saw high levels of domestic abuse, drug and alcohol dependency, and frequent experiences of violence, separation and bereavement. If we think of the homeless women and their experience around pregnancy and motherhood, again we have high levels of domestic abuse, drug and alcohol dependency, and frequent experiences of violence. There are likely to be separations – partners who abandon them during pregnancy – and bereavements for these women too. Remember, they are also homeless. They may even be sleeping rough on the street (in one case I know, a pregnant woman with no recourse to public funds because of her nationality was sleeping on the street, and the third sector outreach team working with her fought a huge battle with social services to try to get them to house her; in the end, she was not housed, and was admitted directly to hospital from the street when she came to term). Homeless pregnant women, or women experiencing 'severe and multiple disadvantage', or whose partners are experiencing are in the SMD2 or SMD3 categories (Lankelly Chase, 2015), are likely to be experiencing high levels of stress, anxiety and depression, and probably fear: fear of their partners, and/or of and for themselves, and/or of and for their babies-to-be, and/or of social services who may come and take their babies away (again). These feelings may be amplified as the hormonal changes of pregnancy, and the psychophysiological preparations for becoming a mother, take place. Their ability to regulate their affect – to keep their emotional reactions within a comfortable range – may well be severely impaired. The women may increase their drug and alcohol intake, or their GPs may increase their prescribed medication intake (anti-depressants, anti-psychotics, painkillers, sleeping tablets), to help cope with the impact of these amplified feelings and the surrounding social stresses. They may even attempt suicide. The baby in the womb shares some of this experience; without the context of meaning or understanding, it is pure experience. To the baby, this is what life is like: exciting/arousing, calming/soporific, unpredictable.

Then s/he is born. Among her/his first experiences may be withdrawals, whether from illicit drugs and/or alcohol or from prescribed drugs – it really doesn't make much difference to the baby, without meaning or understanding: it is an experience that will become part of their vocabulary of experiences. Or s/he may have experienced withdrawals already, when her/his mother gave up drugs/alcohol/medication when she found out she was pregnant, though often the mother will have been given other drugs by her GP or dependency doctor to help her get through the withdrawals, so the baby's experience will still be of unpredictable mood and stress activation changes.

I won't go any further with the process for the baby here, as we will look at that later in this chapter. What I want to focus on here is the impact of very early trauma on the baby/child and how this carries through to adulthood.

The key point here is that the early period of development for a child is extremely important, and influential throughout their childhood, adolescent and adult lives. This has been known for a long time: 'Give me a child for his first seven years and I'll give you the man', Ignatius Loyola, the founder of the order of Jesuits in the Catholic Church, is reputed to have said (Eduqna, 2017); or 'the Child is father of the Man', as Wordsworth put it (Wordsworth, 1807); and psychoanalysts from Klein onwards have proposed that early infantile relationships are fundamental to understanding our development and behaviours as adults, and this is the cornerstone of modern object relations theory (Greenberg and Mitchell, 1983; Klein, 1998). However, they were talking about 'character' or what psychologists would probably call 'personality'. We now know that the early period of development is extremely important for much more than that: it affects us physiologically and psychologically throughout our lives. As Ruth Lanius puts it, 'Time does not heal the wounds that occur in those earliest years; time conceals them. They are not lost; they are embodied' (Lanius *et al.*, 2010, p.xiv); and she goes on to say, 'Only in recent decades has the magnitude of the problem of developmentally damaged humans begun to be recognised and understood.'

Just a brief word here about 'physiologically and psychologically' – they are aspects of one and the same dynamic system. Mind and body are not in any way separate. Freud, to be fair, always argued for a biological/physiological basis to psychological development and activity (see Freud, 1915). We live, and experience ourselves, and live in and experience the world around us, with a mind–brain–body system (Lanius *et al.*, 2010; Siegel, 2012; Van der Kolk, 2015). Therefore, there is an 'of course' element to the statement that what happens to and around us in our early development affects us physiologically as well as psychologically: it cannot be otherwise in a system.

The primary process of an organism is to draw material from its environment, process the material so as to extract nutrition and expel waste or toxic material; it is a more developed organism, i.e. not a single cell structure, then it has a second process as well, which is to interact with another organism of the same species so as to reproduce. Both of these processes require the organism to be an 'open system with strong but permeable boundaries'; Vega Zagier-Roberts goes on to say:

> In complex organisms, there will be a number of such open systems operating simultaneously, each performing its own specialised function. The activities of these different sub-systems need to be co-ordinated so as to serve the needs of the organism as a whole, and complex superordinate systems are evolved to provide this co-ordinating function... (Zagier-Roberts, 1994)

The mind–brain–body system evolved to be the 'complex superordinate system' that provides this 'co-ordinating function' in human lives (Panksepp and Biven, 2012); it is also the system that provides the co-ordinating function in our social lives, our lives as part of families and as part of a wider society (Schore, 1994; McGilchrist, 2009; Fiske and Taylor, 2013).

As a result, we are biopsychosocial: our self-actualisations in all three domains – the physical, the psychological and the social – are related to each other, and each of them informs the way each of the others, each aspect of our selves, develops. Of course, there are significant genetic drivers: we tend to develop with two arms and two legs, ten fingers and ten toes, and with five senses and a set of bodily organs, from gut to brain, that keep the whole thing running in a relatively co-ordinated way. Equally of course, this is not always the case, and we are becoming increasingly aware of the interaction between these developmental processes and environmental factors: high levels of pollutants, for example, or inadequate food or water, or high levels of radiation – or lack of nurture or the impact of trauma. Gene expression is increasingly being seen as environmentally conditioned; epigenetics is perhaps going to be the driver of the next big explosion of knowledge and understanding of human development, as neurobiology has been over the last 20 years (Ebrahim, 2012). Epigenetics too appears to confirm the importance of early experience: a study in Glasgow showed double the epigenetic impact of childhood socio-economic deprivation compared to adult socio-economic deprivation (Borghol *et al.*, 2012).

If we apply these perspectives to the concepts of complex needs and poly- or multi-morbidity, then I think that they shed some considerable light on what is going on. What I think we are seeing is that the impact of early deprivation and early adverse childhood experiences/infantile trauma – trauma compounded into compound trauma in fact – becomes manifest in many ways in adult life: in mental health problems, in social and behavioural difficulties, in substance dependencies and in physical health problems. It is not so much that they are all caused by compound trauma; it is probably more exact to say that compound trauma lays the pre-conditions for the later development of mental and physical health problems, social and behavioural difficulties, and substance dependencies. As Lanius puts it:

> Many of our most intractable public health problems are the result of compensatory behaviours such as smoking, overeating, promiscuity, and alcohol and drug use, which provide immediate partial relief from emotional problems caused by traumatic childhood experiences. That relationship is [relatively – my addition] straightforward: early trauma to depression or anxiety, to obesity, to diabetes, to heart disease; trauma to smoking to emphysema to lung cancer. But…the chronic life stress of the underlying life experiences is generally unrecognised and hence unappreciated as a second and separate etiological mechanism underlying many biomedical diseases. (Lanius *et al.*, 2010)

The impact of chronic life stress arising from compound trauma opens the door, as it were, for other diseases, and reduces the capacity for resistance to other environmental stresses and attacks. In Zagier-Roberts' terms, it weakens the 'strong but permeable' boundaries of the organism, both in terms of its auto-immune system and in terms of its self-realisation and self-definition. People who have experienced compound trauma live with a hyper-aroused stress response (Van der Kolk, 2015); the stress response, normally deactivated in small infants by 'love and relaxation responses' from their caregivers (Stefano, Stefano and Esch, 2008), continues in a state of alertness and arousal more or less continuously in those who have experienced compound trauma. The relationship between heightened and prolonged stress arousal and biomedical illnesses is only just beginning to be explored; an example is in breast cancer where an environmentally interactive molecule associated with stress management turns out to be highly influential in whether breast cancer outcomes are death or recovery – the implications of their findings being that prolonged exposure to heightened stress increases the likelihood of death from breast cancer (Wolford *et al.*, 2013).

We can add to this the finding that social exclusion activates the same pain responses and neurobiology as physical injury (Eisenberger, Lieberman and Williams, 2003; Kross *et al.*, 2011), and so is equally traumatising in the physiological sense as it is in the psychological and emotional sense; it would not be so surprising, then, that we might find a physiological expression of stress/distress caused by social exclusion. We also find that social isolation, which is the personal experience of social exclusion, is associated with a larger effect size in increased morbidity and mortality than any one of obesity, smoking or alcohol consumption (Holt-Lunstad, Smith and Layton, 2010), the areas that continue to be the main focus of public health.

It seems to me that there is very significant evidence now for early adverse childhood experiences coupled with compound trauma to be seen as underlying conditions that predispose the person affected to what we call complex needs. Complex needs have their roots in the experience of early deprivation and trauma, compounded by later experiences of further deprivation and trauma.

We cannot effectively tackle complex needs without working with and responding to the trauma that lies underneath it.

Furthermore, we can propose that complex needs are a bio-psychosocial continuum, a single but multifaceted response to early deprivation and trauma. Just as in the argument with the term complex trauma, the complexity lies in the multiplicity of responses required to deal with the multifaceted expression of underlying over-heightened stress conditions and developmental disorders and dysregulation, not in the aetiology of the condition. However, behaving as if all these multifaceted expressions of distress were all separate and nothing to do with each other – which is what happens with our ultra-specific and specialism-driven services – again does the client/patient a great disservice. It mystifies the meaning behind their situation, and does not enable a coherent integrated response to both the underlying trauma and the ways it manifests in the person's behaviours, psychology and physiology.

Therefore, not only can we not effectively tackle complex needs without working with and responding to the trauma that lies underneath it, neither can we effectively tackle complex needs in a piecemeal, fragmented way. In the aetiology of complex needs, one thing leads to another; in our responses to complex needs, one thing undone can lead to the unravelling of the others.

Bearing in mind our overview of the interconnectedness of complex needs and their relation to compound trauma, we will now turn our attention to the processes of social exclusion.

References

Baradon, T. (2010) (ed.) *Relational Trauma in Infancy*. London: Routledge.
Borghol, N., Suderman, M., McArdle, W., Racine, A., *et al.* (2012) 'Associations with early-life socio-economic position in adult DNA methylation.' *International Journal of Epidemiology 41*, 1, 62–74.
Ebrahim S. (2012) 'Epigenetics: the next big thing.' *International Journal of Epidemiology 41*, 1, 1–3.
EduQnA (2017) Accessed February 2017 at www.eduqna.com/Quotations/499-Quotations-7.html
Eisenberger, N.I., Lieberman, M.D. and Williams, K.D. (2003) 'Does rejection hurt? An FMRI study of social exclusion.' *Science 302*, 290–292.
Fiske, S.T. and Taylor, S.E. (2013) *Social Cognition: From Brains to Culture*, 2nd edition. London: Sage.
Freud, S. (1915) 'The Instincts and Their Vicissitudes.' In P. Gay (ed.) (1995) *The Freud Reader*. London: Vintage.
Greenberg, J.R. and Mitchell S.A. (1983) *Object Relations in Psychoanalytic Theory*. London: Harvard University Press.
Holt-Lunstad, J., Smith T.B. and Layton J.B. (2010) 'Social relationships and mortality risk: a meta-analytic review.' *Plos Medicine 7*, 7, http://dx.doi.org/10.1371/journal.pmed.1000316
Klein, M. (1998) *Love, Guilt and Reparation and Other Works 1921–1945*. London: Vintage.
Kross, E., Bermana, M.G., Mischel, W., Smith E.E. and Wagerd T.D. (2011) 'Social rejection shares somatosensory representations with physical pain.' *PNAS 108*, 15, 6270–6275.
Lanius, R.A., Vermetten E. and Pain C. (2010) (eds) *The Impact of Early Life Trauma on Health and Disease: The Hidden Epidemic*. Cambridge: Cambridge University Press.
Lankelly Chase (2015) *Hard Edges: Mapping Severe and Multiple Disadvantage in England*. Accessed February 2017 at http://lankellychase.org.uk/multiple-disadvantage/publications/hard-edges
Liotti G. (2016) 'Infant attachment and the origins of dissociative processes.' *Attachment 10*, 1, 20–36.
McCluskey, U. and Hooper, C-A. (2000) *Psychodynamic Perspectives on Abuse*. London: Jessica Kingsley Publishers.
McGilchrist I. (2009) *The Master and his Emissary*. New Haven, CT and London: Yale University Press.
Panksepp, J. and Biven L. (2012) *The Archaeology of Mind*. London: Norton.

Roos, L.E., Mota, N., Afifi, T.O., Katz, L.Y., Distasio, J. and Sareen, J. (2013) 'Relationship between adverse childhood experiences and homelessness and Axis I and II disorders.' *American Journal of Public Health 103*, Suppl.2, S275–281.

Schore A. (1994) *Affect Regulation and the Origin of the Self: The Neurobiology of Emotional Development.* New Jersey: Lawrence Erlbaum.

Siegel, D. (2012) *The Developing Mind*, 2nd edition. New York: The Guilford Press.

Solomon, M. and Siegel, D. (eds) (2003) *Healing Trauma.* London: WW Norton.

Stefano, G.B., Stefano J.M. and Esch T. (2008) 'Anticipatory stress response: a significant commonality in stress, relaxation, pleasure and love responses.' *Medical Science Monitor 14*, 2, 17–21.

OUP (2017) Dictionaries. Accessed February 2017 at www.oxforddictionaries.com

Van der Kolk, B. (2005) 'Developmental trauma disorder.' *Psychiatric Annals 35*, 5, 401–408.

Van der Kolk, B. (2015) *The Body Keeps the Score: Mind, Brain and Body in the Transformation of Trauma.* London: Penguin.

Wolford C., McConoughey S.J., Jalgaonkar S.P., Leon M., *et al.* (2013) 'Transcription factor ATF3 links host adaptive response to breast cancer metastasis.' *Journal of Clinical Investigation 123*, 7, 2893–2906.

Wordsworth, W. (1807) 'My Heart Leaps Up.' In Poems, In Two Volumes. London: Henry Froude.

Zagier-Roberts V. (1994) 'The organization of work: contributions from open systems theory.' In A. Obholzer and V. Zagier Roberts (eds) *The Unconscious at Work.* London: Routledge.

3

THE PROCESS OF SOCIAL EXCLUSION

DR PETER COCKERSELL

We left our baby, in Chapter 2, having just been born and having withdrawals from drugs/alcohol or prescribed medication. We will now follow the baby's progress to becoming a rough sleeper.

To do this we will look at our baby's developmental processes, and the interactions between them and their environment and how they affect what happens, and we will follow the child through adolescence to adulthood. Although of course each individual rough sleeper and homeless person has their own unique story, I hope that what I describe here will build up a picture of a typical process of social exclusion. My purpose is not to tell a specific story, but to illustrate how some of the interactive dynamic processes between individual psychology and environmental stresses come to shape the person we meet; essentially the rough guide to how experiencing compound trauma leads to complex needs and social exclusion and the behaviours we associate with many rough sleepers and homeless people.

For that reason I am inventing a 'case study', a story of someone who experiences compound trauma that leads to social exclusion. The story is not of one person, but is a composite of events that have all happened to people I have met and/or worked with since I began working in homelessness. I have chosen to portray a woman, who I have called Bea, but it could equally easily be a man. I have chosen a woman because socially excluded women tend to be even more invisible than socially excluded men. What happens in the story is a composite, but that all of it happens to one person is not an unlikely fiction; indeed, many of the people I have worked with have had far more trauma in their lives than in this story I will tell. In working with people who have been or are homeless or rough sleepers, I am often left with a sense of profound admiration for the men and women who have experienced so much trauma and so many damaging relationships and yet can still recover, and get on with finding fulfilment in their own lives; they are amazing.

The baby and the development of a sense of self

We will begin with our baby, just born. However, first we will look at some developmental psychology. As the paediatrician and psychoanalyst Winnicott put it, 'there is no such thing as a baby…meaning that if you set out to describe a baby, you will find you are describing a baby and someone. A baby cannot exist alone, but is essentially part of a relationship' (Winnicott, 1960, p.587). This tremendous insight has now been very clearly reaffirmed by the findings of neurobiology: the development of a sense of self takes place in the relationship between the baby and someone (Schore,1994).

Humans are deeply and fundamentally social, and our neurological development reflects that (Schore, 1994; Panksepp and Biven, 2012), and so does the way our mind works (Heard and Lake, 2009; Siegel, 2015). The baby only understands itself as existing at all in interaction and relationship with another, and the quality of this relationship and interaction determines *how* the baby understands its self.

In thinking about human development and the very early development of the self, we are always thinking about two interactive systems: the internal world and the external world. The external world is made up of the environment the baby finds itself in: the people who stay in it and the people who come and go, how hostile or benign it is, its stability or its changeability, its responsiveness or unresponsiveness. The internal world is made up of the baby's experiences, via its senses and via eating, of itself and of its environment: feelings of being warm or cold, hungry or satisfied, tired or active, being awake or not being awake (which is rather like not being at all), being held and loved and cared for, or not. Gradually, the baby develops a sense of itself as an individual self though the accumulation of related experiences and consistency – Winnicott called this a sense of 'continuity of being'. If the baby's caregiver is consistently there for the baby, and responsive, then the baby develops a sense of the continuity of its own existence over time, and a sense of the continuity of its relationship with its caregiver, which Winnicott called 'ego-relatedness'. These are some of the intrapsychic processes of self-formation going on at the same time, in the first few years, as the development of the baby's attachment system, and they underpin a sense of secure attachment and the ability to take an exploratory approach to the world. A strong sense of continuity of being and of ego-relatedness give you what John Bowlby, a psychiatrist and psychoanalyst who was one of the people who developed attachment theory (the other being Mary Ainsworth), called 'a secure base'.

There are some basic biological drives, called motivational systems, four of which are in play in a child's early development and throughout our lives (Heard and Lake, 2009; Panksepp and Biven, 2012); the fifth activates later, circumstances permitting. They are:

- defensive/fear system – fight, flight, freeze
- seeking system – food, shelter, relationships
- attachment system – care-seeking and caregiving systems
- hierarchical system – status recognition and behaviours, equality/inequality
- reproductive system – sexual-partnering, sexual activity.

These are biological urges, but they are regulated by a series of 'super-ordinate systems', including:

- homeostatic systems – temperature, blood flow, heart-rate, pain, pleasure and emotions
- affect regulation/social interaction/stress systems – hyper- and hypo-arousal, shame and pride.

These systems are in turn also regulated by, and regulate, physiological developmental stages such as brain development: the evolutionarily earlier parts of the brain, the so-called 'reptilian' and 'mammalian' brains, develop first and dominate our mental functioning before the 'human' brain gets fully functional (Heard and Lake, 2009); the emotional and survival-critical right brain dominates for the first three to four years before the rationalising, verbalising left brain really kicks in, though it always remains second fiddle (McGilchrist, 2009). All of these physiological developments are also subject to environmentally sensitive epigenetic triggers, so there are always the feedback loops between individual psyche and external environment in an interactive and dynamic interplay.

Increasingly, as we go through these early physiological development processes, guided by the interaction between fundamental biological motivational systems and environmental stimuli and feedback, another factor comes into play – mind. Bizarrely, mind has never been defined by the psychiatric profession or the psychoanalysts (though psychoanalysis has developed detailed concepts of our psychic processes, of how our minds work). However, mind has now been defined by Dan Siegel, another paediatrician and Clinical Professor of Psychiatry at UCLA. He describes mind as having three aspects:

- 'personal subjective experience'
- 'consciousness with a sense of knowing and that which is known'
- 'a regulatory function that is an emergent, self-organising process of the extended nervous system and its relationships…'.

(Siegel, 2012)

It is the third of these that interests us here, the 'regulatory function' that is 'an emergent, self-organising process of the extended nervous system and its relationships'. Siegel portrays mind as working by a 'flow of energy and information' (Siegel, 2012, p.1–11, A1–51) between and within individual people; this activates and energises, and is activated and energised by, the extended nervous system, the 'embodied brain' (Siegel, 2012). This activity, this emergent self-organising process, comes to have a more and more significant management role in regulating our responses to the motivational systems, our mental states, and our physiological processes. As Schore puts it, 'an emergent property of hierarchically-organized cortical-subcortical systems is the capacity to regulate the transitions between various internal states that support affect, cognition and behaviour' (Schore, 2015, p.xxx). Mind, in inevitable interaction with our drives, our physiology and our environments, becomes a big player in the way our lives develop.

Of course, most of this is unconscious: the processes we have been thinking about in this chapter are almost all unconscious or predominantly unconscious. The great majority of what is going on in our minds, brains and social relations is unconscious: this idea, originally of Freud's (Freud, 1915), has been confirmed by neurobiology (Schore, 2013). Social psychology is also moving towards a recognition that quite complex social communications and individual decision-making occur at an unconscious level (Bargh and Morsella, 2008). As Freud put it:

> to require that whatever goes on in the mind must also be known to consciousness is to make an untenable claim. We can go further and argue…that at any given moment consciousness includes only a small content, so that the greater part…must in any case be for very considerable periods in a state of latency, that is to say, of being psychically unconscious. (Freud, 1915, p.574)

Inside the baby's mind: object relations

So, we have a picture of our baby, getting on with what life presents to her/him, unconscious of processing her/his interactions with, and reactions to, the environment through the filters of motivational systems, regulatory systems and a dawning sense of her/his own mind. But before we follow our baby's trajectory towards rough sleeping, let us first spend some time thinking about what is going on in her/his mind. What is the baby's experience?

The answer is that we don't know exactly – and our own memories of this period of our own lives are embodied now, and unconscious, and unavailable to our explicit memory systems, which developed too late to capture the news from the front line of infantile self-experience anyway. But the psychoanalytic/psychodynamic project, since its origin, has been 'a systematic enquiry into the inner workings of human experience' (Guntrip, 1977, p.5); and, by using a critical examination of clinical material and testing it against ever-evolving theory and further clinical observation, in a hermeneutic process not unlike that of physics, it has come up with quite a refined model of early human experience. This model, which has been found to be quite consistent with the neurobiological understandings of the mind (Schore, 2013) is called 'object relations theory'.

Eve Caligor, an American psychiatrist, gives a relatively succinct account of what 'object relations' are:

> cognitive-affective units consisting of an image of the self, interacting with an image of another person, with the entire interaction linked to an affect state, are considered to be the most basic psychic structures… These internalised relationship patterns are referred to as internal object relations…internal object relations are the building blocks of higher-order structures, and they are also seen to organise subjective experience. (Caligor, Kernberg and Clarkin, 2007, p.9)

Furthermore:

> internal object relations emerge from the interaction of inborn affect dispositions and attachment relationships; from the earliest days of life, constitutionally determined affect states are activated in relation to, regulated by, and cognitively linked to interactions with caretakers. (Caligor *et al.*, 2007, p.10)

So essentially, internal object relations are images of the self in interaction with another linked by an affect state, which is also how Bowlby described inner working models in his attachment paradigm; he himself said that 'attachment theory was developed as a variant of object-relations theory' (Bowlby, 1988, p.29). Object relations are the basic 'building blocks of higher-order structures'; these higher-order structures are mental organisations such as the perception of self, the capacity for thoughts and thinking, and the way we perceive and understand and give meaning to, 'organise', 'our subjective experience'. They are the core of our personalities. They are also organised within our minds by affect: basic object relations (cognitive–affective units) link together because of similar emotional values, i.e. similar intensities and types of feeling. This is really important when we come to think of the impact of compound trauma on our baby, because it is where her/his capacity to manage, process and think through difficult feelings will come from.

As Caligor noted above, echoing Schore, 'from the earliest days of life…affect states are activated in relation to, regulated by, and cognitively linked to interactions with caretakers': if our interactions with our caretakers are not consistent and regular and within a certain range of emotional and arousal intensity, leading us towards continuity of being and ego-relatedness, then it will be very hard for us to link together our object relations, our basic units of thinking and being.

So, let's go back to our baby and her journey through life in interaction with her environment. She spends the first few days with her mother and some nurses in a hospital; she's fed and cleaned and kept at a regular, quite warm, temperature, which all feels quite nice and comfortable, and the baby feels the world is OK and part of her own sphere of self. At this stage, the baby can't distinguish clearly between what is or isn't self because all she's experiencing are a series of self-in-interaction-with-another-in-an-affect-state – that's what life's all about. There's also this funny feeling of not-quite-rightness, a sort of twitchy tetchiness that comes sometimes from somewhere but not from somebody, and then the nurse comes and the baby drinks something, and the twitchy-tetchy feeling disappears, and that forms two experiences: a twitchy-tetchy feeling that doesn't seem quite connected to anything else – it's not me-in-relation-to-an-other – and then a warm nice-woman-nice-being-held-nice-drink-no-twitchy-tetchiness feeling, which does feel good.

The baby's sense of self coalesces around these experiences, and they gradually build up inside into an inner world, what Bowlby called an inner working model through which the rest of experience is then perceived and framed, and allocated meaning. These experiences, the 'units' of object relations, link through related affect states: where the affect states are significantly different, they do not link, they remain separate. Classically, feelings of satisfaction and frustration (being fed vs being left hungry) don't go together; feeling love and feeling fear (being held and soothed vs being shouted at or near, being hit, or not being responded to at all) don't go together. This experience leads to what in psychology theory is known as 'splitting' – the baby experiences the mother/carer who comes and holds and soothes and feeds her/him as one person, and the mother/carer who shouts or doesn't come at all when the baby cries as another person altogether. Indeed, the baby tries (unconsciously of course) to keep these two apart, and to deny the reality of the mother/carer who is frightening and unresponsive: the baby wants and needs to rely on an environment that is benign because s/he is completely dependent, and feeling dependent on a hostile environment is the first deeply disturbing and anxiety-provoking experience that is 'too hard to think'. As we remarked earlier, the baby experiences the environment as part of him/herself at this stage of development, so the 'good' experience' and the 'bad' experience are both part of the baby him/herself, but the baby cannot incorporate or own the bad part because it is too difficult to think (Fairbairn, 1994).

I would like to draw attention to two things potentially arising from this stage of development and this situation: the capacity for thinking, and the capacity to form stable relationships.

First, the capacity for thinking: thinking basically begins as the linking together of these object relations, these fundamental units of experience of the self-in-relation-to-the-other-within-an-affect-context (Bion, 1984; Panksepp and Biven, 2012; Schore, 2013). Thinking for the first three years or so is deeply and strongly defined by emotional processes (McGilchrist, 2011), and throughout life, despite the development and apparent dominance of left-brain verbalised rationality, continues to be emotion led (LeDoux, 1999; McGilchrist, 2011). This is because, as we have seen, the affect state is the key 'glue' of the primary fundamental unit of thinking. As we have also seen, these units – experiences that become thought–feelings that become thoughts as our brain develops over the first four years or so – link to others because of similarity in affect values. Very disparate values, whether in mood or affect or intensity, are less likely to link up, or link only tenuously, or do not link at all. Making sense of whole experiences, 'making it all add up', depends on our capacity to link our thoughts and feelings and for our thought–feeling units to be able to link up. For someone without emotional language and with widely disparate and unregulated emotional experiences, this kind of joined-up thinking – thinking of the whole picture within a broad context over a period of time – becomes very difficult.

The other potential problem with thinking is that the mind/brain/body system works as efficiently and ergonomically as possible: so rather than thinking everything through each time, it uses anticipation to predict and direct responsiveness, and it uses pre-experienced 'mental states' – sets of object relational units joined together by similar affect – to respond emotionally to situations. Through emotion, we move between mental states associated with particular sets of situational responses: this can be a smooth process if we have experience of good self- and interpersonal affect regulation, or we can 'flip' suddenly between mental states if our experience has been very disjointed. As noted, this is a very efficient way of doing things, but it does mean that we approach every situation with a preconceived perspective, that of our inner working model, or more appropriately, models; we unconsciously pick the one we most expect to meet the requirements of the situation, using unconscious emotional signals and interpersonal communication as our guide as to which is the appropriate response. It is fairly obvious from this that, if your early experience, when you are forming your inner working models and when your mental states are coalescing, is one of regular hyper-arousal of anxiety or fear states, these responses will come to dominate your anticipatory responses and responsive mental state. At least severe, you will be a 'glass half-empty' person; at most severe, your world will seem populated almost entirely by 'bad', and even existence-threatening, situations – 'the whole world's against me'.

As well as affecting our capacity to think and the way we think, our 'default mode' if you like, these very early object relations also affect how we relate to people and to ourselves; after all, they are formed of our self-in-relation-to-the-other-within-an-affect-state. This works fine where the infant is raised in a benign situation with relative stability of care; it is more problematical where the infant is raised within a volatile environment, with unpredictable care, with moments of good care and moments of terror, or with severe neglect or emotional unavailability of her/his carer. As we noted earlier, the infant experiences these different experiences as emanating from different people, because they are in different object-relation sets, because these are determined by values of similar intensity and mood of affect, and because thinking that the environment is hostile is unthinkable. As another psychiatrist and psychoanalyst put it, 'splitting of the object in the struggle to cope with unhappy real life experience leads to a splitting of the ego in the struggle to maintain relations with both the good and bad aspects of the mother and other family figures' (Guntrip, 1977, p.98).

This is the tendency to idealise or denigrate others, another aspect of psychological splitting. This has implications for relationships which are quite functional when you are an infant or a child, when maintaining a relationship with your primary carers is essential to survival, but less so for an adult. If you idealise one relationship or set of relationships, then you have to denigrate some other part of your relationships, because both 'good' and 'bad' are there inside you, they are part of your inner working models.

As we have seen, because it is so difficult to think the 'bad' part, because there is a self-preservation element in denying the hostility of the environment when that hostility arises from the primary relationships upon which one is dependent, and because the infantile experience is that all of this is happening within them – and is therefore their fault – the difficult experience has to be psychically disowned.

This, we noted, is called splitting. This leads to another psychic process which psychology calls 'projection'. As we disown the 'bad' part of our inner worlds, we have to find a place for it – experience, rather like energy in physics, cannot be destroyed (despite our best attempts with large amounts of drugs, alcohol and positive thinking!) – and what we do, again unconsciously, is attribute our 'bad' object relations, feelings, thoughts, to others and external situations. Of course, the others and external situations may lend themselves to this purpose very well, and one of the processes of social exclusion is that the negative projections of the person who has experienced compound trauma, their negative view of the world as a hostile and aggressive place, and their perception that their mental state is a true representation of reality (Bateman and Fonagy, 2006), are often confirmed by real oppressive experiences. As the old joke goes, just because I'm paranoid it doesn't mean they're not out to get me.

The baby's journey to social exclusion and rough sleeping

Now we can return to our baby, Bea, with all this going on in her mind, with her sense of self just beginning to come into being. So far, she only really has the first part of Siegel's definition of mind, 'personal subjective experience'. She goes home, to wherever home is: her mother's environment, which, let us imagine, is a small social housing studio flat in a big city. What happens next is going to have a big impact on her: this is when the rest of her mind is developing, when 'consciousness with a sense of knowing and that which is known' and 'a regulatory function that is an emergent, self-organising process of the extended nervous system and its relationships' (Siegel, 2012, p.1–11, A1–51) is coalescing around her experience, following the processes that we have just been looking at.

As Winnicott remarked, when we think of the baby we think of the baby in relation to someone else. What is happening with the mother/carer is critical here: it is in this relationship that the baby will develop their capacity for affect regulation and for thinking, and their sense of self (Schore, 1994; Fonagy *et al.*, 2003).

What may be happening for Bea is that, over the first few weeks and months of coming back home, her mother has these experiences:

- Bea's mother's mother dies, and she hears about it despite the fact that they haven't actually seen each other for years.

- Her partner turns up or is still hanging out at the studio, he's there with his friends drinking or taking drugs, he's pleased to see her and the baby because it makes him feel like a big man, and he gives her drinks and drugs; they get out of it, and don't pay attention to the baby crying, and they don't really even notice that the baby's crying.

- Her partner becomes violent, and starts shouting at her, they have a row, he hits her, makes her bleed, she screams while he's doing that; the baby's crying, but she's trying to protect her face.

- The baby keeps crying, they've run out of food and they haven't changed the baby's nappy for ages, and the baby is hungry and sore, and the partner can't get any sleep and is drunk/hungover, and she can't deal with it because the partner's in a rage and the baby keeps crying and she doesn't know what to do and she's slapped it and it still cries, and her partner's screamed in its face and shook it and it's gone silent, thank heavens…

The baby grows into a little infant and then a toddler, becomes a quiet child usually, a little bit withdrawn, but doesn't cry much and 'isn't a bother', though she does throw a temper sometimes, but everyone says it's just the 'terrible twos' and if she gets really out of hand – like screaming or smashing things or having a complete tantrum – then she responds to a sharp slap. The violent partner, the baby's father, isn't around any more – for all she knows, he's dead now – and that's better, but money's really tight and mother's got a bit of a habit now, mainly crack, it cheers her up when she's feeling depressed, which she is most of the time, and she's started prostituting herself a bit to make ends meet and feed her habit.

Sometimes she has to leave the baby with a neighbour, but he's a nice bloke – quiet, helpful, an oldish bloke, never any trouble in his place. He sexually abuses Bea. Mother doesn't really notice: the child doesn't want to go next door and be left there, but then she often kicks up a tantrum when she's left alone anywhere; and she's sullen and quiet when she comes back, but then, she's prone to being sulky when she hasn't had her way. Things could be worse, for the mum; for the child, they couldn't be much worse, but she loves her mum, she's the best mum ever when she's there, it's the neighbour and the father who left, it's the men who are the problem, the men who come round and take her mother away from the child, or the men she is left with who break her boundaries, hurt her, terrify her, and threaten to kill her if she ever says a word to her mum.

Bea has got to school now. It's hard at school: she often hasn't had anything to eat before she goes, and she has to find her own clothes in the morning and they're not always clean, and she begins to notice that she's different to the other kids, her life is different; she hasn't got what they've got, and she can't invite friends back to her house – not that she'd want to, she'd be ashamed. Some of the other children start to tease her – they call her poor, dirty, smelly – and she's noticed that the ones she did make friends with are keeping away from her a bit because she's always got nits and lice, she can't get rid of them herself and mum's not very good at it, she tried, she washed Bea's hair in lice-killing shampoo, but it didn't work. Some of the kids tried to bully her too, but she knew what to do about that, she'd seen her dad, and she hit them; it didn't quite work how she expected, though, because, like, this huge rage rose up insider her and she really hurt the other kid. She got excluded for that. It didn't really matter, the headmaster was a creep anyway, reminded her of the man next door; though he wasn't abusing her any more as she didn't go round there any more, though she still felt frightened of him and disgusted with herself when she saw him.

School was getting difficult because she couldn't keep up with the work; how could they expect her to do homework when at home she was looking after her mum, or keeping out of the way of her mum's 'friends'? She knew what they were up to when they weren't just taking drugs and drinking. She began truanting, no bother really, and better to hang out in the park, as long as you kept out of the way of the creepy adults, especially the men, and she could always lash out or run if they tried to bother her. It all came on top though, because the school noticed her truancy, and her mum turned up to see the school when she was out of it, and someone then came round to the house and it was dirty and there was evidence of drug-taking, and her mum was out of it then too, and then social services got involved and she was taken into foster care. Her mum was really upset, and said it was all her fault;

she felt really bad about that. Her mum said it was going to break her heart to lose her.

She felt bad about that, but the first foster carer was lovely, and they looked after her in a kindly way, and got rid of the nits and lice, and fed her well (she even got out of the habit of hiding a bit of food under her bed, to make sure she had something for the morning). Mum didn't keep up the contact meetings though, that was hard; but she tried to be brave about it, and didn't cry. She started going to school again, and made some friends, and even found that she could manage schoolwork and do her homework, it began to seem as if she wasn't as stupid as she'd always thought; maybe school was something she could do.

Unfortunately, she couldn't stay there, with those foster parents, for the rest of her childhood, it was only a temporary placement. Social services had been doing some work on her case, and they'd found that her mother had a brother up north, and he was willing to take her. He had a family already, with two children, both boys, and though his wife had died of cancer a while back, it looked like a stable, blood-related family all the same. It was decided to place her there. That was hard.

She cried a lot, but only when no-one was around. She had to change schools as well, of course, and lost all her friends. Nobody seemed to worry about that: they all told her just to put a brave face on it, to cheer up, not to think about the past, and they took away her phone and her electronics so she couldn't keep in touch with anyone, and returned any letters that came for her, so as not to upset her and make her pine. She tried to believe everybody hadn't forgotten her, even her mother, but it was difficult. She wondered sometimes just what was so awful about her, that nobody wanted to stay with her ever. However, she got on with life – she might even have made a go of it: it was difficult at the new school because everyone knew each other, and she was an outsider, and a bit quiet and then a bit quick-tempered, and they thought she was 'snobby' because she was quiet, appeared aloof, and because she came from 'down south'. She might have managed all this because she was still managing school and doing quite well, and even felt a bit proud of herself, but then the elder of the two boys started to abuse her. He came into her bedroom and raped her, and told her that if she ever told anyone about it, he would kill her. Just like the man next door. Just like men. She wasn't going to tell anyone anyway, and not just because the boy would kill her. Like she was going to talk to her step-father/uncle about it, he was a man; like she was going to talk to social services, who'd taken her from her mum and broken her mum's heart; like she was going to talk to the school, they didn't really care. Nobody cared. She would go and find her mum. She ran away.

They took her back, when they caught her, and she ran away again; they took her back, she ran away; they took her into care. She learned to take drugs there, and had her first consensual sexual relationships – not great, but not forced, and the situation was eased by girlfriends being around and a bit of drugs and alcohol. She ran away from the care home once or twice too, but really to go off and find excitement with her friends and their friends outside: sex, drugs, hanging out, it felt kind of alright, like being a bit in control. Certainly a bit more in control than being in the care home – *they* tried to control her there: they even took her to a psychologist, and she got some labels which said there was something wrong with her because she didn't pay attention to anything and didn't do what she was told to do. Why would she do what they told her? Nobody understood her, they didn't know what she felt, she hated most of them – there was one who she loved, and would do anything for, but the rest, they were all just creepy or doing their jobs, interested in themselves and not what she wanted. Not that she really knew what she wanted when it came down to it; if she thought about what she wanted, it came down pretty much to just not being where she was.

She got caught with drugs, rather a lot; she was carrying them for a bloke. She didn't say that because he'd probably kill her if she did, so she went to a young offenders' institution. She was bullied there, but she also made some friends and she met up with them when she got out. She didn't have anywhere to live when she was discharged, but they offered to let her stay with them. Where they lived was chaotic, with lots of men, drugs and alcohol going through the place and through its inhabitants, but on the whole the other women were friendly and kind enough in their way, and she felt OK. It was almost like being at home with mum again. It was almost too like home, because one of the women had this boyfriend who would get drunk and violent and beat her up, sometimes in the flat, and they'd try and defend her, and they'd chase him off, but they'd all take a hit or two. The woman still went back to him. He really beat her up one time, and even got arrested, but they let him out on bail and he kept coming round; the woman was terrified, but still went with him. She got depressed and killed herself. All the women were a bit upset, but Bea didn't cry, not when she was with anyone anyway.

Then there was this young man who was quite powerful in their social group, and she kind of looked up to him, and he kind of liked her, and she felt good that this powerful young man paid her attention; and he was quite slow, as in gentle, and quite kind to her, and that was new. They became an item. She went to live with him. It was good, she was special, he loved her. The idea seemed silly to her, but she thought he loved her like she would've wished her mother had – like she was the most important thing, and that there was no room for anyone else. He was a bit jealous, which was alright, good even, but after a while he became really jealous; this felt good sometimes, because it made her feel precious and special, but it became more and more difficult: he would get into rages about her going out, think she was seeing someone else. He knocked her about when he got into one of his rages. She forgave him: it wasn't really him, something came over him to act like that, and he was always really sorry. Anyway, it was as much her fault, because when he got angry she'd get angry too, and she'd go into a rage and she'd hit him; he hit her harder, that was all. After he put her in hospital the second time, though, somehow she managed to summon up the courage to run away even though she still loved him. Good old running away: she'd lost count of how many times running away had seemed to be the best option.

It wasn't her intention to go on the streets: but she couldn't go back to the flat where she had been before her relationship, because most of her friends were no longer there – they'd moved on, died, gone to prison. And of course, he'd find her there. She didn't have any real friends any more anyway, as she'd hardly been able to go out alone or talk to anyone because he'd got so jealous – it had been like being back in the care home, except without the other girls. She knew a couple of his mates, but that was obviously no good. So she slept on the streets for the first time (apart from the occasional night with her friends from the care home, but that had been different: now she really was homeless). People offered help: drug dealers, pimps, men looking for sex. She wasn't going to do prostitution, she'd seen her mum do that and seen what it had done to her: if it wasn't for that, her mum would've looked after her all right, and none of this would have happened. And for the same reason she wouldn't do crack. She did drink as much as she could though – it helped to get her through the cold of night and the loneliness of day. She begged for money; on the whole the police were OK, though sometimes they'd move her on or warn her; she moved about, so she wasn't too much of a nuisance or a target anywhere, and so outreach services couldn't find her. They'd only want to put her in an institution again, a care home, a prison.

She drank as much as she could, and found she had to have a drink by her when she woke up or else she started to shake, and get this strange twitchy-tetchy feeling; so what, that's life. She was a bit dirty, and a bit smelly, and she had lice again: it didn't feel that strange, it kind of said something about how she felt, and it helped keep the men away. Not enough though. She still got raped while she was drunk, by a homeless man who was drunk too. She didn't want sex, and she'd said no, and he threatened her with a knife, and carried on. She hadn't felt like fighting anyway – she somehow hadn't had the energy to hit him or rage at him or do anything, she'd gone into that funny sullen, quiet space she used to go in when she was little. It felt like nothing much really mattered. What was she going to get from life anyway? Who would hear if she cried?

This story is told about a woman experiencing the process of social exclusion arising from compound trauma; it could be told about a man. There would be some differences, probably more violence and more crime, perhaps more travelling greater distances, perhaps a suicide attempt either directly or by overdose; there'd still likely be neglect, and physical, emotional and/or sexual abuse. Rape too, though the levels of male rape are not known, and men find it even harder than women to disclose rape. But overall, the story of a man experiencing the process of social exclusion arising from compound trauma is likely to be similar. There could, of course, also be more trauma in the life of 'Bea', whose story I have told: many homeless women have had multiple abusive relationships as well as serially abusive childhoods, and something which I have missed out in Bea's story which is also very common for homeless women, is the loss of a child, usually to care and/or adoption. The point of the story is not to cover every eventuality: it is simply to illustrate how social exclusion is a process that happens between a person experiencing severe and multiple disadvantage and the society in which we and they live.

The psychological impact of compound trauma and social exclusion

From what we have looked at in this chapter in terms of infant development and the development of the infant's mind, we can imagine the impact of Bea's story on her mental states, her inner world, her object relations, and her perception of the people she meets and the situations she finds herself in. We can begin to understand how she might feel. So we are able to make some sort of assessment of her psychological and emotional state, how she typically reacts to people and situations, and what she might be thinking about them; we can also guess a bit at how she might think, feel and experience life. I would like to do this in the next chapter, as a precursor to thinking about the psychology of recovery. Here, however, I want to have a brief look at the psychological processes likely to arise from Bea's story to highlight how the social process of social exclusion plays its part.

Bea has her first experience of positivity: she is fed and nurtured in the hospital, and gets to be with her mum a lot. The only downside is her experience of withdrawals, and of administered psychoactive substances to relieve her 'twitchy-tetchy' anxiety feelings; these anxiety feelings, we note, are somewhat divorced from the people she's in contact with, because they come from her own bodily processes. However, as a baby she isn't able to distinguish clearly between her own bodily processes and the external world – it's all one experiential whole – and so her anxiety is also felt as environmental but generalised, unfocused.

Then we have her experience after returning home. As we saw at the beginning of the chapter, it is in her first two years that she will be forming her fundamental attachments, and her basic object relations; her initial sense of herself as a person will begin to be laid down.

When she gets home, however, things change and she has her first experience of sudden environmental change, with no meaning. She still gets some attention from her mother, and is cleaned and fed sometimes (otherwise she'd die), but it is no longer regular. In particular, her crying often or at least sometimes goes unanswered, and sometimes goes answered by an attack. Babies cry to activate their mother/carer's attachment caregiving system; it is their primary way of alerting the environment to their needs. For Bea this attachment care-seeking behaviour produces unpredictable results: she is likely to have an insecure attachment pattern. It may be ambivalent, especially with her mother, and by transference with other females; it may be avoidant, especially with her father and other men; and it may be disorganised, as her fear motivational system is activated at the same time as her attachment system when she is hit by her mother/carer and her partner.

Her sense of her mother as good is preserved by the perception that men are totally bad: all the bad resides in men. She has a tendency to idealise and denigrate. The uncomfortable reality that her mother ignores her crying sometimes and slaps her sometimes, along with her idealisation of her mother, leads her to the perception that the bad must reside in her, so that she comes to think that she isn't good for much and deserves poor treatment, a self-perception which becomes apparent more and more as she develops and matures. She struggles with her sense of boundaries, having had them broken; and has little or no trust, because she doesn't experience herself as heard and important, and she experiences others as unreliable and often abusive. But she continues to look for relationship because that is a primary drive, and because she has had a little bit of experience of what good relationship is like, with her mother for a few days and occasionally thereafter, and with one set of her foster carers, and even with her abusive boyfriend at first. However, relationships become abusive or are ruptured, and don't last; and fear, and running away once she can, are core experiences. Of course, when she was very little and couldn't physically run away, she had to psychically run away, and stopped crying and became sullen and quiet.

She 'flips' from mood to mood, and suffers from rages that surprise her, but don't really feel like hers; she allows and even expects others to behave in this way, because it's 'normal'. She feels done to, and disempowered to take control of her own life, and when she does try to take control in fact she attempts to replace the deficit in the love she received from her mother – trying to control the object, rather than her relationship with the object. She finds self-soothing deeply attractive, having not been soothed by her mother (and learned affect regulation), and having already had experience of psychoactive substances, withdrawal anxiety, and the way of life where high levels of drug and alcohol intoxication are, again, normal. She has learned to hide her feelings, hide the reality of what is happening to her; and, from earlier still, she has learned that an angry silence is safer than crying out, so she turns her anger inwards in the form of depression and self-neglect. She becomes an alcoholic. She ends up in an adult version of a state very much like the state she was in when she was taken away from her mother, and her mother's 'heart was broken'; she seems to be unconsciously re-enacting her childhood experience – in the hope that this time she will get the maternal love and care she so sorely wanted but never quite got.

Bea's is a story of compound trauma, with multiple losses of various sorts, abuse, neglect, and ultimately self-neglect and self-destructivity. The social exclusion that begins with her mother and mother's partner being unable to respond appropriately to her cries and her need for care is compounded through her life. When she has infantile rages, everyone accepts them as normal. When she rages at school, she is excluded; it is treated as behavioural, not communicative. The school only notices anything is wrong when she truants and makes it obvious: and when they do notice, they again see it as a problem, not as a communication – nobody is asking her why, or what's going on for her; their objective is to make sure she goes to school and everyone complies with the requirements of the Education Act. They didn't notice she was covered in lice – school lice nurses were abolished in funding cuts – which might have been a signal of neglect at home.

When they did act, they took Bea into foster care, which might have been the right thing to do at the time as the situation was pretty dire, but they didn't put in large amounts of effort to work with her mother or to ensure regular post-placement contact. In fact, they found a way of placing her with family, a less costly intervention which may be of benefit to the child, and may not: in this case it was not. Bea was happy in the foster home, and didn't want to go to her uncle's, who she didn't even know; again, her views were not considered important enough to direct the course of her life, confirming her view of herself as unwanted and unimportant, and not heard. They then took measures to ensure she was isolated, a form of trauma and an expression of social exclusion, under the guise of wanting her to settle down in her new placement. Their disregard of attachment psychology in general, and the importance of Bea's attachments, confirmed again Bea's damaged attachment patterns. They broke her sense of continuity, again confirming her experience that things just suddenly flip and that she had no control over her life.

By the time she was abused again, she was unable to say anything about it or do anything about it except run away. Her previous violent temper had been lost to her belief that she was never heard, seen or valued; she abandoned 'fight' for her earlier response of 'flight' (that she had learned in response to the attacks by her mother and her mother's partner). She ran away. Again, this was not treated as a communication. Eventually she was put into a care home – probably with people saying she was 'hard to manage' and 'unmanageable' in her placement with the uncle; there she was in a situation of multiple adults with no real attachment to any of them except for one idealisation, a situation she found herself in throughout her life. Again, no attention to her attachment needs, or to her developmental needs: she saw a psychologist, but they focused on behavioural issues, and gave them labels that suggested there was something wrong with her. This of course reaffirmed her view that she was the problem, that she was somehow bad and undeserving.

In prison she met other women who had probably had not dissimilar stories, and with whom she could relate, in a context of institutional bullying that she was familiar with and could respond to by withdrawal of engagement. No rehabilitation there. On the contrary, she was discharged to the care of the socially disadvantaged friends she had made inside; it's a common story that the person waiting outside the prison gates is not a helpful social worker, housing or support officer, but a dealer or a pimp – they offer money, drugs, somewhere to stay. Bea got to live in a house that replicated something of the chaos of her home of early childhood, with women who she could relate to, and see through the lens of her idealised mother-view. She was exposed to trauma, but it continued to be normal. She then entered an abusive relationship herself, having found someone strong (at last, strong and protective) who seemed to love her and think she was really special (at last, someone she was special for); when she was hospitalised, she was not able to take advantage of any offers of support around the domestic abuse because her partner offered her something she needed, she held a negative self-view as 'deserving it' because of her volatility, and because of her distrust of institutions and 'officials'. She was no doubt described by the agencies involved as 'unwilling to engage' or a 'non-engager'.

By the time she ran away from that, she had run out of social relationships to turn to: she had become truly isolated, and socially excluded. She slept on the streets, and avoided people and regular contact with anyone, police or outreach workers or even other homeless people; her damaged attachment patterns were now more like shattered ones. Her desire for love and being cared for was unbearable, and her belief that it could never be fulfilled unshakeable. Nobody comes when you cry. So she drank a lot, and neglected herself, and people walked past her and either ignored her or looked at her with disgust, as she had the quiet old man next door. And she came to share their feeling of worthlessness and self-disgust, so she couldn't even fight when the drunken homeless man raped her.

Bea became socially excluded through a long process of compound trauma and psychological damage in interplay with social neglect, indifference and ignorance, and sometimes downright hostility towards those who are experiencing trauma and deprivation.

Lankelly Chase averaged out the people who experience SMD3, their highest level of severe and multiple deprivation, to over 1500 per local authority in England (Lankelly Chase, 2015). Bea's story may be made up, but similar stories are being enacted right now in every town and city in Britain.

References

Bateman, A. and Fonagy, P. (2006) *Mentalization-Based Treatment for Borderline Personality Disorder.* Oxford: Oxford University Press.
Bargh, J.A. and Morsella, E. (2008) 'The unconscious mind.' *Perspectives on Psychological Science 3*, 1, 73–79.
Bion, W. (1984) *Second Thoughts,* London: Karnac.
Bowlby, J. (1988) *A Secure Base,* London: Routledge.
Caligor, E., Kernberg, O. and Clarkin, M. (2007) *Handbook of Dynamic Psychotherapy for Higher Level Personality Pathology.* Arlington, VA: American Psychiatric Publishing.
Fairbairn, W.R.D. (1994) *Psychoanalytic Studies of the Personality.* London: Routledge.
Fonagy P., Gyorgy, G., Jurist E.L. and Target M. (2003) *Affect Regulation, Mentalization, and the Origin of the Self.* New York: Other Press.
Freud, S. (1915) 'The Unconscious.' In P. Gay (ed.) (1995) *The Freud Reader.* London: Vintage.
Guntrip, H. (1977) *Psychoanalytic Theory, Therapy and the Self.* London: Karnac.
Heard, D. and Lake, B. (2009) *The Challenge of Attachment for Caregiving.* London: Karnac.
Lankelly Chase (2015) *Hard Edges: Mapping Severe and Multiple Disadvantage in England.* Accessed February 2017 at http://lankellychase.org.uk/multiple-disadvantage/publications/hard-edges
Le Doux, J. (1999) *The Emotional Brain.* London: Phoenix.
McGilchrist, I. (2009) *The Master and his Emissary.* New Haven and London: Yale University Press.
Panksepp, J. and Biven, L. (2012) *The Archaeology of Mind.* London: Norton.
Schore, A. (2013) *The Science of the Art of Psychotherapy.* London: Norton.
Siegel, D. (2012) *Pocket Guide to Interpersonal Neurobiology.* London: Norton.
Siegal, D. (2015) *The Developing Mind.* London:Norton
Winnicott, D.W. (1965) 'The Theory of the Parent-Infant Relationship.' *International Journal of Pscho-Analysis 41,* 585–595.

2

SOLUTIONS
PRINCIPLES OF PRACTICE

4

A PSYCHOLOGICAL PERSPECTIVE ON RECOVERY

DR PETER COCKERSELL

I am going to look in this chapter at the psychology of recovery.

We looked earlier on, and continue to look throughout this book, at the impact of compound trauma on the emotional and psychological development and behaviours of the affected individual; we looked at how these are socially compounded, and the sort of social interactions that arise from them, and from not treating them appropriately.

This book also contains various accounts of psychologically informed or psychotherapeutic treatments that have been found to be effective with people who have experienced compound trauma and social exclusion. These chapters, written by a range of clinicians and clients, highlight how much it is an approach and attitude in working with people who have experienced compound trauma rather than a specific set of techniques that makes the difference: the understanding is psychodynamic – because it's based on human experience, and psychodynamic theories are the best explication we have so far of how human minds work – but the techniques are psychologically informed human interactions, or humanly informed psychology. This isn't a book about individuals' pathology but about social interactivity and pathogenic social experiences. If compound trauma derives from bad experiences and damaging relationships, then healing originates in good experiences and positive relationships: if social exclusion derives from a particular set of socially contexted experiences, then so does recovery.

For this reason, this chapter is not really about psychological treatments at all, though it has a bearing on all treatment – all therapeutic activity – including psychological and psychosocial 'treatments': this chapter is about 'recovery'. If, in our roles as psychotherapists or other clinicians, or support workers or peer mentors, we are going to support our clients to embark on or progress in their recovery journey, it helps if we understand the emotional and psychological processes of recovery.

The meaning of 'recovery'

First I will define what I mean by 'recovery'. In common language, recovery has two main meanings, 'recovery of' and 'recovery from': 'recovery of' is, for example, when we have lost something and find it again; and 'recovery from' is, for example, when we have regained our strength after a gruelling bout of exercise, or our wellbeing after an illness. In both these cases it has a meaning of getting back something that we had before, either as a possession or as an inherent quality or condition.

The word 'recovery' in the context of substance dependency and mental health continues to have this meaning of getting something back, in both the 'recovery of' and 'recovery from' senses, but it has an additional meaning of getting something or somewhere new or different, of achieving something that the person hadn't achieved before. This is how homelessness services have also taken to using the word recovery. Recovery is often described in terms such as 'taking (more) control of your life', 'achieving (more of) your potential', or being 'more yourself', becoming 'more self-defining'. Recovery in this sense is not just about getting something back; indeed, it may not mean getting anything back at all – it is aspirational. So, when I talk about the process of recovery, either as a professional working to support or facilitate someone else's recovery journey, or as an individual making my own, I am talking about reaching out, beyond, and above my current position or condition into an aspirational world as well as reaching deep down, within, and back to where I am coming from, the places I want/need 'recovery of' or 'recovery from'.

I would also like to note what 'recovery' does not mean – it does not mean returning to the state that preceded whatever it is that the person is 'recovering from': poor mental health, substance dependency, homelessness, the experience of compound trauma. In this aspect, this socially contexted meaning of recovery is very different to the meaning of recovery in biological illnesses: if you have flu, you may well hope to return to the physical condition you had before you had flu; or if you have hepatitis, with the right treatment you may well hope to return to the same physical condition you had before hepatitis. It is more like recovery from physical trauma: if you have a broken leg, you will recover the use of your leg, but it will never be as strong as the unbroken leg, and will feel sore or stiff if stressed well into the future; if you are bitten by a shark or involved in a serious car crash, you will bear the scars forever, and your injuries may well be life-changing. In these high-trauma cases you may well recover – be alive, 'get your life back', achieve all sorts of amazing things (just think of the Paralympians) but you will recover to a different place from that which preceded the event. Recovery from social exclusion is much more like recovery after traumatic injury; in at least most cases, it *is* recovery after traumatic injury. The neurological processing of social exclusion activates the same systems as the neurological processing of physiological trauma (Eisenberger, Lieberman and Williams, 2003). This is often compounded by a deep shame response, which reinforces the trauma response and activates many of the same 'shutting down' neurological systems (Schore, 2013): when you have a physical injury, people often rally round and are deeply sympathetic; when you have a psycho-emotional injury, a 'mental health problem', then people often shun you.

In addition, there is an added way in which recovery from psycho-emotional trauma (often accompanied, of course, by physical trauma as well) is about not getting back to the state that preceded the trauma. The state that preceded the trauma is, almost by definition, vulnerable to trauma: 'recovery' in this circumstance really means the development of a higher level of resilience, and so an increased capacity to process potentially traumatising situations and protect yourself against potentially traumatising relationships in the future.

These different aspects of recovery – 'recovery of', 'recovery from', recovery as 'enacted aspiration' and 'recovery as not getting back to where you started from' – are all crucial because they affect what is going on at an intersubjective and often unconscious level in the therapeutic endeavour, whatever technical form that endeavour actually adopts to support the beginning or enhancement of the recovery process.

The differences are crucial because there are different sets of biopsychosocial processes at play in these different aspects of recovery

– 'recovery of', 'recovery from', 'enacted aspiration' and 'recovery as not getting back to where you started from'. Just as, when working in the Cycle of Change model (Prochaska and di Clemente, 1982), there is little point in urging to 'action' the person who is in 'pre-contemplation', so in recovery work we need to understand what is going on inside the person so as to most effectively engage with them. In effect, this means engaging with as many of the processes of recovery as are in operation, and as we can. These processes of recovery, how they play out in the therapeutic encounter and therapeutic relationship, and what the 'therapeutic encounter' and 'therapeutic relationship' actually are, will form the main topic of this chapter.

The nature of 'therapeutic'

Let's start with the 'therapeutic encounter' and 'therapeutic relationship', or rather, let's start with just 'therapeutic'. The word 'therapeutic' means, the dictionary tells us, 1. 'of or relating to the treatment of disease or disorders by remedial agents or methods', or 2. 'having a beneficial effect on the body or mind' (Merriam-Webster, 2017a). If we do something that is 'beneficial [to] the body or mind', then that activity is therapeutic. This means that we can do something specifically 'relating to the treatment of disease or disorders', and those of us who are clinicians tend to do just that, but it isn't the only therapeutic activity, and indeed it may not be the most important in either quality or quantity, and it is not a necessity in all situations. It also means that we can be almost accidentally therapeutic, without even thinking about it – 'having a beneficial effect on the body or mind' of someone through very ordinary interactions, such as giving someone who is thirsty a glass of water, or just smiling at someone.

'Therapeutic' is an adjective, i.e. 'a word…typically serving as a modifier of a noun to denote a quality of the thing named' (Merriam-Webster, 2017b). I think it's helpful to remember this, and to think of therapeutic as an adjective, as 'a quality of the thing named', because it means that therapeutic can be applied to pretty much anything. What 'therapeutic' describes is a quality brought to bear on or within that thing, whatever that thing is. So a therapeutic environment, or a therapeutic encounter, or a therapeutic relationship are environments, encounters and relationships that have a particular quality to them: they are a particular type of environment, encounter or relationship with specific characteristics. Further, we can argue that these particular and specific characteristics are something that we can intend, that we can encourage and foster: they describe a quality that we can, to a greater or lesser degree, bring to the environments, encounters and relationships. We can take a situation or encounter and make it therapeutic. It is not an inherent quality of situations or encounters: just because something happens in a hospital, for example, that something is not necessarily therapeutic. Just because something happens in a hostel or the street, that something is not necessarily not therapeutic. We can add therapeutic to the situation or encounter.

The fact that we can add therapeutic to the situation or encounter, I suggest, also implies that we can be more consciously, and potentially more effectively, therapeutic if we think about it, and if we use 'remedial agents or methods'. There is no reason to believe that only clinicians can use 'remedial agents or methods', as the dictionary suggests by linking them to 'treatment of disease and disorders', to enhance the therapeutic quality of their interactions: clinicians of different sorts may use different 'remedial agents or methods' and may think about them in terms of diseases and disorders, but hostel staff, social workers, police and peers can also use 'remedial agents or methods', while thinking about them in terms of functionality, usefulness, or just 'getting themselves together' or 'getting a life'. These too are beneficial to body or mind. The examples and experiences of practice in this book are examples of people using 'remedial agents or methods' to create therapeutic environments, encounters and relationships.

So what is this 'quality', this mysterious ingredient, that transforms any situation or encounter into a therapeutic one? Put simply, it is interacting in the situation or encounter in such a way that it enables or enhances the other person's recovery. The quality, the specific characteristics, of a therapeutic interaction are such that they enable or enhance the other person's capacity for either 'recovery of', 'recovery from', recovery as 'enacted aspiration', or 'recovery as not getting back to where you started from', or all of these.

J's story

Let's just think about these aspects of recovery, and perhaps the best way to do that is to think of someone's life story, a client I worked with who we'll call J. J's mother died suddenly of a heart attack, in front of him, when he was very young (six), and the drunken father used to be violent to the children and couldn't/didn't look after them. J was taken into care, as were most of his siblings; they were separated and placed in different homes and foster families. J was abused in the foster family in which he was placed, and became 'difficult' and violent, and passed through several care homes, in one of which he was abused again, before moving on to young offenders' institutions; as a young adult he became a heavy drinker, occasional criminal, episodically violent, and a rough sleeper (it could be argued he had been homeless for many years already by then). When I met J he had a shattered sense of self, he thought he was worthless, dangerous, a victim, a decent man, and nothing much at all; he was deeply angry with and ashamed of his past, couldn't think about his mother, hated and admired his father (who taught him to fight, and 'to be hard', by punching him randomly), and didn't believe there was much in life for him except drunkenness and the hostel/prison/rough sleeping circuit; he didn't trust institutions, indeed hated them, and he couldn't stay away from them. He didn't believe in recovery: it hadn't crossed his mind.

We can think of the different aspects of recovery in J's situation. There's 'recovery of': J had a 'home' once – not a great one because of his father's drunkenness and violence, but a place he felt loved, with his mother he loved, siblings who looked out for each other, and a neighbourhood where he felt he belonged, or was at least known, somebody, but it gave him a core sense of himself in relation to others and to a specific space. There's 'recovery from': the trauma of his mother dying (he was actually playing with her when she died), the violence of his father, the neglect, the separation from his siblings, the abuse, his criminalisation and punishment for reacting to the abuse (the first time he was sent to a young offenders' institution was because he hit and hurt the care home manager who tried to abuse him), and then the myriad traumatic experiences of being part of a drinking school, on and off the streets, in and out of hostels and prisons, social exclusion and social nobody-ness.

Then, perhaps the beginning or seed of the change process for him, there's 'recovery as not getting back to where you started from': J did not want to be a victim, or to be so angry and volatile, and did not want to go on in a world of drunkenness, violence and the 'revolving door' of multiple deprivation and exclusion. And finally there was recovery in the sense of 'enacted aspiration': J came to value himself and others, and began to volunteer and do some work within homelessness services, and made positive contact with some of his siblings, and stopped being an out-and-out drinker, though he still went on binges, and he stayed in one place, though he still found that really testing and would periodically really struggle not just to drop everything and go off (but he would talk about it, and struggle with it, and generally not do it, and at least returned).

In the rest of this chapter we will look at the different processes that were in play in J's story of recovery, and how the 'remedial agents and methods' of the different people and agencies he encountered interacted with these processes to enable and support a 'beneficial effect on body or mind' to take place, and J to achieve more of his potential. I think it's important to note here that the work done by the services he encountered was to enable and support, it was to provide the environment and nutrients that J could use to take on his own recovery journey. When it comes down to it, recovery is something that each person does for themselves, supported more than hindered by the services they encounter (see the clients' experiences in this book to see how much of a fine balance that often is), but their own action. As clinicians or hostel or other staff, we can provide more or less positive inputs: the outcomes are achieved by our clients, with their determination, perseverance and courage.

The processes of recovery

If we look at the processes of recovery that we identified in the story of J – the 'recovery of', 'recovery from', recovery as 'enacted aspiration' and 'recovery as not getting back to where you started from' in his story – then we can begin to identify some of the processes of recovery.

Let's start with 'recovery of'. We identified that J had had some sense of himself in relation to others and to a social space, and some socio-environmental personal sense of home; we also identified that that had been shattered. We looked, in Part 1, on the processes of social exclusion and the impact of compound trauma, how early experiences, compounded by later ones, of negative events and damaging relationships impact so damagingly on a person's sense of self, and their ability to self-regulate and self-manage. This inability to self-regulate and self-manage in turn further undermines the person's social inclusion and their sense of an integrated, coherent and valued self: in J's case, becoming violent, usually drunk, 'always messing things up', overreacting and 'exploding' at the slightest real or imaginary attack, not trusting anyone, not looking after himself, hating institutions and ending up in institutions all the time; and they don't understand why, except that it must be because they're either bad, or mad, or both. (Interestingly, the colloquial way of putting this, and the way rough sleepers often put it, is that they're 'really fucked up': this expression has a dual meaning – that they are in a serious mess inside and out, and that they have been seriously done over – which actually reflects the true situation they find themselves in, and the true experience of what's happened).

'Recovery of' for J requires a process of recovering a sense of a stable self, a self that has a valued and valuable place in a set of relationships and social spaces. As noted in Chapter 2, our internal self-representation is created by an accumulation of experience of ourselves in relation to others within an affective context (Bowlby, 1988; Fairbairn,1994; Schore, 1994; Siegel, 2015). This is both an internal and external process: internal through our experience of ourselves in terms of neglected, hurt, angry, excited, frightened or terrified, hyper- or hypo-aroused; external through the interaction with environmental and social factors, particularly initially our primary carers, and then those who later become closest to us in whatever social circles we move in (in J's case, damaged – trauma-impacted – individuals in care, in the prison system, and in the rough sleeping and drinking circuits). 'Recovery of' means that there was a state before now when the desired quality was present; as we have noted in J's story, he knew a time (and still cherishes the memory of that time, even while recognising its far-from-perfectness) when he felt integrated into a socially and environmentally contextualised sense of a self that he could enjoy being, and that could consider the world a place with positive possibilities.

So, in some ways, work with J in the 'recovery of' is work to help him get back in touch with his emotional memory of being that person. Different techniques, 'remedial methods', can be used for this by different professionals, peers and peer professionals, 'remedial agents', working with him. A psychodynamic psychotherapist might explore the reality of that time in more depth – what was good, what wasn't good, how it felt to be part of that family in that place at that time, what the experience was and what it means for J now. A cognitive therapist might want to encourage thinking about what positive skills and attitudes he learned from those times (amongst others), and what negative thinking patterns/coping strategies he may also have learned that he can seek to avoid in his here and now behaviours. A hostel or outreach worker may seek to re-create in reality or ideation some of the positives: a sense of place or 'home' (or an aspiration to have a place or home – outreach workers often have to work significantly on the client's capacity to think of a place as a positive, and to internalise the idea of 'housedness') (Adlam and Scanlon, 2006), a steady and trustworthy relationship with some affection and respect, or perhaps encourage supportive relationships with some of his more together peers in the hostel or day centres or wherever J uses. But underneath these technical interventions a process is happening which is the creation of a new experience of positive relationship and (I hope) positive environmental events for J which he can internalise as a new, or renewed, experience of himself as a positive and positively contextualised self: someone who has intrinsic value, and is externally valued and validated. The key processes are those of early development: positive regard, boundaried care, respect, non-retaliation, responsiveness and interactivity, recognition of and validation of experience, the containment of complex, challenging, and just plain horrible experiences and feelings, the containment of anger and rage, having some good times together, and offering support and encouragement. This process can often start, though, with the staff member or clinician (see the chapters on practice, and particularly John Conolly's chapter, in this book) holding the belief and hope until such time as the client can see it within themselves: as someone who was well on their recovery journey said at a St Mungo's homeless women's conference, 'I didn't believe in myself, but it seems that other people believed in me; through their belief I could begin to do things' (personal communication, 2013).

'Recovery from' for J is about recovery from compound trauma and social exclusion. We looked at the impact of compound trauma and social exclusion in Part 1 of this book; as we saw then, compound trauma impacts on the psychological and physiological level (we will look at this further in Chapters 13 and 14 of this book, on complexity and multi-morbidity). The basic motivational systems driven by our neurophysiological processes – the attachment (caregiving and care-seeking), seeking (exploratory–withdrawal/'shame'), fear (flight–fight and freeze), and hierarchical (dominant/submissive) systems – are deeply interactive with the environment (Porges, 2011; Panksepp and Biven 2012; Van der Kolk, 2014) and deeply damaged by compound trauma; once damaged, they in turn motivate the trauma-impacted person to behave in ways that are often triggers to further exclusion (Van der Kolk, 2011; see also Chapter 3). These basic motivational systems are integral to our sense of ourselves and our 'personality', because they drive much of what we do, how we react, what we feel like inside, and indeed our health and vitality (Heard, Lake and McCluskey, 2009; Lanius, Vermetten and Pain, 2010; Porges, 2011). So, there is a 'recovery from' that takes place at the neurophysiological level.

However, our actual experience of the neurophysiological happens in the realm of meanings and relationships, the 'real' world of interactions between ourselves and others, our understanding of ourselves and others, and where we find (or lose) ourselves in the context of culture, society and personal history. It's tautological, but experience is first and foremost experiential; and then it is contextualised by our meanings, which themselves derive from our personal history of experience, our cultural and social environment, and our meaning-making capacity (learned and developed). Therefore, we can say that the physiological process in 'recovery from', and the meaning-making process in 'recovery from' are inevitably and inextricably intertwined.

This means that psychosocial 'remedial methods' make absolute sense in 'recovery from'. In terms of the 'psycho' part of psychosocial, psychotherapy, whatever the modality, it is always about remaking meaning and reinterpreting experience, whether done directly as in narrative therapy (see Roberts and Holmes, 1998), in the indirect way through self-exploration in dynamic therapy, or through trying to change patterns of thinking in the cognitive approaches. As well as being about making changes in the meaning–constructs of the inner world, rearranging the object relations in psychodynamic or psychoanalytic terms, psychotherapy affects the neurophysiology underpinning those meaning constructions (Schore, 2013): it is a neurophysiological intervention (Stahl, 2012). Psychotherapists reframe meaning by validation (witnessing, testimony) and by allocating responsibility more appropriately, by stimulating mentalisation (Bateman and Fonagy, 2006) and the capacity to understand one's own and others' mental states and see the role they play in action and interaction, by stimulating the linking of thoughts and feelings, and by enabling the experience of a different kind of relationship, one that reflects a more benign caregiver/careseeker relationship and which can stimulate 'learned secure attachment' (Bowlby, 1988) and help develop better regulated, and so less volatile, affective and motivational systems (Solomon and Siegel, 2003; Porges, 2011).

It is not just formal, or informal, psychotherapy that can do this, of course: Psychologically Informed Environments (PIEs) (see elsewhere in this book for theory and practice) are also designed to support this kind of 'recovery from'. Central to them is the idea of thoughtful and reflective interaction rather than reaction, of containment and non-punitive engagements, of behaviour as communication and understanding as enabling, and the creation of an environment where people feel 'emotionally safe' as well as physically (Keats *et al.*, 2012). Managing relationships is one of the central principles of PIE, and is so in recognition of the fact that healing relationships are an enormous factor in recovery from compound trauma (Solomon and Siegel, 2003), and from homelessness (Groundswell, 2010). The therapeutic relationship is central to 'recovery from': if trauma results from bad experiences and damaging relationships, then healing arises from positive relationships and good experiences.

Of course, managing relationships is not the unique province of the PIE approach, and has been a central tenet of 'keyworking' and homelessness staff's interactions with homeless people for a long time. 'Engagement' and then trying to form a trusting relationship with rough sleepers and homeless people are central to outreach, day centre, shelter and hostel staff practice. In many cases, the way the staff enable this relationship and foster and develop it is by doing things with their clients: trying to get some of the things the client wants or is entitled to, things that would help them materially (whether benefits, sleeping bags, a shower or a bed) or with, for example, pressing health needs (medical treatment, podiatry, decent shoes) or legal support (especially for those with debt or legal status issues). This 'doing things together' creates shared experience and an opportunity for the homeless person to experience a different kind of relationship, a benign one, just as psychotherapy does; and not being psychotherapy, it can often be done in a way that feels less threatening and more informal to the homeless person, whose experience of clinicians and the sort of institutions they tend to inhabit is often quite negative. These relationships with workers through activities are part of clients' re-experiencing themselves in a positive way, and at best it again stimulates learned secure attachment (though there is an unfortunate push, usually from senior management or commissioners, often done in the name of 'efficiency' and a throughput model, to shorten or break relationships 'so that they don't become dependent'; see Chapter 14 in this book for more on this). Relationships are crucial to 'recovery from' (Groundswell, 2010; Cockersell, 2012).

For J, there was accessible psychotherapy available at the day centre he attended, good enough workers and a good enough environment in the hostel he lived in to contain his volatility and drinking, and there was a keyworker able to support him in developing and furthering his wish to do something for other people, a big step forward in recovery from homelessness and social exclusion (Groundswell, 2010), and becoming a volunteer.

Then there is 'recovery as not getting back to where you started from': for J, life really seemed to go wrong when his mother died and his father couldn't look after the children, and he was taken into care. As a psychotherapist, I would suggest it went back before that, because the home he lived in was already rocked by periodic drunken violence, and his father was already violent towards him even though he was barely of primary school age, and his mother's premature demise may well have been linked to the stress and poverty under which she lived; however, we could both agree (he and I) that it really went wrong after he was separated from his siblings and then abused by the foster carer, which seems to have happened in relatively quick succession (certainly in his narrative): he responded with 'bad' behaviour – rebelliousness, refusal to do what he was told, rudeness, truancy, and so on (he would probably have been given a load of diagnoses and drugs nowadays, but in his day the response was behavioural and reactive rather than pharmaceutical and reactive). This behaviour resulted in him being moved from place to place and beginning to get himself a label of 'unmanageable'; it also got him to a children's care home where the home manager (or 'home father' as he apparently liked to be called) tried to abuse J. J, then in his teens, hit him quite hard and several times and injured him, and J was sent to a young offenders' institution (where he was bullied, as it had a culture of bullying and being 'hard', not unlike where he had originally grown up; this began the cycle of offenders' institutions, petty crime, drinking, hostels and rough sleeping. Getting back to where he started his journey into homelessness would have meant going back to this hurt, inarticulate (because his voice was silenced rather than because he had no views), angry, volatile, 'unmanageable' person. J didn't want to be this, and neither did his workers, his 'remedial agents'.

This is the place where enhancing recovery begins to look very like developing resilience. J, as described above, and as the angry, volatile, rough sleeping drinker, was not resilient: he was reactive. And not only reactive, but reacting in any situation to his whole history, not to what was actually happening in the here and now. Having done, with support, a bit of 'recovery of' and 'recovery from', as described above – so his sense of himself as worthwhile was a bit enhanced, and his ability for affect (and therefore behaviour) regulation was also a bit enhanced – J was beginning to become more resilient.

Resilience is the ability to 'bounce back' after adverse events. It is 1. 'the capability of a strained body to recover its size and shape after deformation caused especially by compressive stress' and 2. 'an ability to recover from or adjust easily to misfortune or change' (Merriam-Webster, 2017c). As an American psychologist put it, 'Resilience does not come from rare and special qualities, but from the everyday magic of ordinary, normative human resources in the minds, brains, and bodies of children, in their families and relationships, and in their communitie' (Masten, 2001, p.235). The 'everyday magic of ordinary, normative human resources' was scarce in J's childhood, and it would have been very difficult for him to develop resilience given his story; however, the creation of a good enough network of relationships and some stability in his hostel, through his volunteering, and through psychotherapy, put him in a situation where he could develop this ability to 'bounce back' or to 'recover [his] size and shape' after 'compressive stress' (or more commonly in his life, and the lives of most rough sleepers, 'oppressive stress'). He began to see his own agency, and how what he did and thought made a difference to what happened to him in the world, and that not everything and everyone was out to get him, and that he, with the help of others when required, could make things better again, or at least survivable, when they went wrong. In psychology terms, he had a stronger ego or sense of self, a greater capacity to contextualise both his own feelings and actions and those of others, and a longer time perspective and a reduced tendency to globalise his feelings (if it's not OK now, that doesn't necessarily mean that it's never going to be OK, or that nothing at all is OK). He could tolerate the failings of his hostel more, and the stresses of his life (which were not inconsiderable – after all, he was still homeless, though living in a hostel; still in poverty; still estranged from his siblings; and still had many feelings that were hard to manage; and he still got drunk sometimes when it began to get a bit too much for his developing resilience to manage).

Resilience – the quality that is missing from the place that 'recovery as not getting back to where you started from' is concerned with – develops from experiencing the necessary ingredients for a 'secure base' (Bowlby, 1988), and the developmental interactions that underpin the ability to regulate affect and motivational systems (Schore, 1994; Van der Kolk, 2011). It requires stability, positive interactions, a good, sustained relationship with at least someone, sometimes psychotherapy, and opportunities for self-development and self-expression: client involvement is another of the key pillars of PIE, though not explicit in the original guidance, and participation in group activities, and 'giving something back' are part of the *Escape Plan*, an outline of what helps people recover from homelessness written by homeless people who have moved on (Groundswell, 2010). Again, psychosocial interventions – provided they are truly 'psycho', i.e. psychologically informed and including access to psychotherapy (see Chapter 3), and social, i.e. clients are respected and treated as equals, not 'done to' and subjected to rigid or arbitrary power dynamics – are ideal for 'recovery as not getting back to where you started from'. Or 'moving on with your life', as it could also be termed.

Finally, let's think about recovery as 'enacted aspiration'. J had often wished that his life was different. But wishing doesn't get you anywhere.

One of Freud's earliest ideas was about the struggle we experience between the 'pleasure principle' and the 'reality principle' (Freud, 1911): according to this theory, before we are born we live in a 'hallucinated reality' where our wish is met with satisfaction as we wish it – so that the idea of wanting food and the receiving of nutrition from the mother's womb coincide for the foetus. This remains pretty much the case when the baby is born, as long as the mother is well attuned to its needs; as Winnicott put it:

> The paradox is that the environment is part of the infant and at the same time it isn't…we know that we won't ask the baby, 'Did you create that object or did you find it?' because we know that the two

things are true and that he wouldn't have created it if it hadn't been there, but that he did create it... (Winnicott, 1989, p.580)

Freud went on to suggest that the ego was formed in the 'negotiation' between the pleasure principle and the reality principle (Freud, 1911): that is to say, the ego develops to psychically manage the space between the infant's hallucinated reality of wish satisfaction and the real reality of an external environment that might or might not afford satisfaction of the baby's wish. If the gap is too large, and the level of what Freud called 'un-pleasure' too great, then the infant (and infant ego) struggles to accept reality, or in the worst case does not align with reality at all (which he saw as the root of psychosis).

I go into this here because it has a bearing on the idea of recovery, and particularly the idea of recovery as 'enacted aspiration'. 'Recovery of', 'recovery from' and 'recovery as not getting back to where you started from', as described above, all have an element of being able to negotiate with and accommodate 'real' reality in them: they start off with having real relationships in the here and now with real workers or psychotherapists or psychologists, and end up with having real relationships with a range of people and situations, and being able to adapt to and get enough from situations that are, as the North Americans say, 'sub-optimal'. It means accepting and aligning with a real reality that gives you something, but is not likely to – no, let's be straightforward – will not ever just grant your wish.

An aspiration, according to the dictionary, is 'a hope or ambition of achieving something' (Oxford University, 2017). Similarly, an aspiration, in recovery terms, is not a wish. Wishes, and wish fulfilment, belong to the infantile/psychotic realm of denying or degrading reality, and belong to the pre-recovery stage, where the alcohol/drug dependent guy sits on the side of the street and wishes he could see his long-since-adopted children or that his mother had really been able to love him properly, and goes and buys another can/wrap. An aspiration – something that you hope and plan to achieve, and I would add 'in some timeframe in your lifetime' – implies a reasonable level of acceptance of external realities, and a certain amount of self-awareness of your current position in relation to reality, and a certain belief in your ability to influence reality (in the terms of Freud's idea, a certain ego strength). This is even more true when we think of the idea of an 'enacted aspiration': it is not merely 'a hope or ambition of achieving something', it is taking action in the hope or ambition of achieving something by your actions.

So in recovery as enacted aspiration, the processes are about the capacity to accept reality as it is, to be resilient, to manage affect and motivation systems, and to manage relationships, something which the client may have learned/be learning through the example of their keyworker, PIE workers, and/or psychotherapist or psychologist. It is about developing ego strength, sensitivity and awareness of others' needs and wants, and being able to negotiate with reality so that your own needs are met and those of others are respected.

This is a huge step in recovery (Groundswell, 2010). The 'remedial agents and methods' supporting it, through our therapeutic encounters with our clients, and within our therapeutic environments, are again the psychosocial interventions we have been talking about. This time, though, there is perhaps more emphasis on the social, though with continued support from the psycho because if ego strength is behind the ability to aspire, then sustaining ego strength is crucial to successfully achieving the aspiration. Workers and peer workers may support aspiration through providing information on or access to opportunities, for example, or mentoring the client in some of the tasks are that the client has identified in thinking through their aspiration, or supporting their self-belief in the face of the inevitable setbacks or stresses that reality throws up, or simply providing an extra mind to help problem-solve; there are ways too numerous to list, as each person's aspiration and what they need to achieve it will be unique. Although the client could at this stage be said to be in the latter stages of their recovery journey, they (like the rest of us) still need support and encouragement. They will still benefit from the therapeutic environment, therapeutic encounters and therapeutic relationships that we began by talking about.

J moved on from being a volunteer, and moved on from the hostel; he now has a paid job in a field he wants to work in, and a flat he calls home. He's a bit overweight and sometimes he drinks too much, though not so often nowadays; his contacts with his surviving siblings are not always positive, and are sometimes quite distressing (one won't speak or respond to him because she thinks of him as 'no good, and you were always no good', but he sees himself as still developing, and he's still hopeful, and patient; he's got some good friends; and he is able to mentor other homeless people who are trying to move on from homelessness themselves through voluntary work.

Last words on 'therapeutic' in terms of recovery

Finally, I would like to add one more thing about the therapeutic approach. I said earlier that any interaction or situation could be therapeutic, because therapeutic is a quality that we can add to any situation or interaction. I would like to just expand on that a little further.

This is a chapter about recovery, and so therapeutic here means enabling or supporting someone to embark on or enhance their recovery journey. I asked early on in this chapter, So what is this 'quality', this mysterious ingredient, that transforms any situation or encounter into a therapeutic one? Put simply, it is interacting in the situation or encounter in such a way that it enables or enhances the other person's recovery.

How do you do that? I think there are so many ways – different ones for keyworkers or outreach workers, peer mentors and volunteers, psychodynamic psychotherapists and psychologists, or psychiatrists or cognitive psychologists: each has skills special to their own field, each has skills and qualities that stem from their humanity and own personal histories and the meanings they've made of them. But there are a couple of things which I think are generally useful in turning any situation or encounter into a therapeutic one:

- If at all possible (and it can be difficult, because of our own abilities to manage our affect and motivational systems), don't react – instead, act with reflection.

- If you can't reflect at the time, take some time as soon as you can afterwards to reflect; and reflect with someone if possible.

- Ask yourself a few questions in any interaction: What is the other person trying to communicate by their action? What is going on from their perspective? What am I trying to communicate? Am I succeeding in communicating this?

- Ask yourself, this intervention or comment I'm making, who is it for? Does it add to their recovery, their development, their learning? Does it relieve their anxiety or help them contain their feelings? Or is it primarily to relieve my own anxiety and assuage my feelings, or to make me feel important, or show them who's in control?

- Think about the environment: Is it enabling, or is it oppressive? Does it encourage social or antisocial interactions? What does it say about power? What can I do to make it therapeutic?

- Think about the power dynamics in everything you do; people who have experienced trauma will be very aware of them.

- Homeless people and rough sleepers are people, and their experiences are real, and often their experiences have been (and sometimes still are) really awful. But they're still just people, like all of us are.

- Anyone can go on their own recovery journey; some will, and some won't, but interacting with hope, respect and care will help either way.

- Most homeless people who have moved on from homelessness cited one person who really made the difference for them (Groundswell, 2010). You could be that one person, and you will be for somebody: never forget how important what you say and do can be.

References

Adlam, J. and Scanlon, C. (2006) 'Housing "unhoused minds": inter-personality disorder in the organisation?' *Housing, Care and Support 9*, 3, 9–14.

Bateman, A. and Fonagy, P. (2006) *Mentalisation Based Treatment for Borderline Personality Disorders.* Oxford: Oxford University Press.

Bowlby, J. (1988) *A Secure Base.* London: Routledge.

Cockersell, P. (2012) 'Homelessness, Complex Trauma and Recovery.' In R. Johnson and R. Haigh (eds) *Complex Trauma and Its Effects.* Brighton: Pavilion.

Eisenberger, N.I., Lieberman, M.D. and Williams, K.D. (2003) 'Does rejection hurt? An FMRI study of social exclusion.' *Science 302*, 290–292.

Fairbairn, W.R.D. (1994) *Psychoanalytic Studies of the Personality.* London: Routledge.

Freud, S. (1911) 'Formulations on the Two Principles of Mental Functioning.' In P. Gay (1995) *The Freud Reader*, London: Vantage.

Groundswell (2010) *The Escape Plan.* Accessed October 2017 at http://groundswell.org.uk/what-we-do/peer-research/the-escape-plan/ www.groundswell.org.uk/theescape-plan.html

Heard, D., Lake, B. and McCluskey, U. (2009) *Attachment Therapy with Adolescents and Adults.* London: Karnac.

Keats, H., Cockersell, P., Johnson, R. and Maguire, N. (2012) Psychologically informed services for homeless people, available at http://www.rjaconsultancy.org.uk/6454%20CLG%20PIE%20operational%20document%20AW-1.pdf, accessed January 2018.

Lanius, R.A., Vermetten, E. and Pain, C. (2010) *The Impact of Early Life Trauma on Health and Disease.* Cambridge: Cambridge University Press.

Masten, A.S. (2001) 'Ordinary magic: resilience processes in development.' *American Psychologist 56*, 3, 227–238.

Merriam-Webster Dictionary (2017a) 'Therapeutic.' Accessed July 2017 at www.merriam-webster.com/dictionary/therapeutic

Merriam-Webster Dictionary (2017b) 'Adjective.' Accessed July 2017 at www.merriam-webster.com/dictionary/adjective

Merriam-Webster Dictionary (2017c) 'Resilience.' Accessed July 2017 at www.merriam-webster.com/dictionary/resilience

Oxford University (2017) 'Aspiration.' Accessed December 2017 at https://en.oxforddictionaries.com/definition/aspiration

Panksepp, J. and Biven, L. (2012) *The Archaeology of Mind.* London: Norton.

Porges, S.W. (2011) *The Polyvagal Theory.* London: Norton.

Prochaska, J.O. and DiClemente, C.C. (1982) 'Transtheoretical therapy: toward a more integrative model of change.' *Psychotherapy: Theory, Research and Practice 19*, 3, 276–288.

Roberts, G. and Holmes, J. (1998) *Healing Stories.* Oxford: Oxford University Press.

Schore, A. (1994) *Affect Regulation and the Origin of the Self.* New Jersey: Laurence Erlbaum.

Schore, A. (2013) *The Science of the Art of Psychotherapy.* London: Norton.

Siegel, D. (2015) *The Developing Mind*, 2nd edition. London: Norton.

Solomon, M. and Siegel, D. (eds) (2003) *Healing Trauma.* London: Norton.

Stahl, S.M. (2012) 'Psychotherapy as an epigenetic "drug".' *Journal of Clinical Pharmacy and Therapeutics 37*, 3, 249–253.

Van der Kolk, B. (2011) 'Foreword.' In *The Polyvagal Theory.* London: Norton.

Van der Kolk, B. (2014) *The Body Keeps the Score.* London: Penguin.

Winnicott, D.W.W. (1989) *Psychoanalytic Explorations.* London: Karnac.

5

APPLYING PSYCHOLOGY AS A RESPONSE TO THE IMPACT OF SOCIAL EXCLUSION

PIE and Psychotherapy in Homelessness Services

DR PETER COCKERSELL

Introduction: why apply psychology?

In this chapter I am going to describe the principles of three overarching ways in which we can apply psychology in order to deliver more effective services for homeless people; however, this begs the question, why apply psychology? What is it about psychology that makes us imagine that it will or can deliver more effective homelessness services?

I think the answer lies in the analysis of the problem. What problem are we trying to solve? First of all we have to decide if it is a problem about housing, or a problem about people: the answer is usually both – fairly obviously homelessness is about people who need housing. But that's only very partial, as we saw in the opening chapter. For very many people, and for the chronically homeless, and for the people we have been thinking about, people who have experienced compound trauma and social exclusion, it's in reality a problem about people having wretched lives, of which homelessness is just a part. This is the problem we are trying to solve: how do we help people to no longer have lives blighted by trauma?

We could try and change society, and change the world: society is often unjust and uncaring, deeply unequal and unfair, and can be extremely hostile and damaging to the vulnerable, especially if their vulnerability threatens society's own sense of what is good and right about itself. And, of course, we should try to change society and the world, and make our culture a more caring one, that values human integrity more than money. But that is a big job, and we're not going to achieve it right away, if ever, and if we devote our lives to doing that then we probably will be too busy to help this person here, the one we stepped over, if not on the way to the opera, at least on the way to catch the train to work.

The problem we are trying to answer then is not how to change the world, but how we help the person on the street here and now, how we help the woman we imagined in Chapter 3, Bea: that requires a more immediate answer. And again, we have to analyse the problem: what is Bea's problem that we can help with? This is essentially what we were doing in Chapters 1–3, analysing the problem. And the thing that we came up with was that the experiences that led to people becoming chronically homeless or rough sleepers was compound trauma: we realised that people affected by compound trauma became socially excluded through psychological and social processes. We also recognised that people who are homeless need housing. So there are two problems we are trying to help Bea resolve: one is that she needs somewhere safe to live, which is relatively straightforward if housing is available; and the other is that she needs some help with the effects of compound trauma, in the short term to ensure she takes care of herself and her health, and in the longer term to support her in (re)covering the capacity to function successfully in interaction with society. This second problem (problem because it's a problem *for* her) has two dimensions, a social one and a psychological one. Housing and social responses of one sort or another to homelessness have been around for a long time, but not so the use of psychology. This seems odd from what we understand; as a respondent report in Focus Ireland's evaluation of psychology in services put it:

> So what you have are clients who need really good high quality psychological services and in truth without the provision of those services it is hard for me to imagine how any other intervention can be effective around housing or stabilising people's lives. It is astonishing to me that it has taken us this long to establish posts like these [Counselling Psychologists] in services like this because it is such an essential part of the jigsaw. (Focus Ireland, 2014, p.62)

Just a note about the word 'psychology'. I am using the word in the formal sense, not the lay sense as in 'you need to use a bit of psychology', especially when trying to motivate or support others to do something they may not immediately want to do. I use psychology as a generic term for the two-pronged scientific task of trying to understand how our minds work, and trying to understand how to use this knowledge for therapeutic ends. There are many different branches of psychology – psychoanalytic, psychodynamic, behaviouralist, cognitive, humanistic, to name some of the more dominant ones – and they are often at loggerheads with each other over things that to outsiders may seem strangely parochial, 'fighting like sharks in a teacup' as my old chief executive put it (personal communication). I am using the term generically to mean all forms of psychology, because I know that different services use different models, though the great majority are psychodynamic. Despite the use of different models, I think that there are principles which are common to all the services that work effectively with homeless people and rough sleepers, and it is these that I will try to focus on principally.

This chapter is divided into three parts, because it seems to me that there are three overarching ways in which psychology is being used in an effort to improve the effectiveness of services working with homeless people and others who have experienced compound trauma. These are through delivering:

1. informal or formal psychotherapy, either in individual or group settings

2. services which use psychologists or psychotherapists as part of their staffing, and work within a psychological model

3. psychosocial interventions which are, essentially, social interventions with a therapeutic purpose and designed with the input of psychology into how the therapeutic purpose is delivered.

I am going to look at the principles of practice and the outcomes, potential and realised, associated with these three different forms of what could be called instances of 'applied psychology'.

The examples are all derived from services which I have either been directly involved with, or have known well, while working as a senior manager and/or as a psychoanalytic psychotherapist in homelessness.

These are services designed to work within the theoretical paradigms outlined in the previous three chapters: they take the understandings from neurobiologically and psychodynamically informed psychology and apply them to effective working with people who have experience of compound trauma and social exclusion, and present with complex needs. The principles I outline are drawn from my own practical experience of these services, informed by my understanding of psychological, and specifically psychodynamic, theory. My understanding of psychology, in turn, has been immensely influenced by working in and with these services. It has also been influenced by my life experience, by my clinical training, and by my own experience of having psychotherapy. Finally, my understanding of psychology and the role it can play has been deeply influenced by my experience as a therapist, and particularly the time I have spent working with homeless people, refugees and rough sleepers, many with histories of compound trauma and presenting with 'complex needs': they have been amazing people to work with, and I have learned a huge amount from them.

Informal or formal psychotherapy, delivered in group or individual settings

I will start with psychotherapy services, because this is perhaps the most direct, or at least the most obvious, application of psychology. People who have experienced compound trauma have psychological and emotional problems, so it seems evidently useful and helpful to make psychological therapy available for them. There are accounts of psychotherapy services of different sorts in different settings in Part 3 of this book: here I'm going to look mainly at the principles I think underpin effective psychotherapy with homeless people and rough sleepers, drawing on the experience of the other authors in this book, other psychotherapy services I know, my own experience as a clinician in a psychotherapy service for homeless people, and as a director setting up and overseeing a psychotherapy service for homeless people.

As a clinician, I worked part time for four years as a psychotherapist within NHS Westminster's (then Westminster PCT's) specialist homeless health provision. I set up a service in a day centre, and also worked some of the time from a specialist homelessness primary care practice. I had previously worked for just over four years in St Thomas's Hospital psychotherapy department, where I had worked long term with some rehoused, ex-homeless people with complex needs. My experiences in these two services, but particularly in the former, deeply influenced what I have done since – including the setting up of LifeWorks (see below) and what I see as the principles of effective psychotherapy with homeless people.

As a service director, I set up a psychotherapy service called LifeWorks for homeless people working with or living in St Mungo's services in 2007; it is still running today, and one of the authors of this book tells of her experience setting up a women's psychotherapy and psychosocial service as a specialised project within the LifeWorks service. LifeWorks is staffed by fully qualified and experienced psychodynamic psychotherapists and has, over its history, been able to offer up to a hundred individual sessions of one-to-one psychotherapy per week. Some of its early outcomes are documented in an article I wrote (Cockersell, 2011). Here, I will focus on providing an outline of the model, partly because it informs the principles I describe further on, and partly because it may be helpful for others who are running, or setting up, psychotherapy services for the homeless.

LifeWorks psychotherapy service model

LifeWorks provides one-to-one formal psychodynamic psychotherapy to homeless people and rough sleepers who are either living in, or in contact with, St Mungo's services. It has also at times provided psychotherapy to other homeless people, or people at risk of homelessness, including for example:

- rough sleepers on London Councils' '209' list, a list of the most 'entrenched' chronic rough sleepers in London

- people working with the South London and Maudsley NHS Foundation Trust's street psychiatric team, START

- people being discharged from a medium secure forensic unit to 'halfway housing' in the community

- people who had been abstinent and working with substance use aftercare, who, at after around one year to eighteen months' abstinence were at risk of relapse because of 'identity crisis'.

STAFFING

The service was and is staffed by a number of highly skilled, experienced and fully qualified (UKCP, BPC) psychodynamic psychotherapists, led by an extremely competent manager, who is also well-trained and deeply experienced in mental health and working with people experiencing mental health problems; sometimes it has had administrative support, especially when trying to do evaluations, and sometimes it has had to manage without. It has high staff retention.

Staff received regular group clinical supervision from long-term qualified and experienced psychodynamic or psychoanalytic clinicians; we always used two supervisors, and they were always external to St Mungo's, either freelance or NHS. The psychotherapists received regular management supervision as well by the service manager, who in turn received supervision with the service director (me, when I worked there).

There was also a regular reflective practice group for staff, which included the manager.

The psychotherapists were paid at a high rate for the third sector, equivalent to NHS Band 8, because we wanted to attract high-quality clinicians; whether the pay was instrumental or not, we succeeded.

CLIENTS

The clients of the service, apart from those specific contracts listed above, were simply homeless people or rough sleepers in contact with, or living in, St Mungo's services. The referral system was either by the client's keyworker or self-referral. The only criterion, apart from being a St Mungo's client, was a willingness to come to therapy. Clients had various diagnoses and none; large numbers of clients had characteristics that would meet the diagnostic criteria of personality disorder, but few had diagnoses (in the hostel where the service was first piloted, a clinical psychologist who had come in to do some research found that around 60 per cent met the clinical criteria for personality disorder, but only 8 per cent had a personality disorder diagnosis); episodic psychosis was common; diagnosed psychotic conditions were around the rough sleeping population average of about 30 per cent; there was a lot of depression, more anxiety, and high levels of drug and alcohol use. There were also many with histories of adverse childhood events, as noted in Chapter 1:

- forty-seven per cent experience of neglect/emotional abuse
- thirty-four per cent early loss of parents through abandonment, separation or divorce
- thirty-one per cent early loss of parents through death (including murder and suicide)
- twent-seven per cent sexual abuse
- high levels of parental alcoholism, drug use, and domestic violence.

LOCATION OF THERAPY

The psychotherapy was delivered where the clients were: first of all mainly in hostels, but when we realised that many of the clients did not want to see the therapists in their own hostel, we also saw people in offices, GP surgeries (where we rented rooms), and day centres and other places where there were therapy rooms (e.g. for a time we had a partnership with a small charity that provided support in getting homeless people back to work: St Mungo's helped them to refurbish a section of their building into therapy/meeting rooms, and then used them for a reduced fee to see LifeWorks clients). It's worth noting that for almost all other health- or wellbeing-related services for homeless people with which I have been involved, to ensure a good take-up it has been crucial to locate the service where the homeless people are. This was true for needle exchanges, substitute prescribing services, primary healthcare, podiatry, TB and other screenings, etc; it has not been true for therapy. Clients often prefer to be a certain distance from their 'homelessness-homes' (hostels, shelters, etc.), it seems, to safely go to the wounded places that they can visit in therapy.

The main requisite of wherever the therapy was held is that it should be private, relatively quiet, likely to be undisturbed for the therapeutic hour, and that it could be used regularly and consistently by the therapist to receive their clients. This was not always an easy thing to achieve. For all sorts of reasons – including unconscious attacks on the space for psychotherapy, to which I shall return later in this chapter – it was and is often a continuing struggle to provide a safe place for the client to engage in regular therapy. The LifeWorks manager had to spend an enormous amount of time, energy and skilful negotiation to try to enable the creation and retention of the therapeutic space.

MODEL OF PSYCHOTHERAPY

When the service was first started, we experimented with the model of concurrent individual and group therapy, following the example of some NHS services working with people with diagnoses of personality disorder. This never worked: the clients wouldn't come to group therapy. The reason they gave was largely pragmatic – it wasn't safe to disclose vulnerability to a group of peers who they would very likely have to have dealings with both in hostels and on the streets. There was more to it than this, of course; we had enormous difficulty at first in trying to establish group reflective practice for the staff as well – we found a generalised resistance to 'groupishness' in staff and clients. We also noticed that stable, regular groups are very much not a pattern among homeless people. There are plenty of groups which may appear stable – drinking 'schools', congregations of rough sleepers in a particular location (called 'hotspots' by outreach teams) but on the whole these groups are formed of transient members: there is always a group there, but it is not made up of the same people. One-off groups, even therapeutic ones, might be quite well attended, but ongoing groups would rarely have more than one, if that, of the same people turn up two weeks in a row. We decided to abandon groups, despite magnificent perseverance by the group therapist we had recruited at the beginning.

Psychotherapists have worked with an extraordinary range of people in an extraordinary range of ways within a psychodynamic framework; engagement in deep therapy has often been a slow and painful process, and perseverance and 'holding hope' have been notable qualities of the therapists.

The length of intervention has become more formally flexible. It was originally, as much for costing purposes as because of any clinical evidence, set up as a 25-week intervention. Analysis of the data from the first three years showed that there were a significant number of people who needed and were using longer periods of therapy than 25 weeks; and also a significant number of people using far shorter periods – three to five sessions. There were relatively few in the 10–20 sessions section of the distribution. Following this, LifeWorks has offered psychotherapy, and the length of the engagement has been part of the negotiation within the therapy itself. In fact, the classical therapeutic 'contract', instead of being something that the therapist imposes from the start, becomes more a part of the therapy – something which I think is clinically positive, and probably a better (i.e more therapeutic) way of working. The transitional space itself is co-created by therapist and therapee, not just what goes on within it.

Fairly consistently over the years, LifeWorks has had engagement rates (people returning after the first session for more) of around 70 per cent, and overall attendance rates of around 75 per cent. Considering the attachment backgrounds of most clients, their busy-ness because of drug and alcohol consumption and the pressures of homeless life (especially rough sleeping), and the natural reticence of people who have experienced compound trauma to want to work through issues of the past, these are amazing attendance rates. They are echoed by other psychotherapy services presented in this book, and elsewhere. There seems to be in some quarters a clinical belief that homeless people cannot engage with formal psychotherapy: that is not the experience of LifeWorks.

However, having said that, the psychotherapists are incredibly flexible, and able and willing to work with the material that the clients bring, and at their pace, and not to set agendas or work to set timeframes, schemas, or seek predetermined outcomes. They are also willing and able to work with clients with their dogs in the room or their cans in the room; they are willing to be in spaces the client feels safe in, which may be outside the normal comfort zone of the therapist; they are willing to work with people who take drugs and who drink; they are willing to work with people who smell; they are willing to work with people who may only engage sporadically, attending every other session, or disappear for a few months and reappear and restart. The psychotherapists are amazingly flexible within the boundaries of psychodynamic thinking, and the boundaries of working *with* the client to enable the client to better think through their situation.

Engagement rates have been consistently high since the service began, with around 70 per cent of those who come for a first session continuing into therapy, and overall attendance rates have been consistently high at around 75 per cent: they have been very high when working with people with diagnoses of 'severe and enduring mental illness', e.g. schizophrenia (over 90%) and lower with rough sleepers, for example the '209' (still around 65%).

The great achievement of the psychotherapists of LifeWorks, it seems to me, has been that they have worked with the people who have come to the service. They have not said, 'You don't meet the criteria',

'You're not psychologically minded', or 'You're not capable', despite very often struggling to find a way to establish a true therapeutic alliance with people so damaged and so wary of supposed 'caregiving'.

The psychotherapists have shown remarkable resourcefulness and clinical skill in not asking the client in effect 'What is your pathology?' as so many services do, but instead asking themselves 'How can I work therapeutically with this person?' This to me is the essence and most fundamental principle of psychotherapy with the homeless.

OUTCOMES

There have been no RCTs on LifeWorks. I spent two years working with the Institute of Psychiatry and the National Institute of Health Research, and talking to various universities including UCL, and we could not see how to devise an RCT – the favoured method of the health leadership, and particularly NICE's – that would not significantly compromise the clinical work of the service. My view is that RCTs are not the appropriate tool for psychotherapy research, a view supported by most psychotherapy bodies (see UKCP, 2011), nor are they necessarily the gold standard for research (Cartwright, 2007). Be that as it may, LifeWorks does have practice-based evidence for its effectiveness.

LifeWorks was originally funded by the Cabinet Office as part of the 'Adults Facing Chronic Exclusion' (ACE) programme. Their funding included costs for an evaluation using the South London and Maudsley's evidence-based Wellbeing Assessment Scale; this showed that LifeWorks improved overall wellbeing in 75 per cent of their clients. If you take the figures for those referred or self-referred to LifeWorks, including those who never made it to the first session, and you take this figure of increased wellbeing as significant of 'moving to recovery' – a more robust measure than the NHS's flagship Improving Access to Psychological Therapies (IAPT) programme's – then the referral-to-recovery rate for LifeWorks is 55 per cent. IAPT, working with a far less damaged population, and using the Department of Health's own figures, achieved a referral-to-recovery rate of just 12 per cent (Griffiths and Steen, 2013).

Positive change in LifeWorks clients' overall social functioning, measured using the Outcome Star, a system for measuring changes in social functioning among homeless people which has become the UK standard measure (Homeless Link, 2017) also increased, in this case in 100 per cent of LifeWorks clients; interestingly, it increased significantly more in LifeWorks clients than it did over the same timescales of other homeless people residing in the same hostels who didn't attend LifeWorks (Cockersell, 2011).

The Cabinet Office evaluation, which sadly was never published, also found that LifeWorks was an economically positive intervention from a health service perspective: the cost of the intervention (based on the 25-week average duration of therapy) was covered within 18 months by reduced use of emergency healthcare by those who had received it; given the disproportionately large health expenditure associated with the chronic homeless (NHS Hammersmith, 2013), this is an important point – accessible psychotherapy services for homeless people will save them money over the medium (>two years) term.

LifeWorks' psychotherapy has not just produced positive outcomes in wellbeing and overall health though – it has produced a wide range of positive outcomes, including 42 per cent of LifeWorks clients taking up employment, education or training opportunities (double the figure for other clients of St Mungo's not engaged with LifeWorks) (Cockersell, 2011), and an 84 per cent improvement in housing situation for the members of the '209' with whom LifeWorks worked (some showed no improvement because they were stable in hostels by the time LifeWorks worked with them; only one person LifeWorks worked with who was living on the streets did not become housed during their therapy).

PRINCIPLES OF PSYCHOTHERAPY WITH THE HOMELESS

- *Accessibility* – Accessibility means that clients can easily get to see a skilled clinician the first time they use the service. It's no use having long waiting lists, lots of preconditions, narrow referral criteria, layers of assessment: psychotherapy for the homeless has to be available directly to be accessible, and the first meeting is part of the therapeutic engagement and has to be done by a skilled therapist. One of the reasons that NHS therapies are so hard to access for homeless people is all the rigmarole preceding an actual encounter with a therapist.

- *No diagnostic criteria for acceptance/exclusion* – Most of the clients have a presentation that could bring about many different diagnoses, depending on the day and the mood of the client, the orientation and interests of the clinician, and the focus of the interview, but successful therapy is about the whole person in their life as it is now in the situation it's in. That never fits simple diagnostic criteria, but particularly not for people with histories of compound trauma and presentations of complex needs.

- *No exclusion because of drug and alcohol dependency* – Many, the majority, of homeless people and rough sleepers with histories of compound trauma use drugs and alcohol, and a significant proportion are dependent (see Chapter 1 for more data). Realistically, as psychotherapists we have to work with the person who comes to see us, not the person we wish they were: that goes for all people, not just homeless people. If many or most homeless people are drug/alcohol users/dependent, then that is part of their experience of life, their inner world and their mental state. My experience is that many alcohol-dependent people really struggled to use as little alcohol as they could survive with before coming to therapy: out of respect, I used to try to schedule their appointments for as early as possible. As Consultant Psychiatrist Anne Read put it, 'even with someone intoxicated, the presence of someone interested, accessible and non-judgemental may be therapeutic. Consistency and containment gradually replace what has been being sought through drug use and thus allow a space to develop in which an individual can begin to explore themselves, their drug use, and its meaning' (Read, 2002). There is evidence elsewhere in this book of various successful psychotherapy interventions with people dependent on drugs/alcohol: in many cases psychotherapy enables the person to seek drug treatment, because what is really their problem, what is causing the distress they are trying to manage with substance dependency, has begun to be attended to.

- *Good boundaries* – Good boundaries are crucial, but this doesn't mean exclusion criteria! Good boundaries need to be held around and within the therapy and the therapeutic relationship: psychic and interpersonal boundaries, professional boundaries and boundaries within the system within which the therapist is working. Good boundaries are multifaceted. They include confidentiality, and honesty. They include being there:

absolutely reliably being there in the place and time you say you will be, and staying there for the whole session even if the client doesn't turn up till the last three minutes. They mean listening carefully and attentively, and protecting yourself and the client from hostile projections and unconscious enactments as far as you can. They mean the therapist holding the boundary in a very direct way, because the room and the setting may not be as inviolate as one would want because of unconscious attacks by the hosts of the setting (see Brown *et al.*, 2011). Holding the boundary may well mean creating the boundary as part of the therapy, much in the same way as creating the contract becomes part of the therapy. However, having a strong but flexible and understanding boundary is crucial when working with people who have experienced major transgressions of their boundaries, or indeed little clear establishment of self-boundaries at all.

- *Qualified clinicians* – Open access psychotherapy means the psychotherapists need to be able to work with whatever the client brings, and that takes a good training in the background, and well-developed skills in the foreground.

- *Eclectic practice* – The work is challenging, and the context is challenging, and strict adherence to and application of any model of standard psychotherapy will miss the complex interactions with the clients and misunderstand what is going on in the therapeutic dyad and therapeutic dynamic. These are not textbook clients, these are the people who are excluded from RCTs because they wouldn't meet the criteria and wouldn't comply with the course of treatment. Therapists need to be able to adapt their practice, within good clinical theory and guidance, to work with what the clients bring in a way that the clients can use – the technique may be from psychodynamic or cognitive approaches, or pretty much any other, as long as it meets the criteria of clinical usefulness: 'Is what I am doing/saying likely to be therapeutic and why?' is the question the clinician needs to ask, continuously. And if it is, good. In fact, whatever their original orientation, and whether psychotherapists, clinical psychologists or counselling psychologists, all the clinicians I have met working effectively with homeless people have used an eclectic practice, with techniques taken from more than one theoretical school.

- *Good staff support and supervision* – The work is extremely challenging, the clients can be very challenging, the context can be very challenging. Regular reflective practice groups and frequent clinical supervision, from clinicians who either have experience of this kind of work or can be flexible enough in their conceptualisations to enable the therapists to critically explore their work are essential. And a base the clinicians can call their own, and retreat to at times, is also important.

- *Good management* – The logistics of psychotherapy within homelessness contexts can be quite complex and threaten to undermine the whole therapeutic endeavour. A good manager helps hold the boundaries around the whole service, both psychically and actually. They protect the psychotherapists.

- *Funding* – This is difficult work and needs skilled people to do it well, and they should be paid. LifeWorks was originally funded by the Cabinet Office as a pilot. Since then it has been funded by a mixture of charitable trusts, local authorities, London Councils, and by St Mungo's itself, with different proportions at different times. It is sadly notable that it has never been funded by either a Primary Care Trust or a Clinical Commissioning Group (CCG). Some CCGs do fund some specialist, accessible psychotherapy for homeless people, but not nearly enough, given the major failure of NHS psychological therapies to work with this client group.

- *Acknowledgement* – Fundamentally, the creation of a psychotherapy service for homeless people requires acknowledgement from the senior management of homelessness service providers, from the clinical leads of CCGs, and from those who fund homelessness services that compound trauma plays a big role in chronic homelessness – it's what keeps the revolving door revolving – and that accessible psychological therapies are not a luxury add-on to homelessness responses. It is cost effective and clinically effective, and helps people turn their lives around.

Psychotherapy isn't the answer to everything, or the answer for everyone; but that is no reason to deny it to people who might well benefit from it. The evidence is that accessible psychotherapy following the principles above produces significant benefits for many homeless people. I believe people who have experienced compound trauma and social exclusion in the way so many homeless people and rough sleepers have should be able to expect – indeed have the right to expect – accessible psychotherapy if they want to try it.

Every homelessness service should have access to accessible psychotherapy, because every homeless person should.

Services which use psychologists or psychotherapists as part of their staffing, and work within a psychological model

In some European countries, employing a psychologist within a homelessness service is seen as standard. However, most do not do much therapeutic work: they are generally used more for assessment to identify or justify referrals along particular routes out of homelessness or into other services. Equally, few that I have seen have been integrated into the daily work of the homelessness teams; rather they provide a sort of parallel service, seeing the same clients, but not acting as part of the team providing support. They are separate, acting in a complementary role rather than an integral one. I am sure this is a useful and valid model: it enables a depth of assessment that lay staff could not achieve (see Castaldo, Filoni and Punzi, 2014), and the assessment then carries the weight of a clinical professional which usually means it opens doors and often funding that a lay assessment cannot. However, I think it underplays the benefits that having a psychological professional in the homelessness staffing set-up can bring.

In Britain, employing psychologists or psychotherapists in a homelessness service has been far less common. Some services have had psychotherapy as part of their provision and have had psychologists or psychotherapists coming into the service to deliver their intervention, but again this has been as a complementary rather than an integrated part of the service. Indeed, psychotherapeutic confidentiality has often been seen to militate against integration in such situations, and the psychotherapy service has been quite separate or split off. I am not intending to criticise this – I think there is an essential level of confidentiality for a psychotherapy service to feel safe for its clients – but to suggest that it is a different thing to what we are considering here.

Having psychologists or psychotherapists integrated into a homelessness service creates a different sort of service. Over the last six years or so, in Britain and Ireland this has been formalised into the kind of service called a Psychologically Informed Environment (PIE).

I will go a little bit into the aetiology of PIEs (because where something comes from is important to understanding it), and then describe the principles of PIE and something of the practice and impact of PIEs. A more in-depth exploration of a PIE in practice is contained in Dr Williamson's account of the Lambeth/SLaM PIE (Chapter 6).

In describing the work linking compound trauma with homelessness in Chapter 1, I mentioned how, under Helen Keats' leadership, *Psychologically Informed Services for Homeless People*, which became known as 'the PIE guidance', was published in 2012 (Keats *et al.*, 2012). Helen Keats was at the time national advisor on rough sleeping to the Department of Communities and Local Government (DCLG). The co-authors of the guidance were Dr Nick Maguire of Southampton University, myself (at the time Director of Health and Recovery at St Mungo's) and Robin Johnson. It is Robin Johnson's part that I would like to draw attention to here, partly because he was the originator of the title 'psychologically informed environments', but mainly because he was a major guiding influence in developing the concept in the way it developed. Without him, PIEs would probably have never been conceived, and certainly not in the way they have been.

Prior to working with Helen's group on trauma and homelessness, Robin, a psychiatric social worker by background, had been deeply involved with Rex Haigh, a psychiatrist, and the Royal College of Psychiatry in developing a set of principles for psychiatric care called *Enabling Environments* (Johnson and Haigh, 2011). The RC Psych has since developed *Enabling Environments* into an accredited quality assurance benchmark (RC Psych, 2017). Rex Haigh himself, then Department of Health (DH) national advisor on personality disorders, came from a background of therapeutic communities for people experiencing severe mental health problems, for which he set out some defining principles (Haigh, 2013). Bizarrely, the *Enabling Environments* work has been more influential in prison services and the criminal justice system than it has in psychiatric services. The prison service had its own tradition of therapeutic communities facilitated by psychotherapists, and it developed an approach based on the principles of *Enabling Environments* and therapeutic communities, with a strong presence of psychology/psychotherapy, which it called Psychologically Informed Planned Environments (PIPEs).

Robin brought his knowledge and understanding of PIPEs to Helen's group, with its expertise in psychology, psychotherapy, homelessness and rough sleeping, the guidance was published (Keats *et al.*, 2012), and PIEs were born. Interestingly, the guidance was launched at a series of events organised by Homeless Link, the National Housing Federation, and the Mental Health Network of the NHS Confederation, a statement of the importance of integrated housing and mental healthcare for homeless people.

Principles of PIE

The guidance proposed five key principles in developing PIEs:

- developing a psychological framework
- the physical environment and social spaces
- staff training and support
- managing relationships
- evaluation of outcomes.

(Keats *et al.*, 2012, p.7)

The guidance expands on each of these 'key areas' in turn:

- 'Developing a psychological framework' is defined as having a 'school of thought on human development and personal change...made explicit to all staff. They should be clear about what changes each approach is designed to enable in the individual, how they themselves will need to work and what support the organisation can offer during this process' (p.8).

- 'Designing and managing the social environment is central to developing a psychologically informed service. Thoughtful design, preferably one with service user input, based on thinking through the intentions behind a service, can result in useful changes in the way a building is used, and how it is valued by staff and clients' (p.17).

- 'Staff training and support is…central to the transition into psychologically aware services…A key element to psychologically informed services is the introduction of reflective practice' (p.21).
- 'A focus on managing relationships is perhaps at the heart of what makes a psychologically informed environment different. In this model, relationships are seen as a principal tool for change, and every interaction between staff and clients is an opportunity for development and learning. Rather than seeing the management or staff role as simply trying to contain, control or even manage behaviours, their main role is to encourage the capacity to self-manage' (p.24).
- 'Evaluations are crucial because they are a cornerstone of reflective practice, which in turn is a cornerstone of psychologically informed environments. If you do not know what impact what you do or say is having, how can you know whether it is positive and how can you improve it?' (p.26).

(Keats *et al.*, 2012)

In discussion, the authors of the guidance agree that two more will be included when there is a second edition (personal communications). These will be:

- client participation
- access to psychological therapy.

Some of the thinking for including them in the new edition is as follows:

- *Client participation.* Client participation was implied in the original guidance, but we feel should be made explicit as it is part of the therapeutic work of the service. If clients feel shared ownership of the service, feel respected as equals, feel that they are heard and that what they say matters and can bring about changes in what happens, then they feel safer and more empowered and responsible. It enables experiencing in practice the sort of internal changes that PIEs seek to promote: changes from fear-based personal strategies arising from compound trauma to strategies that recognise interdependence, reciprocity, respect and negotiation.

- *Access to psychological therapy.* This, we feel, should be included because many, though by no means all, of the people who have experienced compound trauma over many years find it very difficult to come to terms with, and to move on from, without some expert help. Practice-based evidence suggests that various forms of psychological therapy helps them do this, so long as it is accessible and follows the principles outlined earlier in this chapter. It also alleviates the burden on the staff of the service. Homelessness service staff are exposed to a lot of 'vicarious trauma' by witnessing traumatic events, and by listening to accounts of trauma that they do not usually have the time or skills to help the client process effectively – for example, though it is important that a member of staff knows if someone has been the victim of abuse because that helps inform their interactions, it is not necessarily helpful for the staff member to be exposed to the full traumatic reality of that abuse: what is helpful for the member of staff, and for the client, is to be able to refer the client to someone who is able, and has the dedicated time, to work with the processes and reality of past or current traumatic experience. In practice, this usually means setting up specialised psychological therapy services because mainstream services are not accessible, or do not have sufficiently or appropriately qualified staff to work with this client group.

Some key factors in the implementation of PIE

Next, I want to consider some of the key factors in implementing PIE. There are many services run along the PIE principles now, in Britain, in Ireland and elsewhere: services whose target client groups are, for example rough sleepers, homeless families, young people, children, women, women involved in prostitution, people with severe and enduring mental illness diagnoses or people with dual diagnosis. Some have grown organically into PIEs, some have been set up as PIEs, some have adopted PIEs because the idea excited them, some have adopted the PIE approach because commissioners demanded it of them. The way in which PIE has been implemented in all these different circumstances, of course, varies. But there are some key factors which seem to help determine the success, or at least the ease, of the implementation and its impact.

These include:

- *Senior management buy-in and support.* It becomes very difficult to run a service in a psychologically informed way if the senior management are operating to another agenda because they will make decisions and apply procedures and processes that undermine the work of the service. Senior management need to understand the principles of PIE, but also understand something of the implications for their practice: their role becomes supportive of the process of change, which is actually led by the team, local manager and psychologist/psychotherapist in partnership with the clients within the service. Just as the service provides a containing, safe environment for the personal development of the clients, so senior management's role is to provide a containing, safe environment for the service and service staff to do their work. In practice, this often means shielding the service as far as possible from some of the attacks on good care and support enacted in the name of austerity or efficiency. The individual trauma experience of the clients is often mirrored in the collective trauma experience of the services that offer them support, and to a large extent it is down to senior management to mitigate this as far as possible. Some thinking derived from clinical models (in this case, psychologically informed thinking) is required of senior management in effective care organisations, beyond and above business models.

- *Introduction of reflective practice.* Reflective practice is at the core of PIE (and other good practice in care organisations). Ensuring time is set aside for reflective practice, and that a suitable location and external expert facilitation is provided, is a simple but crucial way in which management can support the PIE process. The principles of reflective practice are outlined by Donald Schön (Schön, 2016), who first coined the term in the 1960's. For PIE, I would recommend a clinically trained facilitator, either a psychotherapist or psychologist, with experience of PIEs; this also brings the benefits of embedding PIE training and development within the routine of the service and maximises the impact of initial PIE training. Different PIEs have adopted different frequencies of formal reflective practice meetings, from weekly to monthly; monthly would be a minimum. It takes some time for reflective practice to embed and for the staff to really develop ownership of the meetings, so management needs to allow time (one year plus) for reflective practice to develop. Reflective practice is not clinical supervision: it is a space within which the staff team can develop their thinking around what happens in the service.

- *Psychological support.* Psychologists and psychotherapists, through their training and experience in clinical practice, have a particular expertise and knowledge in the theory and application of psychological insights into the impact of trauma and developmental disturbances, the meaning of behaviours in terms of personal perspectives, and the processes of change and resistance to change. Well-qualified psychologists and psychotherapists have also spent years in their own personal therapy, and have a good understanding of the interplay of emotions and unconscious processing of experience between people, including themselves. They offer the team and the clients an invaluable resource in terms of training, facilitation of reflective practice and direct clinical work; they also offer the potential, through collaborative work with the project management, for service management that is aligned with the dynamic processes of change in play there, rather than (as is unfortunately often the case) at odds with it. In terms of implementation, this requires the recruitment or secondment of a qualified clinician, either part- or full-time, and clear delineation of their duties in respect of service management, service staff and direct client work. A minimum requirement is to have a psychologist or psychotherapist to facilitate regular (at least monthly) reflective practice groups: this is the bottom line for psychological support.

- *Training.* It makes sense for the whole staff team, including management, to undergo training in the PIE approach together: as long as the training is discursive and experiential, this fosters a team understanding of PIE and how the principles are applied to the particular service that is being offered and the specific client group being worked with. Training should not be only for the frontline staff: it is important that middle and senior management have some training in PIE too, ideally adapted for their particular roles in the organisation. PIE works best when it is supported by informed management, not undermined by management focused on other priorities and ignorant of the basic practice requirements of PIE implementation, such as a degree of service flexibility and autonomy, or control of their environment, or space and support for thinking. Training is then reinforced through the reflective practice groups (it is helpful if the clinician responsible for reflective practice either deliver/co-delivers, or at least participates in, the whole-team PIE training).

- *Staff participation/champions.* As one of the purposes of the PIE approach is to encourage a more thoughtful approach from the staff, it is important to allow them some autonomy in making decisions based on those thoughts; a process whereby staff can influence how services are delivered is therefore helpful. A PIE should be able to be responsive. The more the staff take ownership of the PIE approach, the more embedded it will become in the service ethos; one way of doing this is to develop local champions who can support the delivery of PIE by developing particular expertise and a particular interest in one of the key principles (e.g. 'social spaces' or 'managing relationships') and can act as a go-to person for other staff, and can co-ordinate initiatives in that domain. This is also a useful approach where there isn't the budget for a significant clinical presence.

- *Willingness to change.* It is often the case that all the change is expected of the clients of a service, and none from the service itself – this is a strange split, and inefficient in promoting change. Implementation of PIE implies a willingness and readiness of services to change themselves – the service as a whole, and the individual staff and managers who work there, and the management that supports them to do so. It is said that if you want to change the world, first you must change yourself; this applies to wanting to inspire change in your clients too.

- *Not forgetting the environment.* It's not all about training and understanding better the meaning behind interactions and behaviours. It's also about creating a positive environment for social and personal development, including a physical environment that supports increasing self-esteem and positive interactions. This is an area that really lends itself to staff and client co-production, perhaps with the help of community resources too (local colleges, businesses with social responsibility activities): a day centre in Trento, in northern Italy, completely redesigned its interior spaces, including all the furniture and all the signage, in a partnership between their clients and the architecture students from the local university – the end result was beautiful and functional, and the process was deeply enriching for both homeless people and students alike.

- *Letting other people know.* When a service adopts the PIE approach, it will change the way it works with its clients and managing relationships will become more central to its way of facilitating personal change in the clients. The different ethos and practice needs explaining to key stakeholders and other services that the project works with; it shouldn't be assumed that they will understand automatically. This means spending some time talking with the other services, both at a service level and about individual clients; the more other services understand what the PIE is trying to do, the less likely they are to unconsciously undermine it.

- *Allowing staff time to do the work.* A fundamental point behind the development of PIEs was the recognition of the role of trauma in the development and sustaining of chronic homelessness. From psychology, we recognised that trauma was caused by negative experiences and damaging relationships, and that healing trauma requires positive experiences and healing relationships. For staff to use their skills and personal capacities to enable positive experiences for the clients and to develop sustaining and enhancing relationships with them, staff must have the time to do that work. Of course, doing administrative and service maintenance work is necessary but it is not the primary task (look at your mission statement to see what the primary task is). The role of management is to facilitate the staff to have the time to do the primary work – which, in most social care organisations is something like supporting the client in their change and recovery process – and to enable the secondary work, the administrative and service maintenance burden, to be done as efficiently as possible and with the minimum necessary interference in the performance of the primary task.

- *Creating a space to think.* It could be said that this is what a PIE is, a space to think and to enact change, for staff and for clients. It is crucial that this is overt and supported by management. A fundamental step is the creation of regular and protected time and space for facilitated reflective practice groups, and an expectation that all members of the team will attend as often as possible; in other words, apart from emergencies, attendance at reflective practice takes priority over other tasks.

This list is not exhaustive, but if attention is paid to these aspects of implementation, while using the principles to guide the actual work of the PIE, then the service is likely to work more deeply and more effectively to the PIE approach.

EVIDENCE OF OUTCOMES

The PIE approach brings positive outcomes across a range of indicators. I am not going to rehearse them here as I have published a range of data elsewhere (Cockersell, 2017) and ongoing research results are available through the PIElink website (PIElink, 2017). In this book, Dr Williamson also explores in detail the effectiveness of the PIE in which she works (Chapter 8). I will limit myself to saying here that positive outcomes have been reported by a range of organisations using the PIE approach, and that these positive outcomes have been in a range of different domains. Reported positive outcomes include:

- increased staff satisfaction, involvement and understanding
- lower eviction rates
- reduction in serious incidents
- increased positive move-on
- clinically significant improved client mental health

- improved engagement with drug/alcohol treatment services
- improved engagement with other services.

(Cockersell, 2017)

Psychosocial interventions which are, essentially, social interventions with a therapeutic purpose and designed with the input of psychology into how the therapeutic purpose is delivered

The focus of this book is on services for socially excluded people with histories of compound trauma where a significant input from the psychological disciplines creates a different and, we argue, more effective, therapeutic environment within which clients can turn their lives around and achieve more of their potential. For this reason we have focused our attention on psychotherapy services within community settings and on PIE. However, for the sake of completeness, I would just like to add a few words about services that have other forms of input from the psychologies.

Most of these are services where staff receive training either from psychologists, or in interventions that derive from psychology. Examples of these would be:

- training on motivational interviewing, active listening or managing challenging behaviours
- less commonly and more elaborately, the use of psychological formulation to create a team or interagency understanding of a client's interactions
- the use of psychologists for occasional 'masterclass' training on a specific type of behaviour such as self-harm or suicide, and how to work with it
- occasional facilitated case conferences for clients with particularly complex presentations.

There are many more such examples. These are, of course, not incompatible with the more in-depth use of psychological inputs that we are focusing on in this book. Indeed, PIEs and services including accessible psychotherapy also benefit deeply from the non-clinical staff having access to these sorts of interventions. They are part of what makes the skill set of most homelessness staff so invaluable to the process of facilitating positive change in their clients.

References

Brown, G., Kainth, K., Matheson, C., Osborne, J., Trenkle, A. and Adlam, J. (2011) 'An hospitable engagement? Open-door psychotherapy with the socially excluded.' *Psychodynamic Practice 17*, 3, 307–324.

Castaldo, M., Filoni, A. and Punzi, I. (2014) *Safya: Un Approccio Transdisciplinare alla Salute degli Homeless in Europa*. Milan: FrancoAngeli.

Cockersell, P. (2011) 'Homelessness and mental health: adding clinical mental health interventions to existing social ones can greatly enhance positive outcomes.' *Journal of Public Mental Health, 10*, 2, 88–98.

Cockersell, P. (2017) 'PIEs five years on.' *Mental Health and Social Inclusion 20*, 4, 1–10.

Focus Ireland (2014) *Evaluation of Focus Ireland's Therapeutic Service*. Dublin: Focus Ireland.

Griffiths, S. and Steen S. (2013) 'IAPT programme: setting key performance indicators in a more robust context: a new perspective.' *The Journal of Psychological Therapies in Primary Care 2*, 133–141.

Groundswell (2010) *The Escape Plan*. Accessed October 2017 at http://groundswell.org.uk/what-we-do/peer-research/the-escape-plan/ www.groundswell.org.uk/theescape-plan.html

Haigh, R. (2013) 'The quintessence of a therapeutic environment.' *Therapeutic Communities: The International Journal of Therapeutic Communities 34*, 1, 6–15.

Homeless Link (2017) *The Outcomes Star*. Accessed December 2017 at https://www.homeless.org.uk/sites/default/files/site-attachments/Outcomes-Star-3rd-Ed-User-Guide.pdf

Johnson, R. and Haigh, R. (2011) 'Enabling environments.' *Mental Health and Social Inclusion 15*, 1, 17–22.

Keats, H., Cockersell, P., Johnson, R. and Maguire, N. (2012) *Psychologically informed services for homeless people*. Accessed January 2018 at http://www.rjaconsultancy.org.uk/6454%20CLG%20PIE%20operational%20document%20AW-1.pdf

NHS Hammersmith (2013) *Rough Sleepers' Health and Healthcare*. Accessed December 2017 at https://www.jsna.info/sites/default/files/Rough%20Sleepers%20Health%20and%20Healthcare%20Summary.pdf

PIElink (2017) Website devoted to PIE approaches. Accessed March 2017 at www.pielink.net

RC Psych (2017) *Enabling Environments*. Accessed February 2017 at www.rcpsych.ac.uk/quality/qualityandaccreditation/enablingenvironments.aspx

Read, A. (2002) 'Psychotherapy with Addicted People.' In M. Weegman and R. Cohen (eds) *The Psychodynamics of Addiction*. London: Whurr.

Schon, D. (2016) *The Reflective Practitioner*. London: Routledge.

UKCP (2011) *NICE Under Scrutiny*. London: Roehampton University.

3

SOLUTIONS
PRACTICE AND EXPERIENCE

6

PRE-TREATMENT THERAPY APPROACH FOR SINGLE HOMELESS PEOPLE

The Co-Construction of Recovery/Discovery

JOHN CONOLLY

The challenge of psychological therapy

Although there are schools which say that psychological therapies can be delivered with simple adherence to a manual of techniques, that is not the experience of many, or probably most, of the professionals practising in the field. Indeed a clinician as experienced and influential as Yalom noted that, 'Formal texts, journal articles and lectures portray therapy as precise and systematic, with carefully delineated stages, strategic technical intervention... Yet I believe deeply that, when no one is looking, the therapist throws in the "real thing"' (Yalom, 1980, p.3). He goes on to describe what he thinks 'the real thing' is in terms of psychological therapies: 'what are these "throw ins", these elusive "off the record" extras? They exist outside of formal theory, they are not written about, they are not explicitly taught... such qualities as compassion, "presence", caring, extending oneself, touching the patient at a profound level, or – that most elusive one of all – wisdom?' (Yalom, 1980, pp.3–4). It is about implementing some of these 'throw ins' that make up the 'real thing' that I think I am writing about here in describing what I have called the 'Pre-treatment Therapy approach'.

The challenges of counselling homeless people

Homelessness is traumatising. It is said that someone who starts sleeping rough, maybe with no serious problems at the outset, has two weeks before they start acquiring the characteristics of a long term rough sleeper. However, the condition of homelessness itself is usually the end result of a series of prior crises (Department of Health, 2010) such as:

- poverty
- unemployment
- sexual or physical abuse
- family disputes and breakdown
- drug or alcohol misuse
- school exclusion
- poor mental health
- lack of support networks.

There is emerging evidence that psychological disorders strongly predict homelessness, in particular youth homelessness and rough sleeping. Maguire *et al.*, 2009 (cited in Department of Health, 2010) found evidence that behaviours leading to homelessness may be associated with mental health problems such as personality disorder (PD), post-traumatic stress disorder, complex trauma and conduct disorders in children.

The prevalence of PD amongst single homeless people is believed to be as high as 68 per cent (and 58% using diagnostic measures). It is believed to be a reaction to an ongoing and sustained traumatic experience (Keats *et al.*, 2012), and its causes are believed to include childhood abuse, deprivation and neglect (Alwin, 2006).

People with PDs also have increased risks of suffering additional mental health problems (Kane, 2006; NICE, 2009), such as:

- anxiety
- depression
- substance misuse disorders

- recurrent deliberate self-harm
- brief psychotic episodes
- eating disorders.

Therefore, people with PD make heavy demands on local services which are usually ill equipped to deal with them. They evoke high levels of anxiety in carers, relatives and professionals. They tend to have frequent, escalating contact across a spectrum of services including mental health, social services, A&E, GPs and the criminal justice system (NIMHE, 2003).

Early intervention has been highlighted as crucial in preventing major deterioration in PD, which can result in a career as a 'professional patient' or lifelong mental health service user, criminality, vagrancy or even death (Haigh, 2006).

One of the key features of PD is a difficulty in maintaining relationships. Thus, the American Psychiatric Association defines PD as 'relatively stable, enduring, and pervasively maladaptive patterns of coping, thinking, feeling, regulating impulses, and relating to others' (cited in Bleiberg, Rossouw and Fonagy, 2012).

I have come to understand PD as a condition whereby people suffer from a 'traumatised personality'. As the personality was developing in the face of prolonged and sustained traumatic experiences, the person's natural 'trauma response', psychological and physiological, became incorporated into its very constitution. Hence, baseline physiological arousal is extremely high for people with PD, and their 'trauma response' is very easily triggered and prolonged, for some lasting over a period of days, making the person prone to re-triggering and seeking self-medication as an aid to all too temporary coping.

Thus homelessness is the end result of a series of crises and is a further crisis in itself. People are physically and psychologically vulnerable. They have no safe private space in which to recuperate, relax, regroup and think how best to solve their problems. They are isolated, chronically frightened, exposed to the re-triggering of the 'trauma response', desperate and feel shamed about it and its consequences.

Yet mainstream health services insist on a fixed address, regular attendance to appointment-based treatment sessions, and the person to be free of addictions. The chaotic circumstances and stresses of homelessness, the underlying mental vulnerabilities and the coping strategies deployed to survive are not taken into account.

McDonagh (2011) makes the point that complex needs homeless people can be exposed to further exclusion from services which feel that they do not meet their criteria: 'In practice, the interplay between the complex needs that go hand in hand with deep social exclusion is often taken as evidence of "chaotic behaviour" and does not generally trigger any differentiated or enhanced response from service providers.'

Already in 1968, Goffman wrote about how certain groups not appearing to live up to social norms could become stigmatised and their identities be invalidated, especially if their 'condition' was visible, prevented them from contributing and was not understood. This stigma unfortunately then became internalised as a 'negative identity' and further feelings of deep and intense shame arose as a result.

Pre-treatment therapy is the enhanced response which the Westminster Homeless Health Counselling Service (Central London Community Health NHS Trust) has developed over time in the face of homeless people's complex needs (Conolly and Ashton, 2011, 2013, 2014, 2016; Conolly, 2016). Irregular attendance, intoxication and drug addiction will not of themselves be exclusion criteria.

'Pre-treatment therapy – the co-construction of recovery/discovery' explained

The words 'pre-treatment' and 'therapy', form an amalgam of 'pretreatment' (Levy, 2013) and 'pre-therapy' (Prouty, Van Werde and Portner, 2002), two approaches developed to help hard to treat patients: homeless people and contact impaired people (people suffering from dementia, psychosis).

'Co-construction' emphasises the jointly co-constructed nature of a user-defined recovery process, and *'Recovery/Discovery'* acknowledges that for some people, psychological resilience has to be built up from scratch and discovered almost, rather than be recovered.

The words 'pre-treatment therapy' combined reflect the need to offer multiply excluded, homeless, complex needs people, trauma-informed support based on the careful management of 'attachment style', shame, 'false and alien selves' and 'therapeutic dissonance' in order to establish a relationship of trust strong enough to withstand the pain of deep and lasting change. Thus a user-defined model of recovery, and its 'co-construction', with a conversational style of interaction, is very much at its core.

There follows a further brief clarification of each of the building blocks making up 'pre-treatment therapy'.

Pre-treatment is 'an approach that enhances safety while promoting transition to housing, and/or treatment alternatives through patient centred supportive interventions that develop goals and motivation to create positive change' (Levy, 2013, p.2). For Levy, this approach needs an adherence to the following principles of practice:

- *The establishment of safety* – where meeting the safety needs of an individual in crisis is used as an opportunity for further engagement and work. At the Homeless Health Counselling service (HHCS), it is the 'drop-in' counselling sessions which offer the opportunity for crisis stabilisation and progression into more structured appointment-based counselling, via the establishment of a rapid emotional connection.

- *The development of a trusting relationship* – via person-centred and other skills. Recognition, empathy, validation, containment, suspension of judgement, genuineness, limited self-revelation, psychoeducation, support and signposting are all extensively used for this purpose.

- *Common language construction* – for Levy this entails the understanding of the homeless person's world by learning the meaning of their gestures, words and actions. At the HHCS, entering someone's fantasies/delusions in order to connect with them, understand the meaning of their fantasy and then act as an interpreter and link for other services has been found to be very effective. Also, Prouty's 'pretherapy' emphatic contact techniques, to reach people at a sub-linguistic level (contact reflections), have also proved to be very useful.

- *Facilitate and support change* – at the HHCS the processes, stages and levels of change are very much taken into account, and it is recognised 'that particular processes are more useful during particular stages of change' (Prochaska and Norcross, 2003, p.525). Relapses are very much seen as part of the recovery journey, and to be learnt from rather than stigmatised. Thus both the 'drop-in' individual and group sessions are open-ended and available to individuals to make use of as and when needed; some people have used one particular drop-in group for some six years in all, with some periods of absence. However, they have demonstrated steady development, and the group for them has gradually become therapeutic (in the sense of engendering a sense of ownership and responsibility for their reactions to life's challenges), rather than a forum for venting or getting sympathy.

- *Cultural and ecological considerations* – for Levy this is to prepare and support the person for successful transition and adaptation to new relationships, ideas, services, resources, treatment and accommodation. At the HHCS this is mainly achieved by offering people a 'secure base' (Holmes, 2006), and helping them develop trust, emotional regulation and psychological resilience.

Co-construction

Co-construction means the delivering of public services in an 'equal and reciprocal relationship between professionals, people using services, their families and their neighbours' (Boyle and Harris, 2009, p.11).

Recovery is co-constructed and pre-treatment therapy is very much based on a user-defined model of recovery and offers a menu of therapeutic interventions the homeless person can choose from and navigate through at more or less their own pace:

- non appointments-based (self-referral), drop-in individual counselling or group support and discussion sessions
- regular appointment-based individual counselling sessions
- recovery maintenance:
  - honorary co-facilitation of peer support and discussion groups
  - giving personal testimony in writing and/or in person at conferences and workshops, etc.

'Recovery–discovery' acknowledges that although many people are helped to 'recover' psychological resilience, for some that resilience has to be built up from scratch almost. Thus, for people from nominally stable backgrounds, who have experienced one-off only (but overwhelming) trauma, mental resilience can be 'recovered' in that it was in place to begin with.

However, some will never have had the opportunity to have developed psychological resources for resilience (because of childhood neglect, deprivation, physical/sexual abuse) and will have experienced a series of overwhelming traumas which cannot be separated out from each other; links are made from one trauma to the other, and stress levels are so high that processing, making sense of and addressing them is impossible. Here, *building up resilience* is needed and, where 'working on the therapeutic relationship is the most important, constitut[es] a significant part, if not all, of therapy' (Rothschild, 2003, pp.15–16).

The establishment of what Holmes (2006) has referred to as a 'secure base' which is when someone – a carer, a counsellor, a therapist, a friend – has become a safe haven for someone, a trusted comforting person from whom one can derive the confidence to face the world and make new relationships. It is also somebody one can turn to in difficult times. Eventually this becomes internalised and becomes part of the person's mental makeup, an internal resource someone can draw upon in times of stress and by which the person can soothe and calm themselves, manage and regulate their emotions.

For Allen, 'secure attachment relationships provide our best means of ameliorating emotional distress' (Allen, 2013, p.xx).

Pre-treatment therapy very much acknowledges attachment style, the impact of trauma and the defensive strategies this gives rise to like the development of a 'false self' (Winnicott, 1965), 'alien self' (Bateman and Fonagy, 2004, 2006a), 'compromised mentalization' (ibid.), 'shame' (Fonagy and Target, 2003; Herman, 2012) and what I call 'therapeutic dissonance' (based on Bateman and Fonagy, 2006a).

Attachment theory and different styles of interaction

We know from 'attachment theory' (Bowlby, 1997,1998a, 1998b; Fonagy, 2001; Holmes, 2006; Wallin, 2007) that early experiences of being cared or not cared for are internalised in the form of 'working models' – unconscious representations of the self, its worthiness, and how reliable and dependable others are in times of need. These mental representations, by unconsciously guiding attention, interpretation, memory and predictions about future relationships, determine the nature of the individual's attachments throughout their lifespan. Attachment theory is a valuable empirically based clinical framework which can help clinicians make sense of and regulate the 'therapeutic alliance', and is increasingly being used in the NHS, for example see Danquah and Berry (2014).

Secure and *insecure* attachment styles have been identified, the latter including three subtypes: avoidant, ambivalent and disorganised.

Securely attached individuals had caregivers who were attentive and responsive to their need for care and comfort. They will have therefore internalised representations of these as providing a 'secure base' enabling self-soothing strategies, emotional regulation and the attainment of a physical and mental state of relaxation (Holmes, 2006). In the expectation of obtaining help, securely attached people will also readily turn to others for help and support, offering them some degree of resilience in the face of adversity. Their spoken narratives will be coherent, credible and well organised where people, time and place are all clear (Daniel, 2015).

Here mental resilience can be recovered and psychotherapy can be made use of once the crisis and chaos of homelessness has been stabilised. In the meantime supportive 'drop-in' one to one counselling sessions and support/discussion groups can help people feel less isolated and alienated, and also help harbour hope.

Avoidant individuals experienced caregivers stressing independence and reacting in a dismissive manner to their needs. They thus learnt to dismiss and downplay their needs, and will rarely approach others for help. When they do they will often feel shame and be extremely uncomfortable with empathy, leading to all sorts of 'distancing' strategies, like disbelieving it, saying or doing something hurtful or dropping out. Their tones will be hard and they will display little empathy for themselves and others. Their narratives will be stereotyped and accepted as a 'given'. The therapeutic task here is be to open up the rigid narrative and get the person in touch with the underlying emotions (Holmes, 2006).

People with an *ambivalent style* had caregivers who were unpredictable, at times warm and caring, at others absent and preoccupied with their own concerns. They thus learnt to exacerbate their needs in order to get attention, something which paradoxically can discourage others from helping them as their behaviour gets labelled as 'attention seeking' or 'manipulative'. They will be all too accepting of what the therapist has to say; they will be the 'perfect patient', compliant on the surface, but uninvolved at any deeper level. Here the therapeutic task is to help the patient 'find her own investment' (Holmes, 2006, p.17). The narrative in this case is long and rambling with little opportunity for dialogue or the passing of information. The purpose seems more to develop a 'clinging' to the counsellor. The task is to bring shape and meaning out of the overriding unstructured emotions. A cognitive approach emphasising the recognition of the link between thoughts and feelings is useful here (Holmes, 2006). I have worked with several people like this and it seems to me that one of their underlying beliefs about themselves was that they were unwanted, of little value and unable to get things 'right'. I found 'limited re-parenting' (Young *et al.*, 2003) quite useful here in that I supported someone through what for them was an extremely challenging task, but gradually weaned them off their dependence once their self-esteem had begun to increase as a result of the small successes achieved.

Disorganised style people experienced caregivers who were frightening and put them in the double bind situation of needing their support but were made to feel more distressed by them. They will approach people when in great distress but will be unable to believe their genuine motivation to help them. They will be extremely suspicious. I have come across two people with exactly this presentation, and in fact I was unable to help them. It is they who drove me on my journey of exploration regarding PD.

Again, according to Holmes, patients with this style miss sessions, come at the wrong times and drop out of treatment for a while. For Holmes, this has to be accepted and some effort made at maintaining contact until the person is ready. The HHCS drop-in sessions allow for this kind of engagement. According to Wallin (2007, p.96):

> Clinicians know the exorbitant cost of their unresolved [disorganised] patients' efforts to 'exile' past trauma or loss. Such patients feel perpetually threatened from within and without, burdened by an ongoing vulnerability to dissociation, overwhelming emotion, and an external world made dangerous by projection outwards of unbearable internal experience.

Here the logic of narratives is difficult to follow, as there are sudden trauma-related shifts, descriptions of self and others are incoherent, contradictory or suddenly change, and there are sudden changes between dramatisation and downplaying (Daniel, 2015). It took several months for one such person, to build up the courage to tell me that she found my expressions of empathy really disturbing in that she just couldn't believe them. I consciously tried downplaying these, and very gradually as her trust in me increased, I believe, she became more appropriately self-assertive, her speech more coherent and she began partaking of social activities more.

Ambivalent and disorganised styles are especially associated with borderline PD (Fonagy *et al.*, 1996, cited in Daniel, 2015, p.148).

The false self

This concept, first developed by Donald Winnicott (1965), consists of a 'defensive structure created to master trauma in a context of total dependency' (Fonagy and Target, 2003, p.26). It is a façade developed to pacify a hostile interpersonal environment at the cost of true feelings, the expression of needs, joy and spontaneity. This often leads some people to feel quite empty emotionally, and unable to be spontaneous, flexible and creative, especially in the context of intimate emotional relationships. It will be impossible to find meaning and satisfaction in life for them. Self-harm, addictions and/or the pursuit of dangerous activities are often attempts to manage this inner emptiness and sense of meaninglessness.

Some chronically homeless people find surviving on the streets a means of avoiding this inner emptiness, only to find its terrifying resurgence upon resettlement, something Scanlon and Adlam (2006) have referred to as 'housing unhoused minds'.

The 'alien self' identifies with the feelings of the 'caregiver' rather than their own and leads to 'an alien experience within the self' (Bateman and Fonagy, 2004, p.89) and to discontinuities of the self; all this impacts on their ability to relate to and connect to themselves and to other people, including care and/or health workers. Deliberate self-harm and suicide are prevalent here.

Shame

Great attention is also given to the management of shame. The shame of an abused child has little to do with common social shame but rather consists of 'an intense and destructive sense of self-disgust, verging on self-hatred' (Fonagy *et al.*, 2006, p.45). Unfortunately, therapy can inadvertently reactivate this '[b]ecause of the power imbalance between patient and therapist, and because the patient exposes her most intimate thoughts and feelings without reciprocity, the therapy relationship is, to some degree, inherently shaming' (Herman, 2012, p.166).

Because of this, groups may be an especially effective mode of intervention in that group members are all peers in their suffering, and in giving support to each, can come to feel that they are of value and deserving of the group support they receive (ibid.).

Trauma also impacts mentalisation, a key psychological function which develops throughout infancy and childhood and which allows the representation of emotional states allowing for their regulation; the development of symbolic thought, memory, comprehension and communication; and the development of a core sense of selfhood, self-worth, and self-reliance (Fonagy and Target, 2003, p.254).

Mentalisation is 'the ability to see and describe oneself and others as thinking, and feeling beings whose actions reflect intentions and plans' (Daniel, 2015, p.19), i.e. having an understanding of self and others as being feeling and thinking *agents*, understanding that actions are driven by feelings and thoughts, and that our thoughts may well be mistaken. We have representations of the world, ourselves and others, but they are representations only, *not* reality.

Individuals with weakened mentalisation will be prone to reverting back to 'pre-mentalisation' states under stress, those states the child works through before achieving mentalisation:

- the *teological* mode, where only actions are trusted as a means of communication, not words

- *equivalence*, where thoughts are believed to be reality, like 'magical' thinking in children

- the *pretend* mode, flight into fantasy.

It is these 'pre-mentalisation' states which make reciprocal communication and interaction very difficult. They help explain some of the very challenging characteristics of PD – e.g. extremely rigid black/white thinking, the interpretation of someone else's (inadvertent) actions as wilful and personally directed towards oneself (teological mode) and 'mind reading' someone else's thoughts and intentions, whereby because one 'thinks' someone else is having certain thoughts, they 'must' be having those thoughts (equivalence mode).

Cognitive dissonance in therapy

Bateman and Fonagy argue that the 'dissonance' between the patient's and therapist's perspectives in an attachment context can lead to greater instability and result in 'more rather than less mental and behavioural disturbance' (2006a, p.191). This can happen at a psychological level, as discussed above, where someone with a weakened sense of their own subjectivity and limited access to their own feelings and representations of themselves, cannot compare their own diffuse, fragmentary sense of self with that (even if accurate) presented by the therapist. But for me it can also happen at a social level, whereby there is an incredible mismatch in the social spheres patient and therapist inhabit, the different assumptive worlds driving their interpretations of experience, social interaction and behavior, the demarcation between outsider and insider.

Surviving many years on the streets can lead to a process of 're-socialisation', whereby the homeless person operates by the norms and standards of street survival, not the pleasantries of mainstream social engagement, especially with the dynamics of organisational hierarchies and bureaucracy, or the subtleties of engaging and negotiating with authority figures and 'power'.

My challenge as a therapist, for instance, has been to suspend my judgement in the face of the most incredible life narratives, so well beyond my own personal experience or even my imagination, that the temptation to label them as fabrication, manipulation, deception, criminal, delusional, got in the way of my making an 'authentic' connection with the person and not prejudging, dismissing or rejecting out of hand the particular narrative and form in which they expressed their suffering, outrage, distrust or hopelessness.

It is just this which I believe underlies the difficulties of integrating or reintegrating with mainstream services and society. This is the fault line which McDonagh's call for an 'enhanced service response' addresses (McDonagh, 2011), and which the PIE initiative tries to provide (Keats *et al.*, 2012).

All of the above consequences of trauma make it extremely difficult to achieve a genuine, authentic connection in therapy, leading *either* to people wanting to please the therapist and be 'model patients' (especially those suffering from dependent PD), resulting in every form of self-sabotage at the very threshold of progress (in that deep down they never really believe that they can, should, deserve to progress, and this was never explored in therapy), *or* to people disengaging from therapy by attempting to use it for social and entertainment value only, or simply leaving it.

Hence the importance of a user-defined and user-led process of recovery.

User-defined recovery process

It was in the mid-1980s that former service users began writing accounts of meaningful recovery and it in the late 1990s that the concept of mental health recovery became a central tenet of government policy (Faulkner, 2012). Castillo (2016, p.36) notes that 'In January 2005, NIMHE published a guiding statement on mental Health Recovery which characterised recovery as the practice of values and the "how" of service delivery and put service users at the heart of mental health recovery.'

Research also began pointing out that self-agency in recovery had to be allowed for by services and that individuals had to be seen beyond their diagnosis and related to as a whole person (Castillo, 2016). It is in this spirit that pre-treatment therapy adheres to the following enduring definition of 'recovery':

> a deeply personal, unique process of changing one's attitudes, values, feelings, goals, skills and/or roles. It is a way of living a satisfying, hopeful life, and contributing to life even with limitations caused by the illness. Recovery involves the development of new meaning and purpose in one's life as one grows beyond the catastrophic effects of mental illness. Recovery from mental illness involves much more than recovery from the illness itself. (Anthony, 1993)

In research conducted with PD patients on their experience of recovery and the factors associated with it, Costillo (2016) isolated the following as fundamental:

- *a sense of safety and trust* – where trust has to be created in a very concrete manner by the reliable, consistent availability of support
- *feeling cared for* – when someone is made to feel that they are being listened to and treated as being worthy and of value
- *a sense of belonging* – as in being part of a network of reciprocal relationships where common ground can be identified, and decision-making shared
- *learning the boundaries* – where social and ethical limits need to be made clear and, according to Castillo (2016), negotiated. When broken, something greatly desired needs to be taken away, but not all support withdrawn and the door not permanently closed.

It is only when these are established that therapy can take place: making sense of and integrating the past, reframing traumatic experiences, managing shame, allocating responsibility where it rightfully belongs, acquiring new skills, developing and believing in hopes, dreams, aspirations, achievements and recovery.

The paradox is that most services require people to learn the boundaries before trust has been developed. Also, many people, with PD especially, will never have had the opportunity to have learnt appropriate negotiation about boundaries, as transgressions would have resulted in their being severely and disproportionately punished, or they would have been traumatically abandoned, marginalised and excluded.

Boundaries with patients at the HHCS are implemented and maintained via 'limited re-parenting' – 'fulfilling, in a limited way the unmet emotional needs of the patient's childhood' and *'Empathic Challenge'* – 'expressing understanding about the patients' schemas [working models, needs] while simultaneously confronting the need to change' (Young *et al.*, 2003, p.206). Both are used in combination as appropriate.

Great care is taken not to confuse 'boundary crossing' with 'boundary violation' (Gutheil, 2005), where boundary crossing is a temporary, non-exploitative deviation from 'classical/general practice that does no harm and actually helps, and boundary violation is a harmful deviation from the norm. One major helpful distinguishing factor is whether these deviations can be discussed in the public domain, in supervision and with other colleagues.

Homeless health counselling service

As already mentioned, this provides walk-in or drop-in one-to-one counselling sessions, walk-in or drop-in support and discussion groups, appointment-based one-to-one counselling sessions and recovery maintenance activities such as honorary group co-facilitation and the writing or presenting of personal recovery journey testimonies.

Drop-in support and counselling

This consists of two weekly morning half-day sessions just before and after the weekend. They are available at a specialist GP surgery for homeless people in Westminster, the Great Chapel Street Medical Centre. People can walk off the street, be sent by their keyworker at their hostel or day centre, or simply be told by the GP or nurse at the surgery to 'pop in for a chat with the counsellor'. The length of the contact will vary according to how many people are waiting, but also to the person's own tolerance and need.

Most people will present in crisis, and great attention is given to making them feel welcome – for example, they are offered a drink – and relating is on a first name basis, as appropriate. Standard crisis intervention models – e.g. the Seven-Stage Crisis Intervention Model (Roberts and Yeager, 2009) the priority being the establishment of an emotional connection assessing all the while that person's likely attachment style in order to regulate the level of counsellor empathy which may be more or less tolerable for that person. The focus will be on establishing trust and a feeling of being cared for as a human being rather than a case to be managed. Common language construction will have a pre-eminent role. Techniques used will be very much person centred and will include recognition, validation, empathy, containment, limited self-revelation, role modelling, psychoeducation, support and signposting. Transference–countertransference indications will be noted in order to help understand and manage the interaction, but not interpreted (due to the likelihood of problematic power dynamics and 'therapeutic dissonance' that this may engender at this stage). The style of communication will be conversational (NICE, 2009) and will include amongst other things assessment of immediate (and chronic) risk. No attempt at taking a comprehensive history is made at the first encounter, in that the focus here is to establish a connection which will encourage the person to return. Given the prevalence of trauma it is understood that history-taking can retrigger a trauma reaction and that the person may well have to deal with this subsequently whilst out on the streets. Therefore, the agenda is very much patient led. Towards the end of the interaction, the discussion may be briefly summarised and reflected back as a lead-in to describing options for moving forward – thus, mention of the drop-in sessions, both individual and group as well as the availability of regular appointments may be made as apropriate, as well as any signposting for more information and/or support of a more practical nature.

Some people make use of the individual drop-in for a few sessions only; others for a prolonged period. Some also attend the appointments-based sessions and/or the drop-in group sessions.

The anger support and discussion group

The groups are run on the principle that:

> participants are offered opportunities for mining their own pasts for buried themes and alternative interpretations…individuals are not coerced into accepting pre-packaged realities, but rather are encouraged to develop their own stories in a more natural, gradual rearranging of their past lives. (Maruna and Ramsden, 2004, pp.139–140)

This takes place in a 'distinctly social process', which involves 'both shame acknowledgment and forgiveness and reacceptance into a moral-social community (ibid.).

As we saw above with Herman (2012), the power imbalance in relationships between service users and professionals can be 'inherently shaming'. Furthermore, many complex needs homeless people have long histories of 'toxic' help whereby they suffered abuse at the hands of those entrusted with their care, and/or the care delivered by professionals was at best ineffective or actually detrimental (see 'Therapeutic dissonance'). Because of this, groups may be an especially effective mode of intervention in that group members are all peers in their suffering, and in giving support to each, can come to feel that they are of value and deserving of the group support they receive (ibid.).

The anger support and discussion group at Connection St Martins Day Center has been running since 2012. It is an open membership group, of a drop-in nature with no expectation of regular attendance. It is assumed that most people dropping in will primarily be at the 'pre-contemplation' and 'contemplation' stages of change (Prochaska and Norcross, 2003), that is, where people cannot recognise that anger is their problem, it is everyone else's fault, or if acknowledged as a possible issue of their own, ways of changing, belief in change, fear of failure, etc. are very prominent. Some will be at a recovery 'maintenance' stage whereby they seek support in consolidating their gains and struggle to prevent lapses and relapses. Exposure to people at different stages of recovery can be very inspiring as well as educative.

Although it is an open membership group, over time a core group of members has established itself and enables newcomers to be more or less seamlessly integrated. The group offers a safe social space where traumatic experiences, as well as actions, can be expressed, sometimes even enacted, but always talked about, subjected to different perspectives, mentalised and gradually processed.

In the context of social dynamics, like taking turns in a conversation, deciding who and how one holds the floor and the group's attention at any given moment, members learn to negotiate boundaries rather than breaking or imposing them violently. Members receive feedback from others, not only regarding their journeys but also on the impact they have on people in the group. When principles of conduct are broken, as in an argument between members, this is pointed out, and the group is asked to air its understanding of what happened, and most importantly why. The protagonists are then invited to share their reactions and also their understanding of what happened and why. Feelings and words are contextualised in an emotional landscape. Thus the group gets to hear, for example, that one of the angry parties may have just experienced one of the major setbacks of their life and this prompted them to verbally insult a member who had inadvertently triggered them. The other, on the other hand, for the first time in their life, held their ground without reverting to actual violence. This is a major learning experience for all involved. Principles can be transgressed without physical violence and membership of the group is not endangered. A recent such episode culminated in the parties apologising to each other and the group reiterating that as long as no actual physical violence is enacted, every member has a place in it. All shook hands at the end.

The co-facilitators ensure that time is adhered to, that everyone feels safe, that the group more or less remains on task, or returns to it, and wonders aloud sometimes as to emerging themes, or how a member may feel when having related an important personal event and no-one responds, etc.

The group session lasts for 90 minutes, the first 20 or so devoted to social time over snacks. Then all are invited to introduce themselves, and someone is prompted to open up general discussion by sharing an anger-driven experience. The last ten minutes are devoted to everyone 'signing out' by saying what learning points. if any, will be taken away with them. This is when the facilitators draw together the themes which have emerged.

An adapted form of Alcoholics Anonymous principles is used as a template for the group. These, however, are periodically returned to and updated as appropriate.

Attention is given to individual members as well as to group cohesiveness and the 'group mind'. The group is asked for its permission when visitors wish to attend. They are instructed as far as possible to be participants and not simply observers.

Anger group factors

The following generic group factors, as identified by Yalom and Leszcz 2005, very much apply to the drop-in anger support and discussion group:

- a neutral space
- identification
- hope
- universality (not alone)
- expression of emotions, including anger
- group cohesiveness
- corrective emotional experience
- develop social skills
- altruism (advise/help each other – empowerment)

- imitative behaviour
- interpersonal learning.

The following more specifically therapeutic factors also apply, especially as the group matures, members learn to trust each other more and are therefore more able to take risks:

- recognising own social impact on others
- assuming responsibility
- attributing responsibility where it belongs.

Group themes

These in general evolve from feelings of anger, outrage and grievance to the expression of vulnerability and seeking support and advice.

Newcomers to the group will usually remain silent, or 'hog' all of the attention by venting their anger and grievance. However, one or more members will quickly challenge the one-sided nature of the narrative. These may well be taken into consideration if not accepted at that particular time. The co-facilitators refrain from such challenges, even empathic ones, as they are much more tolerable from peers.

Other members may resent their inability to air their own concerns, and this will emerge sooner or later, either of their own volition or because the co-faciliators draw attention to it – e.g. how agitated someone appears. It can eventually be discussed and something be learnt about the difficulties of getting attention without resorting to disruptive behaviour and getting potentially excluded (if only on a temporary basis, initially). The group also learns how important its cohesiveness is and the wellbeing of each and every one of its members, and how difficult it is to notice and respond to members' unexpressed needs. Themes include:

- abuse at the hands of 'entrusted' people
- childhood injustices and lifelong anger
- not being cared for by 'helpers' but managed only
- no families to fall back on

- enduring exclusion/marginalisation
- stigma and prejudice – being invisible – having no voice.

Useful coping strategies shared in the group have been:

- 'walking away'
- making use of humour/sarcasm
- distractions – listening to music
- prayer
- self-expressive activities: drawing, painting
- talking to 'calming friends'
- having something to lose, something of value, an overriding goal, purpose.

The group itself is experienced in the value and the regularity of its weekly meetings, and 'containing', in that some members have reported being able to hang on to their explosive anger in the knowledge they will attend its next meeting.

Some members have referred to the group as:

- 'like the family I never had'
- 'I need this group'
- 'it helps me to know that I can come here and let it all out'
- 'my court order says I have to go to an anger management group, but I also come here'
- 'I pay travel to come here'.

Some of the effects of attending the group have been reported as including more constructive engagement with:

- homeless day centres/hostels
- keyworkers
- housing
- family

- reduced alcohol consumption
- reduced explosive angry outbursts
- reduced difficulties with the law.

The group also helps develop and strengthen mentalisation, those psychological functions enabling social interaction and ultimately social inclusion.

Most, if not all, specialist PD programmes consist of, on average, two-year treatment programmes involving daily activity schedules, which include both individual and group sessions. Although, the HHCS cannot lay claim to being a specialist PD treatment unit, it also has developed both group and individual sessions, which makes for a rich constructive exchange with the people who attend both.

Regular appointments-based counselling sessions

As we saw earlier with Castillo (2016), it is only when someone has developed a sense of safety and trust, feeling cared for, belonging and the ability to accept basic boundaries that therapy can take place.

Attending drop-in sessions does not entail taking responsibility for managing time and the 'other's' (the therapist's) expectations, nor does it involve being part of a broader social network whereby appointment-based sessions, in the face of waiting lists, are a prized resource and not to be wasted at someone else's expense. The transition to appointment-based counselling does entail all of this and therefore needs careful management and appraising. Do the person's circumstances allow this kind of commitment? Is the person ready for this?

NICE recommends no less than 20 sessions (roughly six months) for people suffering from PD. Accordingly, this is the nature of the contract on offer at the HHCS, and non-attendance and cancellations are discussed. The contract can be renewed according to circumstances. Homelessness exposes people to an extremely precarious and transient lifestyle. Some people are resettled and may need transition support or lose the temporary accommodation they were in, some have court cases to face, others may suffer an assault at their hostel, others still may be diagnosed with a severe or even terminal illness, or suffer from bereavement, etc; all of these endanger whatever fragile progress may have been achieved.

There will be much in common with the drop-in sessions: an emphasis on establishing a 'secure base', taking into account attachment style, from which to understand any 'enactments' or 'conflicts', which will, we hope, occur further on in the process, this driving the revelation of 'core beliefs' and assumptions ('working models',' schemas', 'fantasies', etc.) and the possible gradual amendment of these, or at least exposure to the therapist's differing interpretations. Sometimes, both parties have to agree to disagree, sometimes, the therapist's alternative interpretation of what occurred, together with its linking back to previous material, may be experienced as a 'revelation' and drive further change.

This process can be vastly enhanced if both appointment and the group sessions are attended, as interpretations of group experiences and events by the patient and therapist will differ greatly and therefore be even more fruitful ground for development.

Another aspect of HHCS provision is the availability of between-session support via work email and/or telephone. Given the precariousness of homelessness combined with the vulnerability of PD, severe crises are as numerous as they are unpredictable. Just the knowledge of that availability is containing in itself, and to date has not been misused. Several episodes of deliberate self-harm and A&E admissions have been avoided by these means.

Absences, interruptions and counselling terminations are given much attention as most homeless people's life journeys have involved sudden and traumatic separations and losses.

Given this, as well as the chronicity of PD, 'post treatment' is also very much part of HHCS provision. Thus people can always return to the service, especially the drop-in sessions, as and when needed, and they are encouraged to contribute to others what they have learnt from their own journeys. Some people elect to co-facilitate further support and discussion groups, and/or give personal testimony in the form of public speaking at conferences and/or writing, such as Chapter 6.

Conclusion

I opened this chapter with a quotation from Yalom, as it has been my experience that people in distress need most of all a caring, empathic, supportive presence, a presence able to suspend judgement and not impose their own agenda, and be capable enough not to shy away from another human being's distress, a presence who is supported enough themselves (via clinical supervision) and be capable of managing their own, only too human, reactions (countertransference).

Marginalised, excluded and stigmatised people are most in need of human recognition, validation and containment. As Shakespeare's *King Lear* so poignantly demonstrates, under all of the social roles, status, wealth and power are but frail human beings who need to feel recognised and that they are part of the human race after all. One aspect of 'interpersonal trauma' (Sanderson, 2010) is being treated without humanity, as an animal rather than a human being. It falls to us not to repeat that by falling into the trap of treating other human beings only as cases or numbers.

References

Allen, J.G. (2013) *Mentalizing in the Development and Treatment of Attachment Trauma.* London: Karnac Books.
Alwin, N. (2006) 'The Causes of Personality Disorder.' In M.J. Sampson, R.A. McCubbin and P. Tyrer (eds) *Personality Disorder and Community Mental Health Teams: A Practitioner's Guide.* Chichester: John Wiley and Sons.
Anthony, W.A. (1993) 'Recovery from mental illness: the guiding vision of the mental health system in the 1990s.' *Psychosocial Rehabilitation Journal 16*, 4, 11–23.
Bateman, A. and Fonagy, P. (2004) *Psychotherapy for Borderline Personality Disorder: Mentalisation-Based Treatment.* Oxford: Oxford University Press.
Bateman, A. and Fonagy, P. (2006a) *Mentalization-Based Treatment for Borderline Personality Disorder: A Practical Guide.* Oxford: Oxford University Press.
Bateman, A. and Fonagy, P. (2006b) 'Mentalizing and Borderline Personality Disorder.' In J.G. Allen and P. Fonagy (eds) *Handbook of Mentalization-Based Treatment.* Chichester: John Wiley and Sons.
Bleiberg, E., Rossouw, T., and Fonagy, P. (2012) 'Adolescent breakdown and emerging borderline personality disorder.' In Eds. Bateman and Fonagy, *Handbook of mentalizing in mental health practice.* 463–510. Washington DC: American Psychiatric Publishing.
Bowlby, J. (1997) *Attachment.* London: Pimlico.
Bowlby, J. (1998a) *Separation, Anger and Anxiety.* London: Pimlico.
Bowlby, J. (1998b) *Loss, Sadness and Depression.* London: Pimlico.
Boyle, D. and Harris, M. (2009) *The Challenge of Co-Production: How Equal Partnerships between Professionals and the Public are Crucial to Improving Public Services.* London: NESTA.
Castillo, H. (2016) *The Reality of Recovery in Personality Disorder.* London: Jessica Kingsley Publishers.
Conolly, J.M.P. (2016) 'Pre-treatment Therapy for Multiply Excluded Homeless People in Central London.' Masterclass presentation delivered at the Royal College of Physicians in Dublin.
Conolly, J.M.P. and Ashton, P. (2011) 'Staff and ex-service user co-working: a counseling service's enhanced response to multiple exclusion homelessness.' *Housing, Care and Support 14*, 4, 134–141.

Conolly, J.M.P. and Ashton, P. (2013) 'Homelessness and Personality Disorder – A Journey towards Co-production.' Presentation delivered at the 1st International Homeless and Inclusion Health Conference, London.

Conolly, J.M.P. and Ashton, P. (2014) 'Anger Discussion Group: A New Approach to Engaging Rough Sleepers towards Working Together towards Solutions.' Presentation delivered at the 2nd International Homeless and Inclusion Health Conference, London.

Conolly, J.M.P. and Ashton, P. (2016) 'From Symptoms to People, A Counsellors Enhanced Response to Multiply Excluded Homeless People.' Presentation delivered at the 4th International Homeless and Inclusion Health Conference, London.

Daniel, S.I.F. (2015) *Adult Attachment Patterns in a Treatment Context: Relationship and Narrative.* Abingdon: Routledge.

Danquah, A.N. and Berry, K. (2016) *Attachment Theory in Adult Mental Health.* Abingdon: Routledge.

Department of Health (2010) 'Healthcare for Single Homeless People.' London: Office of the Chief Analyst.

Faulkner, A. (2012) 'Participation and Service User Involvement.' In D. Harper and A.R. Thompson (eds) *Qualitative Research Methods in Mental Health and Psychotherapy.* Chichester: Wiley-Blackwell.

Fonagy, P. (2001) *Attachment and Psychoanalysis.* London: Karnac.

Fonagy, P. and Target, M.T. (2003) *Psychoanalytic Theories: Perspectives from Developmental Psychopathology.* New York: Brunner-Routledge.

Goffman, E. (1968) *Stigma: Notes on the Management of Spoiled Identity.* London: Penguin.

Gutheil, T.G. (2005) 'Boundary issues and personality disorders.' *Journal of Psychiatric Practice 11*, 421–429.

Haigh, R. (2006) 'People's Experiences of Having a Diagnosis of Personality Disorder.' In M.J. Sampson, R.A. McCubbin and P. Tyrer (eds) *Personality Disorder and Community Mental Health Teams: A Practitioner's Guide.* Chichester: John Wiley and Sons.

Herman, J.L. (2012) 'Shattered Shame States and Their Repair.' In J. Yelin and K. White (eds) *Shattered States – Disorgnized Attachment And Its Repair.* London: Karnac Books.

Holmes, J. (2006) *The Search for the Secure Base: Attachment Theory and Psychotherapy*, 5th edition. Abingdon: Routledge.

Kane, E. (2006) 'Personality Disorder: New Initiatives in Staff Training.' In M.J. Sampson, R.A. McCubbin and P. Tyrer (eds) *Personality Disorder and Community Mental Health Teams: A Practitioner's Guide.* Chichester: John Wiley and Sons.

Keats, H., Cockersell, P., Maguire, N.J., and Johnson, R. (2012) *Psychologically Informed Services for Homeless People: Good Practice Guide.* London: Department of Communities and Local Government. Accessed October 2017 at https://eprints.soton.ac.uk/340022

Levy, J.S. (2013) *Pretreatment Guide.* Ann Arbor, MI: Loving Healing Press.

Maguire, N.J., Johnson, R., Vostanis, P., Keats, H. and Remington, R.E. (2009) 'Homelessness and complex trauma: a review of the literature.' University of Southampton.

Maruna, S. and Ramsden, D. (2004) 'Living to Tell the Tale: Redemption Narratives, Shame Management, and Offender Rehabilitation.' In A. Lieblich, D.P. McAdams and R. Josselson (eds) *Healing Plots: The Narrative Basis of Psychotherapy.* Washington, DC: American Psychological Association.

McDonagh, T. (2011) *Tackling Homelessness and Exclusion: Understanding Complex Lives.* York: The Joseph Rowntree Foundation.

NICE (2009) *Borderline Personality Disorder: Treatment and Management. NICE Clinical Guideline 78.* London: NICE.

NIMHE (National Institute for Mental Health in England) (2003) *Personality Disorder No Longer a Diagnosis of Exclusion.* London: Department of Health.

Prochaska, J.O. and Norcross, J.C. (2003) *Systems of Psychotherapy: A Transtheoretical Analysis*, 5th edition. Belmont, CA: Thompson-Brooks/Cole.

Prouty, G., Van Werde, D. and Portner, M. (2002) *Pre-therapy: Reaching Contact-Impaired Clients.* Ross-on-Wye: PCCS Books.

Roberts, A.R., and Yeager, K.R. (2009) *The Pocket Guide to Crisis Intervention.* Oxford: Oxford University Press.

Rothschild, B. (2003) *The Body Remembers Casebook.* New York: W.W. Norton.

Sanderson, C. (2010) *Introduction to Counselling Survivors of Interpersonal Trauma.* London: Jessica Kingsley Publishers.
Scanlon, C. and Adlam, J. (2006) 'Housing "unhoused minds": inter-personality disorder in the organisation?' *Journal of Housing Care and Support 9,* 3, 9–14.
Wallin, D.J. (2007) *Attachment in Psychotherapy.* New York: The Guilford Press.
Winnicott, D.W. (1965) 'Ego Distortion in Terms of True and False Self.' In *The Maturational Process and the Facilitating Environment: Studies in the Theory of Emotional Development.* New York: International Universities Press.
Yalom, I.D. (1980) *Existential Psychotherapy.* New York: Basic Books.
Yalom, I.D. and Leszcz, M. (2005) *The Theory and Practice of Group Psychotherapy,* 5th edition. New York: Basic Books.
Young, J.E., Klosko, J.S. and Weishaar, M.E. (2003) *Schema Therapy.* New York: Guilford Press.

7
PSYCHOTHERAPY WITH HOMELESS WOMEN
NICOLA SAUNDERS

Introduction

In 2014, St Mungo's published the *Rebuilding Shattered Lives* report, which highlighted the many and interrelated difficulties women encounter both leading up to losing their homes and whilst homeless. The report identified that women were found to be failing in their recovery because of an inadequate response to their specific needs by mainstream homeless services. Interviews conducted with female clients of St Mungo's found that, amongst other things, women wanted to speak to someone with skills and experience who would understand their experiences, but they were not being offered a space or situation to do this. Although many of the women interviewed for the report described difficulties with emotional and psychological wellbeing, many also said that psychological interventions through mainstream mental health services were inaccessible for them. As a consequence of the report, the women's psychotherapy service was set up within LifeWorks, the established psychodynamic psychotherapy service at St Mungo's, to give women the option of requesting to see a female psychotherapist. In addition, the women's service is developing 12-week closed psychoeducational groups for women. Over the course of the last three years' clinical work we have developed a trauma-informed way of working, which incorporates a psychosocial understanding of the emotional needs of women, and in particular women who have been homeless. The focus of this chapter is on how a gender- and trauma-informed way of working has been put into practice with women who attend individual psychotherapy.

The need for women-only provision

The route to becoming homeless is never straightforward and this is reflected in the stories of the women who come to psychotherapy. Consequently, broad-brush explanations of the ways in which women become homeless do not do justice to the attempts women make to avoid losing their home, or convey the distressing and difficult ways in which it happens. The extent of homelessness in general is probably underestimated, but accurate figures for the number of women who are homeless are particularly difficult because they are hidden or hide themselves away and are therefore not included in counts of people sleeping on the streets, which focus on known areas for rough sleepers. There appear to be two reasons for this. First, evidence shows that women avoid living on the streets if they possibly can because of their fear of violence and sexual assault. Instead, women 'sofa surf' between friends and extended family, often for long periods of time ranging between several months to several years. Second, when women do sleep rough they tend to avoid areas where rough sleepers congregate at night, preferring – for safety, as clients have told me – to keep walking and ride night buses or hide themselves away (Reeve, Casey and Goudie, 2006; St Mungo's, 2014). From the women referred for psychotherapy, approximately a third say they have had periods of sleeping rough before living in a hostel. Generally, these are women who do not have trusted family or support networks they can go to nearby or at all. Lengths of homelessness vary considerably, with a small number of women never having a place they refer to as their own home; leaving institutional or foster care they have moved into a homeless hostel, 'sofa surfed' or lived with a partner. Other women leave their family home as a teenager because of parental violence and substance use, or their mother or father may have a new partner and they are expected to leave home. A mental health crisis and frequent periods of time on a psychiatric ward have meant other women are living in supported housing before moving into alternative accommodation. Or, with the help of an outreach worker, women could stop staying with an acquaintance who provided a place to sleep in return for sex or drugs, and move into a hostel.

Demographics and start of the service

The women's service has led to a lowering of the average age of referrals to the overall LifeWorks psychotherapy service; women in their early 20s through to women in their late 60s are coming to therapy and we have also seen an increase in the ethnic diversity of clients. Information collected from referrals to the service shows that most of the women referred have experienced violence and abuse in their relationships with men, and have been the victim of abuse as children. A high proportion of women say they have attempted suicide, use class A substances and/or drink alcohol. Current and historical use of self-injury is common amongst referrals. A small group of women have been violent and/or abusive to another adult. Over half of the women referred have children, including adult children. We have found that young children of women coming to the service are likely to be in the care of their family members, including their mother, which can prove to be a harsh and painful turn of events for women who believe that their mothers have got away with not looking after them only then to be given care of their child.

The women's service is promoted throughout the organisation. Clients can refer themselves and do on the recommendation of other women who have attended, although most often referrals come via keyworkers based in accommodation projects. Women are asked at the point of referral what they want from attending psychotherapy sessions. Overwhelmingly women say they want to talk about what has happened to them and have help to cope with or make sense of their thoughts and behaviour in the present. This includes wanting to understand why their relationships with men are violent and abusive, their long-term substance use in relation to their life experiences and sometimes in relation to not repeating with their children what happened to them. Some women coming to psychotherapy wish to regain contact with adult children or other members of their family. Expressions of wanting to 'move forward' or 'move on' and hoping that talking to someone about what has happened to them will help them realise this are common.

Over the course of the initial months of the service taking referrals, it became clear that what women were bringing to psychotherapy in their personal histories, emotional and behavioural presentations were the long-term effects of interpersonal trauma, including sexual abuse. Bessel Van der Kolk (1989) describes how people, without conscious thought, repeatedly expose themselves to situations which are reminiscent of the original trauma they experienced. Freud thought this compulsion to repeat the trauma was a way people would master and gain control over the initial trauma. However, clinical experience has established that this is not the case, and contemporary psychotherapy understands that compulsive, repetitious, traumatic re-enactments cause considerable further suffering to the person. Such re-enactments include taking on the role of perpetrator and causing harm to others, repeating a pattern of re-victimisation – victims of childhood abuse and neglect are more likely to go on to have abusive adult relationships and enter prostitution, or harm themselves through self-injury, suicide attempts, substance misuse and self-starvation.

The extent of the layered experiences of trauma throughout the lives of the women we were meeting, combined with their own violence and aggression towards themselves and on occasion others, required a way of being able to think about and work with women who had had such experiences, were living in homeless hostels and attending psychotherapy once a week. Most important was to find a way to engage women in a relationship with their psychotherapist when their experiences of relationships, including those with women, had largely been abusive and neglectful.

Trauma informed

Trauma is a shock, the result of a life experience which penetrates the normal defences of the mind. Observable immediate damage does not have to be present for the event to be traumatising. Indeed the hidden damage trauma causes will only become evident some time after the actual event. People respond to traumatic events differently and whether the event is experienced alone or with others can affect how people react. In the case of childhood trauma, children experience repeated incidents where they have felt endangered as a consequence of the actions of their caregiver, which exposes them repeatedly to extreme stress on a cognitive, somatic and emotional level, causing damage to the developing mind and personality of the child (Van der Kolk, 1989, 2014). The development of women's psychotherapy provision was guided by the understanding that the childhood environment within which women grew up failed them because it was neglectful and abusive and left them unable to trust and depend upon it safely.

Attachment theory (Bowlby, [1969]; Heard, Lake and McCluskey, 2012) describes the baby's predetermined instinct to ensure their survival by seeking the care they cannot provide for themselves by their forming an attachment with their caregivers who are predetermined to instinctively respond to their child by giving them care. When a child's care-seeking is responded to with danger rather than care, fear becomes part of the care-seeking attachment system and the response to experiencing fear which exists in all mammals is the fight and flight reflex; part of our automatic nervous system and out of our conscious control, it develops in the first two years of life and acts as our first line of defence. The child's absolute dependency on their parents and carers means that when they are in danger from the people they depend upon for their survival, the fight and flight reflex – stay and fight or get to safety – cannot be acted upon.

Following Bowlby's (1997) theory that each person develops an 'internal working model' of the relationships they have with other people over the course of their life, Heard *et al.* (2012) write that each person has an internalised hierarchy of internal working models, with their primary attachment figures at the top of the hierarchy. When a person has an internal working model of a relationship with an attachment figure or figures they associate with fear, at the times when they seek care, the fearful attachment figure in their internal working model will come to the fore, displacing other supportive experiences of relationships.

The attachment system of caregiving and care-seeking is present throughout a person's life cycle, and is why the experience of being in a relationship which responds with understanding and care to a person who has previously not experienced this, has such potential for healing. By understanding that a significant number of women who come for psychotherapy, and especially at the start, may well do so in a fearful state, we can expect that a woman's fight–flight reflex will be activated. This understanding enables the psychotherapist to prepare herself for being experienced as frightening and for her to be mindful of how she communicates to the client; this includes her tone of voice, body language and the words she uses. In many cases the process of the psychotherapist making phone contact with women directly and setting up the initial appointment with the client helps ameliorate some of this potential fear. However, the first physical meeting of the woman with her psychotherapist, with the close physical proximity of being in a room together, can be a powerful and overwhelming encounter for some. This has the potential for being a shameful and confusing experience for a lot of women who can be taken by surprise by their fear in this context, especially when they are aware they are becoming aggressive or feel they must leave the session abruptly – the fight–flight response in action. Being prepared that such a reaction might occur enables the psychotherapist to be able to keep thinking in the moment and respond to her client by kindly suggesting what they think is happening and helping her to leave in a way that she feels she can come back.

Another common response of people who have experienced trauma is to falsely take responsibility for what was done to them. Bessel Van der Kolk (1989) says that this is a way for people to replace their unpleasant and destabilising feelings of vulnerability and helplessness, with the illusion of their being in control of what occurred to them. In children who have had to find a way of getting through repeated encounters with carers which evoke overwhelming feelings of helplessness and fear in order to survive, self-blame is found to be highly prevalent. So is the need in children for maintaining an image of their parent as 'good' rather than allowing the feelings of anger and fear evoked in them by the carer to be felt internally as this brings with it the possibility that their carer will see this. The psychoanalyst W.R.D. Fairbairn (2003 [1952]) describes how the basis for a child's early personality development is their identification with their parents; consequently, if a child is treated badly by her carers, she will feel it is she who is 'bad' and feel shameful. Whilst this early intrapsychic course of action secures the child's physical survival it does so at a cost; the abusive control the parental figure has over the child in the external world is continued in their internal world. Women attending psychotherapy frequently hold an intrinsic belief in themselves as being 'bad' and to blame for what has happened to them. The belief that they are to blame has a considerable control over women and it is difficult for the psychotherapist to support women to overcome this. Messler Davis and Frawley (1994) say it is most often a feature of psychotherapy with women who have been sexually abused. Whilst this belief can be an obstacle to engaging women in psychotherapy beyond the initial sessions, by understanding how such an unforgiving and deeply held belief came about, we can think about how a therapeutic relationship may be established.

Relevance of understanding gender development for the work

Fundamental to and interwoven with both the developing attachment system and personality is whether the child is a girl or boy. The thoughts and fantasies of parents and others about the sex of a baby begin before the baby is born and the sex of the baby will influence how he or she will be brought up and mothered. The feminist psychoanalysts Susie Orbach and Luise Eichenbaum (Orbach and Eisenbaum, 2000 [1983]; Orbach, 2005 [1986]) say that mothers not only have the job of emotionally and physically caring for their children, they also have the task of socialising their child into the gender of being a girl or a boy. Because the women we see bring difficulties to psychotherapy which cannot be entirely understood from an attachment and psychodynamic perspective, the women's psychotherapy service is informed by the psychosocialisation of girls and women. This allows us to take into account the influence of culture on gender formation on feminine identity, including women's role as a homemaker with the implication that homeless women are outside the norms of what it is to be a woman. We are curious about the uniqueness of each woman's history and experience in addition to the mother–daughter relationship.

Women, say Orbach and Eichenbaum (2000 [1983]) are raised by their mothers to respond to the emotional and dependency needs of other people, their children, partners and friends, whilst being told they are dependent on others, most often men. Mothers pass on to their daughters, through a process of inconsistently meeting their daughter's dependency needs, what they themselves were taught, that girls' and women's feelings of vulnerability and need for emotional dependency are wrong. Girls experience this sometimes as being responded to and soothed by their mother. At other times their initiatives for receiving care and support are curtailed or even disregarded by their mother completely. This experience becomes internalised within girls as it is they who are 'wrong' to have a need for dependency, which in turn engenders uncomfortable shameful feelings about their own emotional needs. This gets resolved internally by girls denying their need for dependency. At the same time, girls' identification with their mothers teaches them to look outside of themselves to notice and be responsive to the emotional needs of others. The validation and approval they receive from their mothers and other women reinforce this behaviour as being acceptable for girls, whilst at the same time they become increasingly alienated from their own need for emotional nurturance. In the long term, women's role of responding to the needs of others will thwart their attempts at gaining the emotional support they long for. The experience of having their dependency needs inconsistently met means women develop an insecure rather than secure internalised sense of self, which causes women to feel precariously attached in their sexual relationships with partners.

This means that in our work with women we encounter a twofold failure of dependency: an internalised experience of a childhood environment that failed to meet their need for dependency because it was abusive and frightening, and the gendered denial of the girl's need for emotional dependency, internalised as it is she who is 'wrong' to have emotional needs. Where the emphasis lies – the failure of a dependent environment or a denial of her emotional dependency – changes during and in between psychotherapy sessions, and it is incumbent on the psychotherapist to be alert to the presence of both.

Adolescence

'Identity formation' says Erikson (1968) is one of the central tasks of adolescence and this is as much a social process as it is an individual one. An adolescent girl's sense of self is established through her day-to-day life, which will include the influence of peers and gendered images of what is the culturally acceptable feminine identity at that time. A common theme for a teenage girl is that she should be focused on her relationships with others. The life expectations an adolescent has for herself, as well as the expectations others have for her will be influenced by her social class, ethnicity, where she lives and the type of work and income of her parent(s). In relation to the women we see, many have had few opportunities to pursue the wishes they had for themselves, some were expected to leave school to get paid work, others without care and guidance stopped going to school or left due to an unplanned pregnancy. Women do express regrets about leaving school early and some are pursuing their wish to go to college. Hope for the future of the younger generation is present in women's encouragement of their children to value their education, although women tend to attribute their children's abilities to other people. A small group of women attending the service have attended higher education and university.

One of the consequences of women being brought up to deny rather than articulate their emotional needs is that women consciously and unconsciously use their own bodies, and in some cases their children, as a means of communication or a way of overcoming and avoiding what they feel and cannot express. Much has been written on women's use of their body (Pines, 1983; Welldon, 1992; Orbach, 2005 [1986]; Motz, 2008, 2014; Lawrence, 2008), and has contributed to the service's thinking and work with women who come to psychotherapy with eating disorders, mainly anorexia and bulimia, self-injury and substance use. Usually these behaviours begin in adolescence; however, all have their antecedents in early childhood.

Self-harm is one of the ways women endeavour to assert control over their mind and emotions by releasing painful tension and anger, most commonly for the service by cutting themselves. When considering eating disorders, it is highly possible that women are restricting their food intake or are bulimic far more than has been identified thus far in the service. Women who are drinking or using drugs explain not buying food as a financial necessity on their limited income, although it is noticeable that when these same women do stop using substances, they restrict their eating or mention purging after eating due to an upset stomach. Lawrence (2008) describes eating disorders as the way some women stop themselves from thinking. Therefore, there is a very likely connection to women who are abstaining from drugs and alcohol replacing eating disorders as a means of avoiding their anger and distress. Also, like women in general, women who have been homeless are influenced by the cultural pressure on women to be thin. Therefore, increasing our awareness and work with eating disorders is an area for the service to develop. Importantly, in whatever way women use their body, psychotherapy can, through a process of gentle curiosity and linking actions to feelings and thoughts, help women to understand what their actions mean to them in order to learn how to express themselves rather than cause themselves harm.

Understanding the role of adolescent sexual relationships is an important aspect of psychotherapy as they are reflective of the more general failure of childhood emotional dependency amongst our clients (Pines, 1983; Welldon, 1988). The significant physical bodily changes girls go through during puberty bring with them attention and approval from boys although this is primarily focused on their appearance. For the women we see who were deprived of emotional care and attention growing up, and in many cases objectified and sexually abused, the attention they receive, combined with what Pines (1983) calls their 'sexual aliveness', provides them with the means of overcoming a lonely and fearful childhood. What they were also seeking in the attention of boys was emotional care, although the sexual attention they received enabled them to avoid their painful feelings. It is important to be clear that this is not adult sexual desire but young girls craving for the kindness they did not receive as a child. Nor are heterosexual sexual relationships in adolescence an indicator of adult women's sexuality.

Longitudinal research conducted in the US is valuable in highlighting just how isolated girls who have been sexually abused in childhood are when they encounter the turbulence of adolescence. The research found that these girls did not have close friendships with other girls prior to adolescence and did not make supportive friendship networks during adolescence which could help them cope with the potentially confusing and traumatising contact they had with boys. In contrast, girls who had not been sexually abused before puberty were found to have supportive and secure friendship groups which included boys before and during adolescence, who provided them with relief from the stresses of the challenges and changes they faced (Van der Kolk, 2014).

For some of our clients adolescent sexual relationships resulted in unplanned pregnancies, which can also be understood as their attempt to fill up their emotional emptiness (Pines; 1983) with a baby who would love them. By our understanding both adolescent sexual relationships and unplanned pregnancies in this way, the emotional needs underlying such behaviour are available to be understood by the women themselves and used to inform our work with women who clinical experience shows have very little empathy for their adolescent self. Sadly, women's own shame and disproval of their adolescent years has been reinforced by the pejorative judgements they have received from others, including other women.

It is also important that we consider the impact of the intense objectification of women's bodies and in particular the impact the sexualisation of adolescent girls in our culture has on our clients. Stoppard (2000) says that the sexualisation of adolescent girls places all adolescent girls, whether they are having sex or not, at an increased risk of rape and sexual assault. Accounts from women include experiences of unwanted sexual attention as an adolescent, often by men who were older and known to them, which in some cases became a contributory factor to their leaving home. Incidents of rape and sexual assault as a teenager are not uncommon.

Writing specifically about women who use alcohol and drugs, Covington (1997) says women encounter negative and derogatory social perceptions which men who use drugs and alcohol do not. Consequently, women who drink and use drugs are regarded as being sexually promiscuous and available for sex, which then places them at risk of aggression and sexual assault when they are under the influence of substances. Women who drink and use drugs experience higher levels of violence and abuse in general and are more in need of medical and hospital attention for their injuries than women who do not.

In our experience, women's use of drugs and alcohol started during their adolescence, although some women describe the normalisation and availability of alcohol and drugs due to parental substance use as contributing to their use of them at a younger age. Drinking with groups of friends in parks and public spaces or being given illegal drugs by an older male boyfriend is far more common. By the time we see them in psychotherapy the initial benefits of fulfilling their unmet dependency needs by helping them feel more confident and capable rather than lonely and ashamed, has diminished as the frequency and amount of using or drinking increases. When talking about the reasons for their current drug and alcohol use, women usually say it is to stop them from thinking and feeling. This both isolates women and adds to the likelihood they will take risks to get drugs, which in turn increases the likelihood of their becoming victims of violence and abuse. It is a reality for some women who are physically and emotionally dependent on alcohol and drugs that this is far less intimidating and reliable than being in relationship with others, including a psychotherapist.

All the women who do engage in psychotherapy, and especially those with children, have encountered stigma and judgement surrounding their substance misuse, and therefore find talking about it shaming and painful. By far the majority of women we see have made attempts to stop drinking or taking drugs at some time and find the occasions when their efforts have been successful to be double edged. They see pleasure in others and receive affirmation from workers, whilst they are left feeling deprived and out of control of feelings and thoughts substances have helped them avoid. Beside these difficulties they feel controlled by the demands of others which they experience as a repetition of earlier helplessness and abuse.

Brown, Harris and Fallot (2013), writing about trauma-informed care for substance use services, say trauma survivors who use substances require a relationship with a worker which is safe and trustworthy and does not repeat the coercion and control of earlier abusive relationships. However, very often the testing and prescribing regimes of drug and alcohol services result in just that and place both female and male workers in the role of coercive perpetrator to their clients. This re-enactment, where women find themselves in the position again of being 'done to', creates a dynamic within which women react in fearful anger and defiance. In both cases, their actions are often misunderstood. Providing psychotherapy can be neutral and take place outside of any conditions put on women from other services. Women will have, for the first time, the opportunity to talk openly about their substance use and explore their ambivalent feelings around giving up drinking or using drugs without expectations, criticism or judgement.

Parallel to the high prevalence of substance use amongst women using the service is their experience of domestic violence. In a review of the academic literature on domestic violence and the rates of violence from women to men and men to women, Johnson (2008, in Motz, 2014) says that the most severe forms of violence or 'intimate terrorism' are committed by men against women. This is different to 'situational couple violence' which is less severe, and there is evidence of this being committed by women and men within relationships. Because a considerable number of women coming for psychotherapy have been in more than one abusive relationship, it is important that women are able to have what they are asking for. That is psychotherapy, which gives them the opportunity they want to understand how their early childhood trauma is connected to and repeated in the kind of intimate relationships they have as an adult. Violent and abusive relationships reinforce women's internalised belief of themselves as a 'bad' and worthless people. When this is combined with the destruction of their sense of agency, women take on the role assigned to them by the perpetrator to be objects which are controlled and maltreated (Motz, 2014).

Not all women who have experienced domestic violence have substance use problems. Nevertheless, women's role of caring for others does mean that women who do not have an alcohol problem stay in relationships with men who do. It is clear from the women who come for psychotherapy that domestic violence has profound and longstanding emotional consequences for them, the effects of which reach into all areas of their lives. The gendered analysis of the Adult Psychiatric Morbidity Survey carried out by Agenda (2016) shows that women who have been in a violent relationship as an adult have a significantly lower household income and live in worse quality rented accommodation, identified by the report as a home which has mould, than women who have not.

Women, fear and anger

Because women bring to psychotherapy a deprived experience of relationships with their mother, being offered a relationship within which they can feel secure, able to talk to another woman and have an experience of being listened to and understood is a fundamentally important part of the psychotherapy. Essential to this is the psychotherapist's own ability to be reliably present with another woman and alive to unmet needs women bring, rather than rigid and mechanical. Because this is a new experience it is not without its difficulties and women require time to overcome, with the understanding of the psychotherapist, the activated expectation that they will be judged and criticised, that their upset is wrong and evidence of weakness rather than emotional needs which will be met with kindness. Just as significant is the psychotherapist being able to develop a relationship between herself and her client which enables the woman to understand her feelings, including the more difficult and often shameful emotions of anger and aggression which can come from feeling in danger. Mitchell (1993) describes feeling endangered as a subjective experience with no connection to how another person might assess the situation, and aggression is a response to feeling endangered. Supporting women to understand that their anger and aggression are interrelational and began as a child, and how that experience informs their experience of people, including their psychotherapist as an adult, is a complicated and important part of the psychotherapy. The use of psychoeducation, which in this case is the giving of information about the fight–flight–freeze response – a powerful bodily response to fear, repeated and recontextualised as women talk about their current experiences, is vital in helping women to understand the dangers they feel from their subjective experiences.

This creates the possibility that psychotherapy can be a place where the woman can begin to think about her anger rather than be disorganised by it, and to begin to connect in relationship with her psychotherapist to the more difficult feeling states of her vulnerability and unmet need for dependency. Also, that anger is a human emotion: clinical experience shows that women feel a righteous anger about what has been done to them, and this does not have to be acted upon in violence against the self. This part of the therapy takes time and may not be possible for some women in psychotherapy once a week. However, if we want to support women in becoming aware of how they take their anger out on their own bodies when they injure themselves or understand how they avoid their emotional pain and helpless vulnerability by gaining a false sense of empowerment by identifying with both the perpetrator of abuse and themselves as victims in putting themselves in harm's way, it is important that we try.

Conclusion

The clinical experience of LifeWorks women's service shows that women make use of psychotherapy which is gender and trauma informed and is accessible to them. Central to the provision of gender- and trauma-informed psychotherapy is the clinical thinking: an understanding of women's gendered experience of having their care-seeking needs curtailed and inconsistently responded to leads women to deny their own needs. Combined with the fear and neglect of abusive traumatised care-seeking means they have experienced a twofold failure of dependency. Women are subject to social expectations and judgements which men are not and this is especially the case with women who have been homeless. The failure to understand the influence of the social on women's psychology and behaviour leaves women, in particular those women who do not have the social power to respond, being misunderstood. By incorporating a gender- and trauma-informed approach it has been possible to provide women with a psychotherapy relationship where their own emotional needs can be brought into awareness and validated, whilst the long-term effects of their traumas are listened to and understood. Both of these areas are a prerequisite for behaviour change and demonstrate the usefulness of psychotherapy with this client group.

Acknowledgements: Thank you to the remarkable women who have attended the women's psychotherapy service from whom I have learned a lot. Thank you also to my past and present colleagues in LifeWorks for your humour and support: Lydia Adobaya, Suad Ahmed, Christos Christophy, Eric Harper, Anna Learmonth, Lee Murphy, Jake Osborne, Chris Scanlon, Sham Selvaratnam, Ian Simpson, Anja Trenkle, Jo Williams, Ana Valea, Rose Ann Varley, Deirdre Vereker.

References

Agenda (2016) *Hidden Hurt – Violence, Abuse and Disadvantage in the Lives of Women*. Accessed October 2017 at http://weareagenda.org/wp-content/uploads/2015/11/Hidden-Hurt-full-report1.pdf

Bowlby, J. (1969) *Attachment and Loss*. New York: Basic Books.

Bowlby, J. (1997) *A Secure Base: Clinical Applications of Attachment Theory*. London: Routledge.

Brown, V.B., Harris, M. and Fallot, R. (2013) 'Moving toward trauma-informed practice in addiction treatment: a collaborative model of agency assessment.' *Journal of Psychoactive Drugs* 45, 5, 386–393.

Covington, S.S. (1997) 'Women, Addiction and Sexuality.' In L. Straussner and E. Zelvin (eds) *Gender Issues in Addiction: Men and Women in Treatment*. New York: Jason Aronson.

Erikson, E.H. (1968) *Identity and the Life Cycle*. London: W.W. Norton.

Fairbairn, W.R.D. (2003) *Psychoanalytic Studies of the Personality*. Hove: Brunner-Routledge.

Heard. D., Lake. B. and McCluskey, U. (2012) *Attachment Therapy with Adolescents and Adults*. London: Karnac.

Lawrence. M. (2008) *The Anorexic Mind*. London: Karnac Books.

Messler Davis, J. and Frawley, M.G. (1994) *Treating the Adult Survivor of Childhood Sexual Abuse*. New York: Basic Books.

Mitchell, S.A. (1993) *Hope and Dread in Psychoanalysis*. New York: Basic Books.

Motz. A. (2008) *The Psychology of Female Violence*. London: Routledge.

Motz, A. (2014) *Toxic Couples: The Psychology of Domestic Violence*. London: Routledge.

Orbach, S. (2005 [1986]) *Hunger Strike*. London: Karnac.

Orbach. S and Eichenbaum. L (2000 [1983]) *What Do Women Want?* London: Harper and Collins.

Pines, D. (1983) *A Woman's Unconscious Use of Her Body*. London: Virago.

Reeve, K., Casey, R. and Goudie, R. (2006) *Homeless Women: Still Being Failed Yet Striving to Survive*. London: Crisis.

Stoppard, J.M. (2000) *Understanding Depression*. London: Routledge.

St. Mungos (2014) *Rebuilding Shattered Lives: The Final Report*. Accessed October 2017 at http://rebuildingshatteredlives.org/read-the-report

Van Der Kolk, B. (1989) 'The compulsion to repeat the trauma.' *Psychiatric Clinics of North America*, 12, 2, 389–411.

Van Der Kolk, B. (2014) *The Body Keeps the Score*. New York: Penguin.

Welldon. E.V. (1992) *Mother, Madonna, Whore: The Idealization and Denigration of Motherhood*. London: Karnac.

8

PIE-ONEERING PSYCHOLOGICAL INTEGRATION IN HOMELESS HOSTELS

DR EMMA WILLIAMSON

Introduction

If someone is not able to develop an 'internal psychological home' through early care and psychological and physical security they will struggle to find an 'external home where they can feel safe and settle' (Adlam and Scanlon, 2006). The prevalence of early deprivation, adverse childhood events and complex trauma in chronic homelessness have been well documented (Fazel *et al.*, 2008; Maguire *et al.*, 2009; Roos *et al.*, 2013). What needs further attention, however, is how to helpfully intervene with such groups in a meaningful and sustainable way. This chapter will discuss a Lambeth-based multiagency 'Psychologically Informed Environments' model that we feel has been helpful in addressing the impact complex trauma and disrupted attachment have on homeless people's identity development and the ability to exist fully and consequently take up residence. We will recommend that to fully understand how to work with this population we need to focus on the psychological processes that underlie chronic homelessness and understand why 'care' and being 'accommodated' can feel so threatening.

Psychologically informed understanding of homelessness

Research has consistently documented the correlation between homelessness and a profusion of comorbid severe and enduring physical and mental health, and substance use issues (St Mungo's, 2013). There have been numerous recommendations about how services can meet these expansive needs (see Zerger, 2002; Essali, Tarboush and Awad, 2012); however, there continues to be a particular group of the chronically homeless who struggle to take up such care when it is offered. It is this 'revolving door' homeless group that we will be talking about here, who can arguably be differentiated from those who find themselves transiently homeless for economic or social reasons. We have found that the interventions on offer can be in danger of targeting symptoms – such as homelessness, substance use and mood – when what needs to be addressed is a developmental and relational problem. As Masters (2005) powerfully conveys in his biography of Stuart Shorter, 'Homelessness – it's not about not having a home. It's about something being seriously f[***]ing wrong.' Homeless people can appear chaotic in their lifestyle and pattern of service use. They can frequently present in crisis to multiple agencies, demonstrating a genuinely high level of urgent need, only to repeatedly fail to take up the support when offered, complete courses of treatment, reliably attend planned preventative interventions or sustain accommodation.

Within the psychodynamic literature, we have found Rey's (1994) concept of the claustro-agoraphobic dilemma helpful in understanding the intense longing for and yet profound fear of attachment – common in us all to some degree – that we feel underlies this amplified pattern of approach and avoidance in homelessness. We see time and again a desperate and terrifying need for care surfacing within a homeless individual and help being sought with pressure for an urgent solution, only to quickly be experienced as 'too much', overwhelming, intrusive or failing. The individual then retreats, care is removed and the cycle repeats as overwhelming anxieties of deprivation and abandonment build. This relentless pattern generates anxiety and frustration in both the individual and the care system. As Foster (2013), drawing on the work of Britton, explains:

> Any relationship that falls short of the fantasised perfect match between client and worker gives rise to anxieties, described by Britton

as those of being trapped by 'a deathly container, or, exposure in a shattered world...faced with these two catastrophic alternatives, incarceration or fragmentation, some people...remain paralysed at the frontier. (p.91)

The claustro-agoraphobic dilemma, where connection and separateness are equally unbearable, is felt to result from disruption during an early developmental stage when the mother and child are still a 'unit'. Through whatever means – be that loss, violation or neglect – there is a failure to complete the crucial projective and introjective processes between the mother and the infant. If this occurs, the infant can be left in an unintegrated state, with underdeveloped psychological boundaries and lacking a sense of themselves as whole and separate from others. This can result in terrible fears of either engulfment/entrapment (claustrophobic anxieties) or, by fleeing this experience, isolation and abandonment (agoraphobic anxieties). To solve this 'perpetually oscillating psychic dilemma' regarding the distance between 'self' and 'others', the individual can be left functioning in a very restricted emotional range – 'surviving "on the edge" in many senses...a failure of identity development, characterized by being neither fully one thing nor another - a kind of "threshold" existence' (Cooper and Lousada, 2005, pp.31–33). This is of direct relevance to thinking about service design and delivery with homeless people and how to work with the 'threshold existence' so many experience.

Psychologically informed service model

Johnson and Haigh (2010, 2011) and Maguire *et al.* (2009), amongst others, have called on providers to attend to the primacy of such psychological needs and complex trauma in the treatment of homelessness. One crucial vehicle for this has been the evolution of the 'Psychologically Informed Environments' (PIE) initiative (Johnson and Haigh, 2011) as a best practice recommendation by the Department for Communities and Local Government and the National Mental Health Development Unit (Maguire *et al.*, 2010; Keats *et al.*, 2012). A PIE is described as any support setting adopting a coherent shared psychological and relational framework that facilitates growth and enablement for homeless people.

Over the past five years Thames Reach, South London and Maudsley NHS Foundation Trust (SLaM) and London Borough of Lambeth (LBL)

Commissioning Team for Adults and Health have worked in partnership to deliver the PIE Lambeth Psychology in Hostels Project initiative (PiH). This truly integrated mental health and accommodation support service bases a team of National Health Service (NHS) clinical and counselling psychologists, along with some consultant psychiatry time, inside homeless hostels full time to work together with hostel staff teams. The Lambeth PiH has advanced the PIE concept and developed a service that effectively wraps three identified Lambeth hostel sites in a 'psychological envelope' where everything that happens is informed by a psychological understanding of the residents. This includes attending not only to the formal therapeutic interventions on offer, but also the physical environment, shared leadership and management approaches, risk management and level of support provided to staff via group reflective practice, individual clinical supervision and consultation, and regular training. This is important in developing a high degree of expertise and increasing all staff's capacity to manage the work and the anxieties arising from it.

As far as possible, the usual barriers and service exclusion criteria to accessing psychological therapy are removed and the psychologists have an open-door policy, working with anyone living in the hostel. Access is not based on diagnosis and the team work with the real-life complexities seen in this population. Residents who are still using alcohol or drugs are not automatically excluded from formal psychological input and comorbidities beyond mental health and substance misuse are addressed where required, including amongst others: learning disabilities, neuropsychological impairment, chronic physical health conditions and assessment of mental capacity. We have found value in the discipline of clinical psychology for such diverse clinical work and the ability to provide specialist psychometric and neuropsychological assessments or draw on a breadth of life-span and developmental expertise.

The PIH service consciously employs graded interventions of increasing physical and psychological proximity to allow residents to slowly come into contact with support – and consequently their internal world – at a manageable pace. As contact between psychologist and resident slowly moves from smiles in a corridor to chats over coffee and ultimately towards more formal therapy sessions, so too do topics of conversation slowly evolve, from comments on the weather, perhaps to passing remarks on state-of-mind to in-depth psychological work. This progression can take months of careful work. In this way, we work to avoid triggering claustro-agoraphobic anxieties as much as possible. This is an approach that is particularly important for individuals with a history of trauma who have had their physical and emotional boundaries violated and have often experienced a lack of control over their situation. The graded interventions are made possible by the on-site presence of psychology and hostel staff, creating access to flexible familiar specialist support and allowing for close partnership working and care integration. Homeless people can express suspicion of mental health services but by being on site the psychologists become familiar faces, work indirectly via the keyworker or creatively engage residents with informal activities (e.g. dog walking, gardening). This aims to break down barriers, build trust and slowly establish a relationship before potentially progressing towards more formal individual or group treatment options that require greater contact.

A case example – environmental stability to internal stability

We can see the pattern of stabilisation and increasing psychological contact made possible by the PIH model when thinking about Matt's journey. Before we met Matt, a white British man in his late 30s, he had lived on the streets for 15 years, refusing all offers of accommodation and support. He had been raised by a violent father and a 'caring but weak' mother who was unable to protect Matt or herself. Matt was taken into care at the age of eight and moved between different children's homes. By the age of 13 he was using a cocktail of drugs and alcohol to cope and was in frequent contact with the criminal justice system for crimes related to violence and theft. As a result of these early experiences Matt had difficulty forming relationships, trusting others, respecting authority, rules and the law. He was very dismissive of support and struggled to be vulnerable or show distress following a lifetime of violent and unreliable caregiving.

Matt first came to the PiH project for a couple of nights' emergency shelter during a particularly bitter winter snow storm. This offer was part of the local authority's 'Severe Weather Emergency Protocol' to provide temporary refuge to rough sleepers in dangerously cold weather. Upon arrival Matt made it clear that he did not need help or want to live in a hostel and that he would only stay for a night or two until the weather improved. After a few days Matt was invited to stay for longer and warily accepted while asserting that this was temporary and on his terms; and so it went on, gradually extending his stay with constant threats to abandon his place and assertion that he neither wanted nor needed a place. Matt struggled in how to make his needs known or seek support in appropriate ways. Negative attention had always been easy to acquire and had been reinforced by his contact with services. In these early months in the hostel Matt was often highly intoxicated, chaotic and frequently aggressive to staff and other residents, who felt increasingly exhausted by his behaviour.

In group reflective practice staff explored their various experiences of having Matt in the hostel and found themselves polarised, with some feeling compassionate and others persecuted by Matt as he split the team into good and bad. Gradually, by sharing their experiences the team found themselves able to come to a more integrated middle ground and formulate an understanding of Matt's behaviour. They described how Matt continued to push boundaries, break rules and test out the robustness and dependability of the staff team/hostel 'container'. As Scanlon and Adlam (2008) describe, 'cycle[s] of violence and perversity can be understood as an expression of longing for a safe space that [can] survive the attack and contain their rage' (p.540). In an identification with his father Matt seemed to need to control and humiliate others in an attempt to overcome his experiences of the past and take up the position of the aggressor. The team felt Matt's need to feel in control and his inability to back down when boundaries were asserted stemmed from terrible fears of intrusion and the need to keep others at a safe distance. However, other members of the team saw Matt moving from the role of the 'aggressor' to the 'protector', allying with staff to support them in managing other challenging residents or offering support with hostel maintenance, a positive means of maintaining a sense of power and control. Based on this formulation, the staff developed a 'team approach' detailing how to work most effectively and consistently with Matt. They began seeking him out for positive attention, for help with tasks and sought to give him control of his environment as much as possible. The approach was put to the test when Matt began consistently refusing to pay his service charge and was putting his tenancy at risk. It was felt he was not only fighting against authority in these moments but also an internal struggle against rising anxieties around a growing desire to stay. Hostel management met with Matt to explore his reasons for not paying and get his input into a new service charge policy. This helped Matt understand, contribute to and feel more in control of the service charge process, rather than fight against a 'done to' position. He was proud to be asked for his input and gained a sense of importance, which allowed him to begin to pay while saving face and minimising the shame and humiliation so easily evoked by capitulating to authority.

As the team and environmental container held and began to stabilise Matt, he became increasingly curious about the psychologist. The psychologist had held back until now but with a gentle, flexible and informal approach, they began meeting for walks and coffee – activities specifically chosen to feel less intense and overwhelming. As the relationship developed, Matt more readily sought the psychologist out at times of frustration or anxiety. Alongside the flexibility and gradual contact there was recognition of the importance of providing a safe reliable space or 'frame' (Parsons, 2014) characterised by continuity and consistency. This aimed to facilitate a new experience of interpersonal contact that was dependable, boundaried, containing and non-violating. Matt attempted to maintain a sense of control and separateness by choosing when he arrived for his sessions and what was discussed; but slowly they began meeting more regularly, for longer periods and were able to formalise the work. Adopting a mentalisation-based treatment (MBT) approach (Bateman and Fonagy, 2010) Matt worked on his feelings of being under attack, fears of intimacy, being taken over and the use of substances to manage these experiences.

MBT is an evidence-based approach based on attachment theory. It supports the development of emotional awareness, affect regulation, interpersonal relating and recognition of the boundary between 'Self' and 'Other'; deficits felt to both precede and perpetuate chronic homelessness (Winston, 2000). Mentalising is a form of *imaginative* mental activity about oneself and others in which you perceive and interpret human behaviour in terms of *intentional* mental states (e.g. needs, desires, feelings, beliefs). Improving the capacity to mentalise in the therapeutic relationship has been found to be later sustained outside therapy even in moments of high emotional arousal. MBT interventions were consistently adopted across the Lambeth PiH service, within a wider psychodynamic frame. Claustro–agoraphobic fears of intrusion or abandonment result from and contribute to a collapse in mentalising. We have found that mentalisation-based interventions are well placed to help clinicians operate within a bearable sphere of therapeutic proximity. For example, with Matt, close attention was paid to the moment-to-moment fluctuations in his mentalising capacity as an indication of the psychological proximity he could manage at any given time. Adaptions were therefore made in an attempt to be sensitive to feelings of 'impingement'. Despite these efforts, Matt's relationship with the psychologist occasionally broke down due to his sensitivity to psychological contact, but he found himself able to re-engage, with such instances becoming less and less common as he progressed.

Matt made substantial progress during his one-year stay. His violent and chaotic behaviour all but stopped, he had no contact with the criminal justice system, stopped using drugs and substantially reduced his alcohol intake. After several failed attempts and a sustained and coordinated effort by hostel staff, addiction and psychology teams, Matt stabilised enough to face breaking contact with the hostel and reach out to engage with a residential detox programme. Here the emergence of claustro–agoraphobic anxieties and the 'instinctual conflict between making or breaking contact' (O'Shaughnessy, 1999, p.868) again emerged and needed to be worked through. When working with 'endings' and 'move-on' there is important work to be done in understanding the pain of separation following development of an attachment relationship. This client group have commonly experienced multiple losses, relationship ruptures, unsatisfactory endings or even had a striking absence of positive attachment figures. This can make the loss of that object even harder. With this in mind the PiH team offer 'transition support' for a period of time after people move on, conduct joint meetings with new keyworkers to support the establishment of new relationships and finish pieces of therapy where needed. Former residents, like Matt, are also encouraged to return for visits, are offered opportunities to volunteer or to become part of the PiH Peer Mentor Service, allowing the PIH to be a secure base from which clients can venture out. This supports the gradual maturation and separation process and aims to work with the agoraphobic anxieties of abandonment that are stirred up by moving on that so often cause people to collapse and cycle back around the system.

Service outcomes

There are prevailing myths that homeless people are 'treatment resistant', have poor coping mechanisms for managing psychosocial interventions and do not want or engage in treatment when offered. However, we have found that homeless people readily take up and make use of support when it is specifically tailored to meet their needs and informed by a relational and developmental understanding. Our position is supported by Dykeman (2011) who, in a review of the literature, found flexible levels of contact, individualisation, a slower period of initial engagement and on-site access is consistently found in the most successful therapeutic interventions with homeless people.

For people who have experienced severe deprivation and with histories of compound trauma, Cockersell (2016) argues that 'PIEs achieve more positive outcomes than services not run as PIEs'. A growing PIE literature is demonstrating positive change in a range of areas including sustained housing, behaviour, service use and improved mental health, outcomes demonstrated in the Lambeth PiH project. The Lambeth PiH has broken new ground engaging homeless people in a planned consistent way and we are continuing to develop and improve our service model to successfully reach smaller sub-populations that have traditionally been even harder to make contact with such as homeless women and poly-substance users. Standardised self-report and clinician-rated mental health scales demonstrate clinically and statistically significant reductions in mental distress (Health of the Nation Outcome Scales – clinician rated, medium-large effect size; Clinical Outcomes in Routine Evaluation – service user rated CORE, medium effect size). This included clinically significant reductions in symptoms of depression, self-harm, agitation and aggression, substance misuse, relationship problems and activities of daily living. This is noteworthy considering the severe and enduring nature of this group's mental health difficulties. Many of these individuals have never been able to access or make use of mainstream mental health services but as a result of the work have gone on to access other services such as addictions and physical health in planned preventative ways and reduce chaotic crisis admissions. Independent research is underway, with initial health economic outcomes suggesting reductions in hospital admissions, A&E attendance, rough sleeping and a halving of all criminal justice contact, amongst others. Improvements have been noted in positive move-on and resettlement and, like Matt, high-profile homeless cases stabilised who historically have been unable to sustain accommodation. These findings come from service evaluations with further independent research underway. It is clear that PIEs show promise but there is an ongoing need to strengthen research in this area and have clarity around the service models and intervention standards needed to produce the anticipated benefits.

Conclusion

As we have seen – '[a] life lived in the excluded margins of accommodation and society can be driven by this relentless internal need to move, to reside at the edge, and not be able to psychologically stay put' (Williamson and Taylor, 2015, p.33). Here, homelessness can be understood as a developmental and relational issue where solutions beyond symptom and housing management are required for real change. In recent years, the consolidation and refocusing of psychological practice in homelessness has advanced practice nationally. There is no doubt that more research is needed, but what appears clear is that PIE – as a coherent framework of psychological thinking around homelessness – shows great promise. It offers the opportunity for service integration in a parallel process that supports clients' psychological integration, addressing the 'internal state of unhousedness' (Henderson Hospital, cited in Campbell, 2006) which has historically trapped so many on the threshold.

Acknowledgements: Thames Reach: All hostel staff, residents and senior management. SLaM: PIH team – with particular reference to Dr James Peddie, Specialist Clinical Psychologist, for his work with Matt, Psychological Medicine and Integrated Care CAG Management. LBL: Commissioning Team for Adults and Health. Independent evaluation by Southampton University and Resolving Chaos Ltd. I would also like to acknowledge the prior thinking and application of Rey's claustro–agoraphobic dilemma in earlier work with Kathy Taylor (Williamson and Taylor, 2015).

References

Adlam, J. and Scanlon, C. (2006) 'Housing "unhoused minds": inter-personality disorder in the organisation?' *Housing, care and support*, 9, 3, 9–14.

Bateman, A.W. and Fonagy, P. (2010) 'Mentalization based treatment for borderline personality disorder.' *World Psychiatry 9*, 11–15.

Campbell, J. (2006) 'Homelessness and containment: a psychotherapy project with homeless people and workers in the homeless field.' *Psychoanalytic Psychotherapy 20*, 157–174.

Cockersell, P. (2016) 'PIEs five years on.' *Mental Health and Social Inclusion 20*, 4, 221–230.

Cooper, A. and Lousada, J. (2005) *Borderline Welfare: Feeling and Fear of Feeling in Modern Welfare* (The Tavistock Clinic Series). London: Karnac.

Dykeman, B. (2011) 'Interventions strategies with the homeless population.' *Journal of Instructional Psychology 38*, 1, 32–39.

Essali, A., Tarboush, M. and Awad, M. (2012) 'Specialist interventions for homeless people with severe mental illness (protocol).' The Cochrane Library, 12.

Fazel, S., Khosla, V., Doll, H. and Geddes, J. (2008) 'The prevalence of mental disorders among the homeless in Western countries: Systematic review and meta-regression analysis.' *PLoS Medicine 5*, 12, 1670–1681.

Foster, A. (2013) 'The Deprivation of Female Drug Addicts: A Case for Specialist Treatment.' In M. Bower, R. Hale and H. Wood (eds) *Addictive States of Mind*. London: Karnac.

Johnson, R. and Haigh, R. (2010) 'Social psychiatry and social policy for the 21st century – new concepts for new needs: the psychologically informed environment.' *Mental Health and Social Inclusion 14*, 4, 30–35.

Johnson, R. and Haigh, R. (2011) 'Social psychiatry and social policy for the 21st century: new concepts for new needs – the 'Enabling Environments' initiative.' *Mental Health and Social Inclusion 15*, 1, 17–23.

Keats, H., Cockersell, P., Maguire, N.J., and Johnson, R. (2012) *Psychologically Informed Services for Homeless People: Good Practice Guide*. London: Department of Communities and Local Government. Accessed October 2017 at https://eprints.soton.ac.uk/340022

Maguire, N.J., Johnson, R., Vostanis, P., Keats, H. and Remington, R.E. (2009) *Homelessness and Complex Trauma: A Review of the Literature*. University of Southampton.

Maguire, N., Johnson, R., Vostanis, P. and Keats, H. (2010) *Meeting the Psychological and Emotional Needs of the Homeless*. Accessed October 2017 at https://eprints.soton.ac.uk/187695

Masters (2005) *Stuart: A Life Backwards*. London: Fourth Estate.

O'Shaughnessy, E. (1999) 'Relating to the superego.' *International Journal of Psychoanalysis 80*, 861–870.

Parsons, M. (2014) *Living Psychoanalysis: From Theory to Experience*. New York: Routledge.

Rey, J.H. (1994) *Universals of Psychoanalysis in the Treatment of Psychotic and Borderline States*. London: Free Association.

Roos, L.E., Mota, N., Afifi, O.A., Katz, L.Y., Distasio, J. and Sareen, J. (2013) 'Relationship between adverse childhood experiences and homelessness and the impact of axis I and II disorders.' *American Journal of Public Health 103*, 2, 275–281.

Scanlon, C. and Adlam, J. (2006) 'Housing "unhoused minds": inter-personality disorder in the organisation?' *Housing, Care and Support 9*, 3, 9–14.

Scanlon, C. and Adlam, J. (2008) 'Refusal, social exclusion and the cycle of rejection: a cynical analysis?' *Critical Social Policy 28*, 4, 529–549.

St Mungo's (2013) *Health and Homelessness: Understanding the Costs and Role of Primary Care Services for Homeless People*. Accessed December 2017 at http://cdn.basw.co.uk/upload/basw_24522-7.pdf

Williamson, E. and Taylor, K. (2015) 'Minding the margins: an innovation to integrate psychology in a homeless hostel environment.' *DCP Clinical Psychology Forum 265*, 33–37.

Winston, A.P. (2000) 'Recent developments in borderline personality disorder.' *Advances in Psychiatric Treatment 6*, 211–218.

Zerger, S. (2002) *Substance Abuse Treatment: What Works for Homeless People? A Review of the Literature*. Nahsville, TN: National Health Care for the Homeless Council. Accessed October 2017 at www.nhchc.org/wp-content/uploads/2012/02/SubstanceAbuseTreatmentLitReview.pdf

9
PIE
What the People Say
DR CATRIONA REID

Hostels and 'chronic' homelessness: a personal view

When thinking about accommodation for homeless people, hostels are often the first thing that come to mind. In 1834, workhouses were set up to accommodate those who were destitute. Migration to urban areas in the 19th century then led to increased provision of hostel accommodation for single men, the 'spike' described by George Orwell in *Down and Out in Paris and London* being a typical example (Orwell, 1933). For many years and until as late as the mid-1980s, large institutional hostels met only the most basic needs of physical shelter, often providing poor conditions and occupying the workhouse buildings that preceded them (Hutson, 1999). It has since been recognised that accommodation for homeless people can in itself provide an intervention for change and the nature and purpose of hostels have developed into improved environments which support people with a range of difficulties including mental health and substance use (DCLG, 2006).

My first contact with the homeless community was as a volunteer in a day centre in Central London. I found it very difficult to understand why, despite the offer or multiple offers of housing in hostels, a significant group of homeless people continued to 'prefer' to sleep on the streets. The chance of a roof and a bed was often rejected, or accepted and then quickly abandoned in favour of what was a cold, often dangerous and transient existence.

I then moved on to work as street outreach worker with homeless people. It soon became clear that the problem of homelessness was not simply one of the supply of housing. A view sometimes taken in the UK is that long-term homelessness is a 'lifestyle choice' (discussed in Power and Attenborough, 2003) or linked with a romantic idea of a 'traveller' being 'on the road' (Parsell, 2011) – the reality of homelessness being far from romantic. Many people were homeless for a short time for financial reasons or due to relationship breakdowns and were both willing and able to move away from the streets with some help. However, a group of people defined variously as 'entrenched', hard to reach', 'revolving door' (Teixeira, 2010) 'multiply excluded' (Fitzpatrick, Bramley and Johnsen, 2012) were frequently offered and rejected accommodation, and in many cases, any help at all. They chose not to accept, it was argued, and usually lived on the streets for years, sometimes also dying there. Whilst our team were knowledgeable in housing, immigration, the Mental Health Act, the practicalities of drug and alcohol use and had skills to help people in all kinds of practical ways, many of us struggled to understand why, short of coercion, we could not help our long-term clients move indoors. When we were able to get people through the doors of a hostel it was often after months of negotiation; such clients could generally only endure being indoors long enough to complete the housing benefit paperwork, would leave shortly afterwards and whilst we hoped in vain that they would return, they often never even slept in their rooms. It felt as if we were regularly confronted by our failure, when we met our clients day after day still on the streets. When various initiatives were suggested to 'end homelessness', the most notable being Boris Johnson's ambition to end rough sleeping by 2012 (BBC, 2008), it seemed unlikely that this would ever be achieved and indeed this was the case.

The practicalities of the homeless system in terms of commissioning, finances and pathways dictated the work. Our job was to get people 'off the street'. We would engage with them, verify their rough sleeping status, get them emergency help and often house them in an emergency shelter, who would either 'reconnect' them to their area of origin or move them into a first-stage hostel, then to a second-stage hostel and if things had not already broken down by that point, eventually into their own accommodation (again, privately rented and short term). A series of relationships were built and then broken and the prospect of security, had it ever existed, seemed a long way off.

The introduction of PIEs

Evidence about the relationship between early trauma, abuse and neglect and later psychological difficulties has long been established (Felitti et al., 1998). Abuse and neglect in childhood have been linked to disruption in normal emotional, cognitive and interpersonal development (Cloitre, Cohen and Koenen, 2006). Initial guidance about *Meeting the Psychological and Emotional Needs of Homeless People* (Maguire, Johnson, and Vostanis, 2010) cast a fresh light on this in the context of homelessness. This document made explicit links between the prevalence of complex trauma in the homeless population and subsequent psychological difficulties, in particular those relating to emotional regulation and managing attachment and loss, difficulties which commonly attract a label of personality disorder. Further evidence has since supported this, documenting high levels of physical and sexual abuse in childhood in homeless people (Sundin and Baguley, 2015) and correspondingly high levels of mental health difficulties, substance use and an estimate of personality disorder significantly higher than the general population with an upper range of 70 per cent (Fazel, Geddes, and Kushel, 2014; Fazel et al., 2008). Despite these levels of need, the anecdotal and formal evidence suggests that very few homeless people were in contact with or given meaningful care by mental health services (Bramley et al., 2015).

A later document proposed guidance on creating Psychologically Informed Environments (PIEs) (Keats et al., 2012). PIEs were suggested as a means of addressing these complex difficulties. What is a PIE? Johnson and Haigh first proposed the concept (Johnson and Haigh, 2010, 2011a, 2011b), drawing on the theory and principles of a Therapeutic Community, such as the Cassell or Henderson Hospitals: a structured and managed environment where participation in the social context provides the 'treatment' for mental health problems. PIEs were conceptualised as an 'updated' Therapeutic Community 'for the 21st century' (Haigh et al., 2012 p.35). They were proposed as neither a therapeutic model or technique nor the provision of physical shelter, but rather the attempt to provide psychological safety and rebuild damaged attachment relationships through the provision of a professional home and family (Seager, 2006, 2011). This could be applied to any service, 'such as a hostel or day centre where the social environment makes people feel emotionally safe' (Maguire et al., 2010 p.19). A 'broadly therapeutic framework' should underpin this (Keats et al., 2012 p.6).

There is no prescription for a particular psychological model, provided a coherent and consistent approach is taken:

> Wherever...psychological thinking can be translated meaningfully into a carefully considered approach to redesigning and managing the social environment, we have a PIE...the definitive marker of a PIE is simply that, if asked why the unit is run in such and such a way, the staff would give an answer couched in terms of the emotional and psychological needs of the service users, rather than giving some more logistical or practical rationale, such as convenience, costs or health and safety regulations. (Johnson and Haigh, 2010, pp.31–32)

Keats *et al.* (2012) state that PIEs should have five main components:

1. a psychological framework committed to the therapeutic approach underlying the project
2. the physical environment managed in a way that promotes psychological safety and security
3. staff trained in the therapeutic approach and supported to use it in their work with clients
4. managing relationships should be considered the principal tool for change
5. evaluation and monitoring of outcomes at service and individual levels should take place.

Background to the PIEs research

Homelessness as an area in which to work has historically been paid little attention by psychologists. Clinical psychologists are trained by the NHS and many stay within this setting, whereas the majority of homelessness services were set up in and are still the domain of the voluntary sector (Brown, 2015). Despite a theoretical commitment to equality of access to services contained in the NHS constitution, there are few NHS specialist homeless services or those who are both prepared and able to work with people with a chaotic lifestyle (Maguire, 2015). When I was given the opportunity to train as a clinical psychologist I wanted to investigate whether and how PIEs could function as part of the solution to this. A lot was written about the theory, but how did they work in practice? Were they any different to the 'standard' hostels in which I had housed people and, if so, in what way? What was the experience like for staff? Did residents experience them any differently and, if so, how? Most importantly, could they be a more acceptable option for long-term homeless clients than continuing to live on the streets? This was couched in the larger question of what role psychology could play in trying to address the issues we had struggled with during outreach, given that, despite the growing recognition of the importance of the meeting psychological needs, most of my clients were unlikely to have ever come into contact with a psychologist (Timms and Taylor, 2015).

A small scale qualitative study was carried out in two PIE hostels in London, attempting to answer these questions of how PIEs functioned in practice (Phipps, 2016; Phipps *et al.*, 2017). The following reflections are drawn from the findings of this project (unless otherwise specified, all quotations from participants are taken from these sources).

What is a home?

'It's important for our clients that they actually feel safe and they feel someone cares for them and they belong somewhere'

Homelessness is more than the absence of a house or physical shelter. Homelessness can be thought of as not only a state of physical 'unhousedness' but as 'psychological homelessness' (Seager, 2011) or an 'unhoused mind' (Scanlon, 2006), expressed through alienation, exclusion, distrust and extreme difficulties in closeness or dependence on others. My clients who could not sustain accommodation were not doing so through deliberate wilfulness or lifestyle choice but through an inability to tolerate being 'indoors'. There is a lack of a template from childhood of 'home' as a place of safety and security. More often, home is associated with threat and violence from which a child does not have the power to escape (Van der Kolk, 2014). Consequently, 'home cannot be found because home is in a mental space that cannot be reached' (Cockersell, 2012, p.178). It is no surprise that those who have slept rough for the longest most often abandon their accommodation (Homeless Link, 2010). The staff we spoke to in PIEs were struggling with the question of how to create a physical space called 'home' for people who had little physical or emotional understanding of what this could or should be.

The evidence suggested that 'home' should be two things: a valued and a safe space. Interesting comments were made about deliberate neglect and lack of value placed on spaces for homeless people in the past: 'if you just make it nice, they'll [just] ruin it', the distinct implication being that those living within the space were similarly not valued or trusted to take care of either themselves or their surroundings. Cloitre *et al.* (2006) point out that one of the consequences of early abuse is the removal of the sense of agency and the message given is 'you don't exist' or 'you don't count' (p.24). In opposition to this, efforts were made to give residents choice, autonomy and active participation in creating a space that reflected their identity, from choosing how to paint their room to designing and decorating communal areas. The word 'hostel' was deliberately avoided. Davis (2004) explains the importance of providing choice in design for homeless people since 'choice and self-determination are the cornerstones of dignity and a homeless person has few options… [A] place that makes people feel welcome, comfortable and safe signals that someone cares about them and that they are worthy of this concern' (p.21).

The second aspect of the home, that of safety, was raised on many occasions. Safety encompassed both a sense of physical safety of locked doors, privacy and security but also an emotional 'feeling' of being safe. The first part of a phased approach to working with people who have experienced trauma should always be the establishment of both physical and emotional safety and stability (Herman, 1997), regardless of the service setting. Levy (2015) suggests that in relation to homelessness, the promotion of safety has to come before anything else, especially expectations of change.

Interestingly, assumptions about what the physical space could look like did not always translate into such a safe or valued space. Architecturally innovative or aesthetically pleasing designs, despite being meticulously planned and well built, could sometimes be experienced as cold, clinical or not conducive to a sense of safety at all:

> There was a building…that got some kind of architectural award for homelessness that's got transparent walls, glass walls and… you think, well that might be an architecturally inspired thing but what's that like for a homeless person to look at a transparent wall, transparent house with no visible boundaries…that seems to be a complete misunderstanding of what a nice environment would be for this purpose.

Consistent evidence was provided about the differences between current provision and memories of what hostels were like in the past: 'In the 70s it was get them sober, get them washed, get them fed, get them de-loused and kick them out again. That was basically it.' This speaks clearly to the idea that simply putting a roof over someone's head, of any quality, is not in itself a sufficient intervention to bring about any lasting change.

The professional 'family': rebuilding attachments

'Living here has definitely changed me. I'm actually starting to be glad that I'm here, not wanting to be dead, thanks to... the staff here'

If the first part of a PIE is to establish a 'home', the second is to provide a professional 'family'. A secure attachment relationship with a caregiver, usually within the family, is recognised as the foundation of feelings of safety, security and self-worth in adulthood (Bowlby, 1977). Conversely, disrupted early attachments can contribute to having little sense of belonging or feeling safe, difficulties in establishing and maintaining relationships and in regulating high levels of distress. As John Healy writes, recalling the violence of his childhood in his memoir of homelessness *The Grass Arena*, 'I wished my father would die, then I could get rid of this scared feeling' (Healy, 2012, p.7).

However, in the absence of a secure attachment, attachment to an alternative caregiver can have a protective function in adulthood. By providing care, empathy and containment for distress, trust can develop and the revision of early working models about the safety and predictability of the world, other people and worth of self can take place. It is now understood that attachment styles are not fixed but can change in response to this alternative supportive figure in adulthood, forming an 'earned secure' attachment style (Saunders *et al.*, 2011). Caregiving organisations, teams and services as well as individuals can also provide an alternative source of attachment relationship (Goodwin *et al.*, 2003).

It is therefore not inevitable that early trauma or disrupted attachment will lead to later 'disorder' should alternative supportive relationships intervene. The foundation to recovery from trauma is, at its heart, relational or 'reconnecting with fellow human beings' (Van der Kolk, 2014). Judith Herman's key text on recovery from trauma (1997) states that:

the core experiences of psychological trauma are disempowerment and disconnection from others. Recovery, therefore, is based on the empowerment of the survivor and creation of new connections. Recovery can take place only in the context of relationships; it cannot occur in isolation. (p.133)

A key task within a PIE is the creation of these secure attachment relationships between resident and caregiver(s).

Evidence was shown of both the importance to clients and keyworkers of trust in the relationship and how the relationship could break down if this was not present: as one resident stated, 'They're doing the best for you. There's no ulterior motive. Once you get over that, you can start progressing.' In order for attachment style to be moderated, emotional support (the provision of comfort, reassurance, availability) rather than simply instrumental, task-oriented support should be provided (Saunders *et al.*, 2011). This was reflected in stories about the difference between 'doing things' for clients and being there for, giving time to or listening to them. There was some evidence of clients using their keyworker as a 'secure base' (Ainsworth *et al.*, 1978) being the preferred person they would turn to above all others:

R4: She's up front…she tells you how it is and that…and she's straight with you, she's honest, she helps you.

Interviewer: So if you needed help with anything, who would you go to first?

R4: I would go to [keyworker name], yeah, yeah, I would go to [her].

Interviewer: Ok, and if she wasn't here, what would you do?

R4: Well I could ask for her, to phone her, because they'll let me use the phone and phone her.

Impact on staff

'Trauma doesn't even begin to describe what some of these clients have gone through'

Staff are as integral to a PIE as the clients and the physical structure of the building. It has been illustrated how the bond between client and keyworker has the potential to contribute to building a new attachment relationship. However, the emotional cost to staff of doing this should not be underestimated. Evidence from the study demonstrated that staff had strong emotional reactions both to reading and hearing the content of their clients' history and also to their own work with residents, the value they placed on what they hoped to achieve and the outcomes of their efforts. Staff were aware of the need for consistent and supportive relationships with clients, but these could be immensely challenging to achieve, given the chronic nature of many clients' difficulties and the problems with accepting, understanding and making use of 'help' or care. One staff member described how difficult this was: 'You've worked with a client throughout a number of years and you feel that you have a good relationship and [then] they really press the self destruction button.'

As Adshead (2001) notes, from an attachment perspective, many residents in institutional settings lack the ability to self-soothe due to early trauma and that:

> there is a failure to be able to elicit care (or soothing) from professional caregivers in fruitful ways…so often we see people who are longing for a secure attachment that would reduce their distress, but have no idea either how to elicit care productively, or how to use it when it is offered by a competent caregiver. (pp.327–328)

Staff often struggled to make sense of this, particularly when their genuine offers of help appeared to be rejected, echoing my own experiences of the rejection of help or housing offered whilst working in outreach and the feelings of failure attached. One staff member illustrated this point: 'there's one lady…[diagnosed with] personality disorder…you can't engage with her…she won't turn up to sessions, won't come out of her room…he [the manager] can't do it, I can't do it, I don't know who can do it…' Whilst the attachment styles of staff were not explored in the study, it is very likely that insecure attachments in staff themselves will have also had an impact on their approach and responses to work with clients (Dozier, Cue and Barnett, 1994).

Unsurprisingly, 'compassion fatigue' and 'burnout' have been increasingly recognised in caregiving settings, as has vicarious or secondary traumatisation through exposure to traumatic material (McCann and Pearlman, 1990; Stamm, 2010). The emotional cost of futile attempts to quickly 'fix' or 'save' clients and evidence of secondary traumatisation were both detected from staff. Reflective practice was suggested in the original PIE guidance document as a way to mitigate these effects on staff by providing a forum for the processing of these emotional responses, and supporting learning and development by allowing staff to reflect on their actions and interactions with clients. Reflective practice groups were facilitated by trained therapists. The majority of staff who spoke about reflective practice groups reported finding them enormously helpful and beneficial to their professional practice, helping them to see their clients as 'whole people' rather than just a diagnosis or collection of problems. On the other hand, the task of 'reflection' jarred with the voluntary sector culture of 'doing' and going above and beyond in terms of effort. Time spent sitting 'thinking' was regarded by some as an unnecessary luxury.

This led in turn to reflection on the role of the keyworker. Although 'keyworking' is a widespread role within supported housing and social care settings, it has traditionally been a poorly defined or understood role (McGrath and Pistrang, 2007). Its complex and demanding nature often goes unrecognised. Whilst many embraced the opportunity for their role to include a reflective function, some staff were evidently uncomfortable with the idea that their role included going beyond the 'practical'. Others resisted the role being over-formalised or professionalised, particularly in the context of a desire for equality, informality and the sense of 'family' previously alluded to. It was commented that 'we don't want staff to become any kind of "ologist"'. This highlighted the question (set within the broader context of the application of 'psychology') of what is more broadly speaking 'therapeutic' without constituting formal 'therapy'. The core elements of 'therapeutic alliance' (warmth, trust, empathy) – the 'common' or 'non-specific' factors (Asay and Lambert, 1999) are likely to be fundamental to 'helping' relationships, whether they take place in a therapy room or in an informal context (Barker and Pistrang, 2002).

Challenges of the theory of PIE vs the reality

'You've got a job, you're here to care, you're here to do something, but the reality is that you can't do it...adequately'

Despite the theory of the 'ideal' PIE, our research suggested that putting it into practice in the context of the current social care system and political climate raised a series of challenges. The most notable of these is trying to create a psychologically informed service within a structure or care pathway that is contracted out to different agencies, fragmented and far from being psychologically informed (Seager, 2011). As one staff member mentioned with frustration:

> Funders and commissioners seem to think it's like a factory where you come in as a rough sleeper, go through the process, you engage with the service and at the end of it you come out ready for independent accommodation. Now it doesn't quite work like that.

Expectations set in commissioned timescales did not seem to match the reality of what could be achieved, either theoretically or practically, in terms of psychological needs.

Both social and mental health care have increasingly become marketised and contracted out on the basis of cost, targets and outcomes. This leaves people within it falsely constructed as 'customers' with 'choice' about their accommodation and a lack of security for staff in their jobs. Evidence suggests several years in a therapeutic relationship is necessary to change attachment style, even in a relatively well functioning group of people (Saunders *et al.*, 2011). This can only be achieved when both the provider and recipient of care feel secure. Interestingly, the desire to keep people moving through a pathway of care was linked to an anxiety about encouraging 'dependency', viewed as an outdated notion related to institutionalisation. It was suggested that dependency was unnecessarily pathologised and mistaken for the time needed to establish a genuine attachment relationship. As Hutson (1999, p.213) points out, it is not unreasonable for people who consider a hostel to be their home to have 'a legitimate desire to stay in a place to which [they are] accustomed'. However, the result is 'described as a pathological condition' (being 'institutionalised').

Nowhere was the mismatch between psychological needs and economic/practical expectations clearer than in the issue of 'moving on' after a set period of time (usually two years). At this point it is assumed that hostel residents are adequately prepared and ready to move into their own accommodation or another hostel. Much of the evidence from both staff and residents expressed discomfort and apprehension about this. Despite valuable work done within the hostel, the move-on process risks replicating the series of disrupted attachments and feelings of abandonment and rejection already characteristic of most residents' lives (Seager, 2013). This also puts staff in the unenviable double bind both of having to help residents feel safe and cared for but also not to allow them to feel 'too safe' because of the need for them to move on.

PIEs: What's in a name?

The question was raised in the research of whether a PIE was indeed such a novel concept. Hadn't homeless services always sought to build relationships with clients? Was a PIE anything more than a new piece of jargon or initiative commonly introduced in the sector? What did psychology have to bring to the table that wasn't already known? Given the terminology, one could be mistaken for assuming that a psychologist should be central to the task of creating a PIE. However, what emerged was a more general consideration of how human beings can best help each other, rather than particular psychological models or 'doses' of therapy (Seager, 2013). Johnson and Haigh (2011a) critique 'psychology with a big P'. Indeed, psychologists have a reputation for being overly 'wordy', difficult to understand and protective of their knowledge as somehow special or unique (Osborne-Davies, 1996; Connolly and Williams, 2011). They suggest that what is needed in relation to a PIE is not detailed psychological techniques, models (or indeed a psychologist) but a basic understanding of universal human needs and related concepts such as relationships, containment and attachment and training on how to put these into practice.

Conclusions

Hostels have changed and moved a long way since the 1980s. Alongside the advent of PIEs, there have been several other new initiatives such as Housing First and Trauma-Informed Services, focused on meeting the needs of homeless people through accommodation, therapeutic environments and an understanding of the impact of adverse early experiences on human development and later functioning. This suggests that although a PIE is one way of doing this, there is no single way or exclusive 'label' by which to address the challenge of creating an acceptable and workable solution for those who have been chronically homeless. I will never know whether my long-term clients have been or could be successfully housed in PIEs – and the reality is that many may never be able to access one – but my hope is that they will continue to be used and grow in the future into places where people's needs can be met before they reach such a state of chronic exclusion.

The evidence we found suggested that staff were making exceptional efforts to carry out the demanding task of 're-homing' (Seager, 2011). However, a PIE can only function properly within a psychologically informed political and social context, which understands and prioritises human needs and the time necessary for the rebuilding of damaged and disrupted attachments, over and above costs and contracts.

References

Adshead, G. (2001) 'Attachment in mental health institutions: a commentary.' *Attachment and Human Development 3*, 3, 324–329.

Ainsworth, M., Blehar, M., Waters, E. and Wall, S. (1978) *Patterns of Attachment: A Psychological Study of the Strange Situation*. Hillsdale, NJ: Erlbaum.

Asay, T.I. and Lambert, M.J. (1999) 'The Empirical Case for the Common Factor.' In B. Duncan, S. Miller and M. Hubble (eds) *The Heart and Soul of Change: What Works in Therapy*. Washington, DC: American Psychological Association.

Barker, C. and Pistrang, N. (2002) 'Psychotherapy and social support: integrating research on psychological helping.' *Clinical Psychology Review 22*, 3, 363–381.

BBC (2008) *Bid to Clear Homelessness by 2012*. Accessed October 2017 at http://news.bbc.co.uk/1/hi/england/london/7735365.stm

Bowlby, J. (1977) 'The making and breaking of affectional bonds. I. Aetiology and psychopathology in the light of attachment theory. An expanded version of the Fiftieth Maudsley Lecture, delivered before the Royal College of Psychiatrists, 19 November 1976.' *The British Journal of Psychiatry 130*, 3, 201–210.

Bramley, G., Fitzpatrick, S., Edwards, J., Ford, D. *et al.* (2015) *Hard Edges: Mapping Severe and Multiple Disadvantage*. London: Lankelly Chase Foundation.

Brown, R. (2015) 'When it comes to working with people without homes, where is clinical psychology?' *Clinical Psychology Forum 265*, 42–45.

Cloitre, M., Cohen, L. and Koenen, K. (2006) *Treating Survivors of Childhood Abuse: Psychotherapy for the Interrupted Life*. New York: Guilford.

Cockersell, P. (2012) 'Homelessness, Complex Trauma and Recovery.' In R. Johnson and R. Haigh (eds) *Complex Trauma and Its Effects*. Hove: Pavilion.

Connolly, T., and Williams, C. (2011). 'Team members' perceptions of clinical psychology in an adult community mental health service.' *Clinical Psychology Forum, 240*, 22–31.

Davis, S. (2004) *Designing for the Homeless*. Berkeley, CA: University of California Press.

DCLG (2006) *Places of Change: Tackling Homelessness through the Hostels Capital Improvement Programme*. London: Department for Communities and Local Government.

Dozier, M., Cue, K. and Barnett, L. (1994) 'Clinicians as caregivers: role of attachment organisation in treatment.' *Journal of Consulting and Clinical Psychology 62*, 4, 793–800.

Fazel, S., Geddes, J.R. and Kushel, M. (2014) 'The health of homeless people in high-income countries: descriptive epidemiology, health consequences, and clinical and policy recommendations.' *The Lancet 384*, 9953, 1529–1540.

Fazel, S., Khosla, V., Doll, H. and Geddes, J. (2008) 'The prevalence of mental disorders among the homeless in western countries: systematic review and meta-regression analysis.' *PLoS Medicine 5*, 12, e225.

Felitti, V.J., Anda, R.F., Nordenberg, D., Williamson, D.F. *et al.* (1998) 'Relationship of childhood abuse and household dysfunction to many of the leading causes of death in adults.' *American Journal of Preventive Medicine 14*, 4, 245–258.

Fitzpatrick, S., Bramley, G. and Johnsen, S. (2012) 'Pathways into multiple exclusion homelessness in seven UK cities.' *Urban Studies 50*, 1, 148–168.

Goodwin, I., Holmes, G., Cochrane, R. and Mason, O. (2003) 'The ability of adult mental health services to meet clients' attachment needs: the development and implementation of the Service Attachment Questionnaire.' *Psychology and Psychotherapy 76*, 2, 145–161.

Haigh, R., Harrison, T., Johnson, R., Paget, S. and Williams, S. (2012) 'Psychologically informed environments and the "Enabling Environments' initiative".' *Housing, Care and Support 15*, 1, 34–42.

Healy, J. (2012) *The Grass Arena*. London: Penguin.

Herman, J. (1997) *Trauma and Recovery*, 2nd edition. New York: Basic Books.

Homeless Link (2010) *Staying In: Understanding Evictions and Abandonments from London's Hostel*. London: Homeless Link.

Hutson, S. (1999) 'Experience of "Homeless" Accommodation and Support.' In S. Hutson and D. Clapham (eds) *Homelessness: Public Policies and Private Troubles*. London and New York: Cassell.

Johnson, R. and Haigh, R. (2010) 'Social psychiatry and social policy for the 21st century – new concepts for new needs: the psychologically informed environment.' *Mental Health and Social Inclusion 14*, 4, 30–35.

Johnson, R. and Haigh, R. (2011a) 'Social psychiatry and social policy for the 21st century: new concepts for new needs – the 'Enabling Environments' initiative. *Mental Health and Social Inclusion 15*, 1, 17–23.

Johnson, R. and Haigh, R. (2011b) 'Social psychiatry and social policy for the twenty-first century – new concepts for new needs: relational health.' *Mental Health and Social Inclusion 15*, 2, 57–65.

Keats, H., Maguire, N.J., Johnson, R. and Cockersell, P. (2012) *Psychologically Informed Services for Homeless People: Good Practice Guide*. London: Department of Communities and Local Government. Accessed October 2017 at https://eprints.soton.ac.uk/340022

Levy, J. (2015) *Pretreatment Guide for Homeless Outreach and Housing First*. Ann Arbor, MI: LHP.

Maguire, N. (2015) 'Clinical psychology: a rare and essential resource in commissioning quality services for homeless people.' *Clinical Psychology Forum 265*, 23–27.

Maguire, N., Johnson, R. and Vostanis, P. (2010) *Meeting the Psychological and Emotional Needs of Homeless People*. Accessed October 2017 at https://eprints.soton.ac.uk/187695

McCann, I. and Pearlman, L. (1990) 'Vicarious traumatization: a framework for understanding the psychological effects of working with victims.' *Journal of Traumatic Stress 3*, 1, 131–149.

McGrath, L. and Pistrang, N. (2007) 'Policeman or friend? Dilemmas in working with homeless young people in the United Kingdom.' *Journal of Social Issues 63*, 3, 589–606.

Orwell, G. (1933) *Down and Out in Paris and London*. London: Penguin.

Osborne-Davies, I. (1996) 'Awareness and attitudes of other health-care professionals towards clinical psychologists.' *Clinical Psychology Forum, 91*, 7–10.

Parsell, C. (2011) 'Homeless identities: enacted and ascribed.' *The British Journal of Sociology 62*, 3, 442–461.

Phipps, C. (2016) '"Living here has changed me": resident and staff perceptions of psychologically informed environments for homeless people.' Doctoral thesis. University College London. Accessed October 2017 at http://discovery.ucl.ac.uk/1519858

Phipps, C., Seager, M., Murphy, L. and Barker, C. (2017) 'Psychologically informed environments for homeless people: resident and staff experiences.' *Housing, Care and Support 20*, 1, 29–42.

Power, C. and Attenborough, J. (2003) 'Up from the streets: a follow-up study of people referred to a specialist team for the homeless mentally ill.' *Journal of Mental Health 12*, 1, 41–49.

Saunders, R., Jacobvitz, D., Zaccagnino, M., Beverung, L.M., and Hazen, N. (2011) 'Pathways to earned-security: the role of alternative support figures.' *Attachment and Human Development 13*, 4, 403–420.

Scanlon, C. (2006) 'Housing "unhoused minds": inter-personality disorder in the organisation?' *Housing, Care and Support 9*, 3, 9–14.

Seager, M. (2006) 'The concept of "psychological safety": a psychoanalytically informed contribution towards "safe, sound and supportive" mental health services.' *Psychoanalytic Psychotherapy 20*, 4, 266–280.

Seager, M. (2011) 'Homelessness is more than houselessness: a psychologically-minded approach to inclusion and rough sleeping.' *Mental Health and Social Inclusion 15*, 4, 183–189.

Seager, M. (2013) 'Using Attachment Theory to Inform Psychologically Minded Care Services, Systems and Environments.' In A.N. Danquah and K. Berry (eds) *Attachment Theory in Adult Mental Health*. New York: Routledge.

Stamm, B.H. (2010) *The Concise PROQOL Manual*. Accessed December 2017 at https://nbpsa.org/images/PRP/ProQOL_Concise_2ndEd_12-2010.pdf

Sundin, E.C. and Baguley, T. (2015) 'Prevalence of childhood abuse among people who are homeless in Western countries: a systematic review and meta-analysis.' *Social Psychiatry and Psychiatric Epidemiology 50*, 2, 183–194.

Teixeira, L. (2010) *Still Left Out? The Rough Sleepers '205' Initiative One Year On*. London: Crisis.

Timms, P. and Taylor, K. (2015) 'Breaking down barriers: clinical psychology and psychiatry in a mental health service for homeless people.' *Clinical Psychology Forum 265*, 28–32.

Van der Kolk, B. (2014) *The Body Keeps the Score: Mind, Brain and Body in the Transformation of Trauma*. St Ives: Penguin.

10

STREETLIGHT

Homeless Psychotherapy in Britain's Happiest Town

DR SALLY READ

I am an integrative psychotherapist, working at Harrogate Homeless Project (HHP), North Yorkshire. Harrogate was voted Britain's happiest town in 2015. The BBC website, revealing this statistic (BBC, 2015) uses a photograph which could have been taken from the office at our project's day centre. In this office I meet regularly with people who have not experienced the pride, contentment and safety described by the BBC. I am going to write about the experience of setting up HHP's psychotherapy service, Streetlight. I hope that by describing the journey we took to get here, I can show that such projects are needed, and can work, outside the metropolitan areas, even in charming, affluent spa towns. Although cities tend to be where we think of homelessness as being a problem, and where statutory bodies might be more aware of their duties of care, we have shown that meaningful work can be done on a small scale and with a modest budget in areas where homelessness is just as prevalent but perhaps less visible. Through the course of telling the story, I will talk a bit about my personal journey too. Like most relational psychotherapists, I know that a constant awareness of my own process is important. In addition, understanding why working with homeless people is rewarding and worth doing is valuable in answering the scepticism of those who doubt the efficacy of our work, not to mention our motivation for attempting it.

My first contact with people experiencing homelessness was back in the days when I was a GP. I worked for ten years in one of the first specialist GP practices for homeless people. What a great job this was. We had a wonderful team, who practised in what I would now call a reflective manner. I learned so much from my colleagues and patients: about respect, our shared humanity, valuing each other, building teams, developing services, lobbying commissioners and much more. I also learned about the pernicious effects of social exclusion, the impact of abuse and neglect in early life, about hopelessness, anger and violence, about managing risk, trying to measure what cannot be measured, and the power of parallel process and projective identification (Ogden, 1982). Looking back, I would say that we had created the beginnings of a Psychologically Informed Environment (PIE; of which more later), and it was the psychological aspects of our work which most interested me. Much of my work involved the care of people using heroin or alcohol. I found this fascinating, but largely for the meaning people gave to their addictions, and the implications for their relationships. About eight years into my first stint at the practice, I attended a drug treatment conference where the keynote presentation was given by a psychotherapist, Phil Barker (see Barker, 2007; Barker and Buchanan-Barker, 2004). I can still remember my feelings of excitement and relief at what I heard. Instead of the quantitative trial data which informed best practice in 'managing' drug misuse, Phil Barker talked about our clients' *personal* logic', their stories. For those of us trying to help make sense of addiction, it is the story that our clients tell that holds the key, and this story is one of relationships. Listening to Phil was a transformational moment for me. Having for some time felt uncomfortable and somewhat lonely in the medical world I inhabited, it was wonderful to hear from someone speaking in a way I'd like to be able to speak. Could this be possible for me too?

It turned out it was. To cut a long story short, I spent the next four years retraining as a psychotherapist whilst continuing to practise medicine part time. The journey of change was a challenging one, of course. In making it, I travelled through all the stages identified by Prochaska and DiClemente (1982) in their cycle of change, a model central to the psychology of addiction and helpful for considering any change process.

Reducing my medical commitments to make time for studying meant a move from the homeless practice to a drug treatment team, a move that involved loss and triggered a period of grieving. I missed colleagues, patients and a way of life that had afforded me a sense of security – paradoxically, a sense of home. I was sad and often angry. How often we see this in our clients who make steps to move out of homelessness. Moving away from what we have known, however hard that life was, involves loss in diverse ways: loss of shared memories of troubles overcome, memories of people we knew who didn't make it, or those who did, of shared triumphs and frustrations. And more, a loss of a known identity, replaced by a less-than-comfortable new identity. It was a tough time, but the new experience of residential weekends as part of a master's degree in integrative psychotherapy was giving me an opportunity to learn how to reflect, to understand and to talk about my feelings.

Sometime later, I had the opportunity to think in depth about the transition I had made from doctor to psychotherapist, whilst writing a chapter on the therapeutic relationship in helping professions (Read, 2014). Others working across professions, or making the move themselves, might find this helpful. As well as transitions in my sense of self, I needed to think about my relationships with clients and colleagues, how I understood teams and team working, and how it feels to be working in non-statutory settings rather than the NHS. For psychotherapists working in homeless services it is important to be able to think about these things, and I will come back to them below.

I qualified as an integrative psychotherapist with UKCP registration in 2011. By then, I was working as a doctor for the local drug treatment agency in Harrogate. Social exclusion, addiction and homelessness don't jump to mind in many people's image of a wealthy, well-heeled town such as ours. Yet, with only a little thought, surely we're not surprised that poverty is everywhere, and always has been. In Harrogate, as elsewhere, it is relatively well hidden perhaps. But the reality is that homelessness is on the rise here as in most places. Affordable rented properties are very thin on the ground. Public Health England's 2014 Health Profile for Harrogate (Public Health England, 2014) includes lower than national average rates for statutory homelessness. However, having been chosen as a No Second Night Out Pilot in 2012, it has been shown that Harrogate has significant homelessness problems. The 2014 annual headcount of rough sleepers (DCLG, 2015) conducted through Homeless Link showed that, per head of population, Harrogate's rough sleeping problem was four times that of Leeds.

So, moving from my job with homeless people in Leeds to one with drug users in Harrogate, I found similar problems of poverty, joblessness, relationship breakdown and addiction. Loneliness, hopelessness, fear and anger were just as prevalent amongst sections of our clientele. It could even be suggested that feelings of worthlessness and despair are worse in a town where wealth and privilege are so visible. As I began to gain confidence and experience in psychotherapy, I wanted to be able to help my clients explore these feelings. But as a doctor I needed to work towards specific outcomes for clients, 'drug-free exit' from treatment being the pinnacle of achievement for our clients. For this and for other reasons I made the decision to stop practising medicine and devote my working time to psychotherapy.

I had reached the action and maintenance stages of change, surely. I felt like a psychotherapist and had time to build my private practice and continue to develop my integrative model. As well as this, I was able to start thinking about how it might be possible to work psychotherapeutically with people who are homeless. I had met some of the staff at HHP in the course of my work at the drug service. Based on not very much knowledge of me, and after a couple of conversations, they agreed to allow me to start working with their clients. This was a big step for all of us, and I remain so grateful that they had the courage and flexibility to give psychotherapy a go. Like most homeless projects, HHP aims to help its clients work towards becoming independent, and recognises how difficult this can be for those with long histories of chronic and complex trauma (see below). The project runs a 16-bedded hostel, a day centre and a No Second Night Out project. We agreed that I would see anyone using any of these services. We would not advertise my services, but rather keyworkers were made aware of what I was offering and told clients about it, as they felt appropriate.

But why offer psychotherapy within the hostel setting? There is a growing awareness of the need for specialist psychotherapeutic services for homeless people. The Faculty for Homeless Health's *Standards for Commissioners and Service Providers* (2013) states that 'Provision should be made for specialist psychologists and psychotherapists to directly deliver psychological therapies and support all staff involved with those individuals through consultation and the provision of facilitated reflective practice.' The standards go on to recommend that psychological therapies must be *accessible, flexible* and *culturally appropriate. Accessibility* was a problem in Harrogate, where, at the time we started Streetlight, other counselling services either had such long waiting times that people with chaotic lives found them impossible to use, or such strict entry (or exclusion) criteria that they were inaccessible to people with histories of complex trauma and substance use. *Culturally appropriate services* in this context implies an understanding of the specific needs of homeless people, in particular awareness of the challenges of chronic complex trauma, which underlies much of the psychological morbidity of people who are homeless. In their review of the evidence linking homelessness and complex trauma, Maguire *et al.* suggest that 'unless and until the underlying psychological issues behind the presenting problem are identified and addressed, homelessness is likely to be repeated' (2009, p.3). In addition, psychotherapists need to be aware of issues arising from drug and alcohol use, and be prepared to work with clients who use substances, within clear boundaries. But perhaps the strongest evidence of all for the need for effective psychotherapy comes from homeless people themselves. In 2015, in preparation for the General Election, St Mungo's Broadway produced a 'manifesto of hope' in which homeless people asked the new government to 'make sure people who are homeless have access to talking therapies' and 'increase the choice of therapies available in order to help people with experiences of trauma, and people using drugs and alcohol' (St Mungo's, 2016).

In the first six months, seven clients were referred to me. They ranged from a request for one session to talk through a recent, traumatic event to the beginning of a long-term therapeutic relationship where there was still intermittent contact some three and a half years later. Only two of the people referred did not have significant problems with addictions. There was one well-defined, short-term piece of work where the client left in a planned way feeling he had got what he was looking for. The rest were more typical of what I have come to understand as manifestations of the insecure, often disorganised styles of attachment which make our clients' lives so challenging. In practice, this uncertainty about committing to a therapeutic relationship becomes reflected in missed appointments, disappearances from the hostel or an increase in behaviour likely to lead to eviction. Although I had expected it would be like this, I experienced countertransferential responses of anxiety, guilt and shame, hopelessness and anger. I really had no idea if I had embarked upon a fool's errand. But as I wondered this, I would remember the disbelief I used to feel when my homeless patients had been written off as 'untreatable' in a mental health setting. The memory of the anger I felt about this was what kept me going, as well as continued faith in the power of therapeutic relationships to effect change. Sometimes it was more like stubborn narcissistic pride that stopped me from giving up. I found myself trying very hard indeed to find meaning in lives which yielded very little sense at all, and often blamed myself for this. On other days, usually when I stopped trying so hard I suspect, I was able to experience, with my client, a 'moment of meeting' (Stern, 2004) which seemed to be of value. Stern identifies these moments as when real engagement occurs and there is a 'sense of moving or leaning forward' (Stern, 2004, p.34). Surely this is something akin to Buber's 'I-Thou' meeting when 'actual presentness, meeting and relation exist' (Buber 1923, p.18). Later on, one client spoke of how much the *respect* I had given him had helped, and perhaps it is this honouring of the humanity of people who have been so disregarded that has the most powerful impact.

Somewhere around six months into this work, I got together with project managers to review our progress. By this stage, we had only a small amount of 'evidence' of psychotherapy's effectiveness in this setting. But there was some. For example, one client with a long history of involvement with the project was coming most weeks and found that he was being helped to make sense of things which had happened to him over many years of homelessness. Another was making significant changes in their drug use. Even so, for most people the experiences of chronic and complex trauma left legacies of guilt, fear and anger which were to need much longer term work.

Perhaps it would be helpful, at this point, to explain some of the theory which underpinned my work from this point, and continues to do so today.

Adlam and Scanlon's concept of the unhoused mind (2005) has been one of the pillars of my integrative model. Homelessness is understood as a *symptom* of an unhoused state of mind, one which is used as a way to communicate distress. Clear parallels are drawn between inner and outer states, between the experience of self and the experience of being housed, or not. The development of a secure psychological skin, or home, depends upon the presence of a secure enough caring relationship for an infant to be able to learn that she is safely housed within her own skin, and within another's mind. However, if her early environment is violent, chaotic or abusive her internal world becomes similarly unsafe. Rather than feeling safely held in a boundaried relationship, she experiences her inner world as populated by intrusive and alarming objects from which she seeks to escape. Homelessness then becomes an acting out of this internal distress, leaving behind the four walls which represent the dangerous or oppressive inner 'home'. For others, the early home is neglectful and barren. Without meaningful emotional attunement, the psyche closes in on itself and avoids contact. Home now becomes a place of fearful isolation, and homelessness, without the imprisonment of the walls of the room, becomes an escape and a means of contact.

Barbara Dowds (2014) links the early environment, attachment styles (Bowlby, 1997 [1969]) and energy regulation in a model which has become helpful to me in understanding how these two types of experience, the one violent and abusive, the other cold and neglectful, can both result in an experience of self which is too uncomfortable to bear and which is communicated through the language of homelessness. Dowd uses ideas of *boundedness* and *charge* to conceptualise the interpersonal and intrapsychic processes she describes. For many people who become homeless, home was a place where boundaries were lacking. Inconsistent parenting led to an atmosphere of fear and anxiety. Dowd calls the developing psyche *underbound* in these cases, and relates this to an ambivalent attachment style. Others have grown up in rigid or cold environments where there was little understanding of the importance of emotional engagement, or where to express emotion would exact punishment. This sterility can be understood as *overbinding* and manifests in an avoidant attachment style.

Alongside this consideration of the quality of the containment offered to the developing child, Dowds describes the level of charge which arises within, as a result of the quality of engagement between carer and child. In environments where there is abuse or 'severe swings between invasive hostile attention and terrifying abandonment' (Dowds, 2014, p.15), the level of arousal or charge is likely to be high. She calls these individuals *overcharged*. In households where there is more consistent neglect or an absence of parental attunement, the level of arousal is depressed and the child could be described as *undercharged*.

Finding Dowds' elegant model some time into this work was exciting and helpful. But, for a while, I fell into the trap of trying too hard to fit my clients into categories of being under/over bound and under/over charged. This reflected my own internal need to impose order on my complex clients. Just as Adlam and Scanlon describe I was trying to 'squeeze unhousedness out of the system...so as to hold on to order and sanity' (2005, p.2). In reality, many homeless people live with chaotic, disorganised attachment styles formed in early environments which were characterised by 'the polarities of abuse and neglect, intrusion and abandonment' (ibid., p.2). Adlam and Scanlon link this uncertainty to a life lived on the threshold, represented most vividly in the figure sleeping in the doorway. Other ways we see this ambivalence acted out is in the cycle of short-term tenancies and frequent evictions or, as I have heard about on several occasions, the people who secure a tenancy but put their tent up indoors, or continue to sleep on the floor or sofa even once their own bed is available to them.

Now, a couple of years later, it is still hard to sit alongside the uncertainty and internal turbulence of minds which are, to some degree, unhoused. Again, I need to come back to reflect on those aspects of my own psyche which are unhoused, the places in me which, whilst sometimes understood and even worked through, can continue to trouble me. I have learned, in part, and through the help of a CPD group whose members often use the ego-state model of transactional analysis (Clarkson, 1992) to recognise the workings of my own abandoned and frightened Child, the one who sought external order and routine to calm her internal turmoil. Understanding this process helps. I am not protected from the experiences of my Child, who continues to fear disruption and uncertainty. But I am able to bring my Adult awareness to what's going on. Sometimes, I can do this for my clients too. When I do it from a 'purely' Adult, or perhaps a Parent place, it may sometimes be helpful. What are perhaps most powerful, though, are the times when my own Child (with her unhoused feelings) meets my client's, whilst I manage to also retain enough functioning Adult to know what's going on and to contain the situation. Adlam and Scanlon describe it thus:

> if in this process of partial identification we can thereby find some empathy with their plight, we may enable them gradually to feel a parallel process that there are parts of their own more disturbed personalities that could also, at last, find some kind of a home. (ibid., p.2)

We know from so many studies (see, for example, Charura and Paul, 2014) that the therapeutic relationship is a powerful agent of change. For those of us working with clients with such complex needs as many homeless people experience, understanding the relationship, in particular recognising our countertransferential responses (Maroda, 2004) is an equally complex business. It helps to remember that, when our clients have started life in damaged and damaging relationships, relationships that really *don't work*, relationships will go on *not working*. Cockersell (2015) reminds us of this, of what he calls the 'significant negative transferences' (ibid., p.16) over which we need to take great care for our clients and ourselves.

Recognising our own processes, and the ways in which our 'housed' minds relate to the unhousedness of those with whom we meet, is essential to our work if we are not to perpetuate the patterns of abuse and neglect in our clients' lives. In my experience, it has also been important to know why I do this work in order to answer the interested questions, sometimes scepticism, of other psychotherapists. Because homeless people have been seen as difficult, even untreatable, by mainstream and statutory services, those of us who have chosen to attempt this work challenge the perceptions of many professionals. As we have seen above, Adlam and Scanlon observe the discomfort created for our housed minds in encountering the unhousedness of others. Blackwell (1997) similarly observed how those who work 'on the margins' may have a fraught relationship with those occupying more central ground. How do we respond to this potential dislocation? Do we stay within the secure centre of our professional registration, teams, outcome measures and evidence base? Or does time spent with people on the margins leads us to vicarious experiences of our clients' powerlessness and distress? And if we do find ourselves out on the margins alongside our clients, how do we relate to the power at the centre? I have struggled with these questions and come to only incomplete answers as to why I do this work and how I relate to colleagues who do not. I know, for example, that one of my early experiences, following the death of my father when I was seven years old, was to feel different from my friends. For me the lack of a father became an internal state of mind, a state of exclusion which became a part of my identity. More recently, I have discovered how powerfully I adapted to what I felt to be an injunction not to feel, not to complain, but to compensate for grief by assiduous application to studying and conforming to what I though was expected of me. This overboundedness led to an inner fear and loneliness which sometimes made relating a threat. And sometimes still does, of course. So I need to be aware of the need that I am seeking to meet when I sit down with a homeless person. As I try to meet their lonely, excluded or abandoned parts, am I also seeking to meet my own? If my client chooses not to respond, to decline the invitation, what will be my reaction? The more some of these dynamics can be brought into awareness, the less the chance I might risk a repetition of earlier, damaging, object relations (Gomez, 1997). Often, Karpman's (1968) model of the drama triangle is a useful and immediate way to work out what's happening. One of the classic patterns of behaviour in those of us working with homeless people is helpfulness or, in drama triangle terms, rescuing. In a paper on helpfulness amongst people working with refugees, Blackwell (1997) suggests that when the therapist adopts a rescuing position, he may be unconsciously projecting out, or disowning, his victim or persecutor roles (typically, the victimhood is projected into the passive client, while whichever agency *isn't* helping becomes the persecutor). But if the client declines to take on a victim role, might the psychotherapist resort to persecutory blame? I have been helped to address drama triangle interactions by thinking about equivalent but autonomous positions. Instead of rescuing, I can ask myself what response I choose, or where my responsibility lies. Rather than viewing myself or others as victims I try to recognise vulnerability, which may or may not be amenable to change. Finally, if I find myself projecting a persecutory role into another, I have learned to ask myself what the power of this person actually amounts to, or indeed what power I myself choose to exercise. All of this thinking benefits from being informed by compassion, both for myself and the other.

So, after this detour into some of the theoretical thinking involved in this work, it is perhaps time to catch up with Streetlight, and what happened next. My growing therapeutic relationships with some clients had got me into thinking about unhoused minds and the connections between our early relationships; in particular how they influence whether home becomes a safe, threatening or even meaningless place for us. For many, home and the relationships within had indeed held uncertainties, sometimes dangers and neglect. Subsequently, their lives became a series of challenges which perpetuated the feelings of unsafety within, making the outside a safer place to be. For those with whom I was able to continue working for many months, the developing relationship promoted an internalised sense of safety, allowing some to keep themselves safe in tenancies which had otherwise seemed too threatening.

Meanwhile, more clients were being referred. We decided it was time to explore sources of funding for the project. After discussion with the charity's trustees it was agreed that the project would employ me on a part-time basis once funding was established. We had explored other models, including one where I offered psychotherapy as an independent contractor. Now that I have been employed as a member of the project team for two years, I feel that employment has offered the structure, boundaries and support that have helped us embed the therapeutic work into the project's culture and practice, in a way in which sessional work may not have done.

The search for funding took just over a year, during which time I continued to work on a voluntary basis. The issues around counsellors and psychotherapists engaging in unpaid work are complex and controversial. I was sometimes challenged by colleagues as to why I would do this difficult work for no financial reward. I was already thinking about my motives anyway, and the issues of the work being voluntary added to the complexity of this. I knew that whatever my underlying desire to engage with people on the margins, I needed to invest my time in building up the evidence that by situating this work within the hostel and day centre setting, we could make a difference. In turn, I felt that the project's staff and trustees were investing trust and support in me.

Where would we look for funds? We considered applying to statutory bodies. I tried to build links with the Local Authority and the local Clinical Commissioning Group (CCG). It was clear that supporting the wellbeing of vulnerable people fitted into the Health and Wellbeing Board's Joint Health and Wellbeing Strategy, as well as the Strategic Plan of the CCG. But translating this into meaningful, focused discussions as to whether either of these groups would commit funds to a small and innovative project like Streetlight was very difficult. In short, there *were* no funds to commit. Although I knew this, there were many times when 'small and innovative' felt more like 'inconsequential and experimental'. It was disheartening. I knew that colleagues in cities like Leeds and Bradford had set up some amazing projects using public money. I felt the lack of both my own local links and what seemed like a different set of priorities in our largely rural county. However, HHP was well supported locally and had a lot of experience in applying for non-statutory funding. We decided that, at this stage, we needed to concentrate our energies in applying to charitable trusts. I began by researching funders who had an interest in supporting mental health projects, supported by one of the trustees who had a lot of knowledge of who was likely to be interested. Once we had identified possible sources, I spent a lot of time in making the clinical case for our bids, whilst our trustee and chief executive put together the business case. I had some experience of bidding for money for projects from my time in the NHS, but no real knowledge of how to put a business case together. It was hard work, not least in finding time to do it all, and to meet with colleagues who were already very busy. At times, I did wonder if I was deluding myself. Our service looked very small and its outcomes uncertain. Were we really going to make a difference in the big scheme of things?

As I look back now over that year of making applications, and review the clients I was seeing at that time, I can see how that sense of uncertainty and ambivalence must have been echoed in the client work. There was, for example, Paul, a young man whose sadness and anger gave rise to a vulnerability and aggression that divided staff and provoked a sense of helplessness in those who tried to relate with him, including me. Other clients helped me believe it was worth continuing. When clients had experienced family relationships which could be relied upon, at least some of the time, they were more able to use psychotherapy to give expression to turbulent feelings and achieve a sense of autonomy and hope. Over the course of that year, several clients made planned and hopeful endings. Others drifted off from therapy, went to prison or returned to chaotic drinking. All in a day's work, but when was that work going to be remunerated? Eventually, as the summer of 2014 was drawing to a close, we received *two* expressions of interest! Just like the proverbial buses. In October, we began our two-year relationship with Lloyds Bank Foundation (LBF). This offer of funding came with a tremendous amount of strategic and business support for the project as a whole, and helped our chief executive build links both with the local banking sector and national charities. One of the first exercises was to write a sustainability plan. LBF was concerned about Streetlight's dependence on just one psychotherapist. We needed to set the service on a firmer footing, and so my first months as an employee (with some paid development time, as well as my clinical hours; luxury!) were spent in writing policies and procedures which a new worker could pick up, as well as working with hostel and day centre staff to embed the provision of psychotherapy within the everyday functioning of the team. Our sustainability plan also included goals for evaluation and dissemination of our model, as well as how we would seek to bring in more funding, possibly even generate our own income.

I will pick up here the thread I left hanging earlier: that of how the psychotherapist 'fits' in a multidisciplinary team, particularly one outside a traditional health setting. Whether working within a hostel, day centre, counselling or mental health team, there will be dominant paradigms, which have a profound impact on therapeutic relationships. One area of potential conflict is that of power dynamics. How are power relationships understood in your service? As a psychotherapist, how do you understand and exercise power, and is this different from, say, your hostel worker colleagues? Issues of autonomy are fundamental to our work with people who have experienced the relative powerlessness of social exclusion (Cockersell, 2015). How we work with these in therapy needs thinking about. To disavow our power as psychotherapists could mean that we are unconsciously exerting it. Larner (1999, p.41) writes that 'therapists can be powerful, but sacrifice themselves for the sake of the other [and this] allows the power of the other to emerge'. This represents one of the most profound lessons that I am still learning, from the doctor who had no choice but to wield the power of safe prescribing guidance or evidence-based protocols to the psychotherapist who spends time allowing the voice of the client to emerge. Similarly, my hostel staff colleagues have to juggle exercising their powers of applying rules for the safe running of the hostel and allowing their residents to take autonomous steps on the road to independence. Sometimes I have found points of difference with support workers. For example, the autonomy encouraged in psychotherapy clients means that some will choose to leave therapy before support workers feel they are 'ready'. This can be a tough dilemma to work with. Brown *et al.* (2011) have written about homeless clients who decline to accept psychotherapy 'on our terms' and they question the whole idea of exclusion and resettlement, recognising the homeless person's right to exercise the power to walk away from therapy and conformity.

Another challenge to us as psychotherapists working in services with other professionals is monitoring. It is incumbent upon us all to demonstrate effectiveness by keeping track of the 'progress' of our clients. LBF have given us a lot of support to integrate the use of the

Outcomes Star[1] into the work of the hostel and Streetlight's work in that setting. They also measure our work along their own transition and progression outcomes.[2] But monitoring is not without its challenges in a psychotherapeutic model which is relational and exploratory. Evidence of effectiveness is essential, clearly, but equally important is how we incorporate monitoring into our clinical practice and the effect it has on our relationships with clients, as well as the need to consider the reductionism involved in trying to capture internal intrapsychic changes with quantitative measures. We are pleased that LBF welcomed a mixture of quantitative and qualitative evidence, which has enabled us to use case study and some client testimonies in our annual reporting.

LBF funding allowed us to pursue another of our central aims: to create PIEs within our services. PIEs have been implemented in many services for homeless people and take many shapes. In her essential document, Ritchie (2016) explains that a PIE is one where the psychological worlds of all its participants are taken into consideration. This means that, for example, staff in a homeless hostel should have an understanding that residents' past lives have a significant bearing on their current feelings, thoughts and behaviours. In turn, staff will seek to understand and support one another by paying heed to their own responses to their clients and to one another. Central to this awareness of psychological process is reflection, and one of the ways this can be achieved is through the reflective practice group. More and more teams in health and social care are finding reflecting together on their work helps staff to build personal and collective resilience. I was fortunate to find some training given by Psychotherapy for Healthcare,[3] which enabled me to get started with facilitation of a group for staff in the hostel. We are still at the early stages of establishing this, and it would be fair to say that some team members remain unsure of its value. But others have expressed appreciation of the value of taking an hour out to think about a difficult incident, a challenging client or the effect of a new policy. At one of our first meetings, one of the team had an idea for how to change the weekly team meeting so as to better consider clients' needs, which has now become normal practice. At another, a small group discussed how our boundaries on what is sexually or

---

1   www.outcomesstar.org.uk
2   www.lloydsbankfoundation.org.uk/how-to-apply/outcomes
3   www.psychotherapyforhealthcare.co.uk

culturally appropriate may differ from our clients', and how we respond to this.

The reflective practice group facilitation has also allowed me to begin exploring another of the ideas of LBF, our funders; that of selling our expertise. We are now offering group facilitation to other teams and have had a regular contract with another homeless service for several months now. Recently, I have attended another training day given by Psychotherapy for Healthcare, this time in how to conduct a debriefing session after a critical incident. This is, I hope, another service which can be useful to our own team and can be offered to other organisations.

So, we draw near to the end of the chapter, as at Streetlight we draw to the end of our first two years of greater security as a funded service. Our relationship with LBF will come to an end for the time being. The trustees of HHP have recognised the benefits of taking a psychologically informed approach and have made a commitment to continue the service. New funding is part-way in place. There is still a lot to do. We have yet to arrange some meaningful external evaluation. Although we have had some good examples of joint working with colleagues in statutory health and housing services over individual clients, we haven't yet established a more secure relationship at a higher level, and certainly no promise of funding. We haven't given up hope. Perhaps one thing (evaluation) might lead to another (funding). But there remain the clients, and the need for relationships which can help them believe in themselves and find hope. In my current caseload are people who have lived lives shaped by abuse, neglect and recurrent loss. And yet two of them are now established in council tenancies that they are managing well, and two more moved on into more independent living. Perhaps we can dare to hope that relationships are starting to work better for them. The question of endings hovers over us. With most clients who have engaged for more than a couple of sessions, endings have been able to happen in a planned way to suit their needs. On a few occasions, when clients have settled into a new home and we have worked at an ending, there has been difficulty and ending has perhaps been too early for the client. But mostly, we have been able to work with open-ended contracts, negotiating endings as we go. My supervisor and our service manager have helped a lot with this. Supervision has been just as important as one would expect. Sometimes it has brought me back from the brink of entering into my client's unboundaried chaos, at others helped me to continue to hold onto hope for a client whose sense of hopelessness was profound. Thinking back to what I wrote about my own process above, the supervision and peer support process help me to maintain contact with both my unhoused Child ego states as well as my nurturing and critical Parent, whilst holding on to Adult awareness, as much as possible. And so I end with motivation, and think again of the cycle of change. We'll go on changing at Streetlight and at HHP, no doubt. The questioning and ambivalence will continue to challenge us. But, we are, for the most and at the moment, maintaining our service. I hope this chapter has given a flavour of how we got here.

References

Adlam, J. and Scanlon, C. (2005) 'Personality disorder and homelessness: membership and unhoused minds in forensic settings.' *Group Analysis 38*, 3, 452–466.

Barker, P. (2007) 'The Person, Not the Drug.' Presentation at SMMGP conference, Birmingham. Accessed June 2016 at www.smmgp.org.uk/download/rcgpconference/rcgp12/rcgp12p19.pdf

Barker, P. and Buchanan-Barker, P. (2004) 'Beyond empowerment: revering the story teller.' *Mental Health Practice 7*, 5, 18–20.

BBC (2015) *Harrogate Named as Happiest Place to Live in Britain.* Accessed October 2017 at www.bbc.co.uk/news/uk-england-33794154

Blackwell, R. (1997) 'Holding, containing and bearing witness: the problem of helpfulness in encounters with torture survivors.' *Journal of Social Work Practice 11*, 2: 81–89.

Bowlby, J. (1997 [1969]) *Attachment and Loss, Volume 1 Attachment.* London: Pimlico.

Brown, G., Kainth, K., Matheson, C., Osborne, J., Trenkle, A. and Adlam, J. (2011) 'An hospitable engagement? Open-door psychotherapy with the socially excluded.' *Psychodynamic Practice 17*, 3, 307–324.

Buber, M. (1923) *I and Thou.* Translated by Gregor Smith. London: Continuum.

Clarkson, P. (1992) *Transactional Analysis Psychotherapy: An Integrative Approach.* Hove: Routledge.

Charura, D. and Paul, S. (eds) (2014) *The Therapeutic Relationship Handbook: Theory and Practice.* Maidenhead: Open University Press.

Cockersell, P. (2015) 'The processes of social exclusion.' *Clinical Psychology Forum 265*, 13–17.

DCLG (2015) *Rough Sleeping in England: Autumn 2014.* Accessed October 2017 at www.gov.uk/government/statistics/rough-sleeping-in-england-autumn-2014

Dowds, B. (2014) *Beyond the Frustrated Self: Overcoming Avoidant Patterns and Opening to Life.* London: Karnac.

Faculty for Homeless Health (2013) *Standards for Commissioners and Service Providers*, Version 2.0. Accessed October 2017 at www.pathway.org.uk/wp-content/uploads/2014/01/Standards-for-commissioners-providers-v2.0-INTERACTIVE.pdf

Gomez, L. (1997) *An Introduction to Object Relations.* London: Free Association Books.

Karpman, S. (1968) 'Fairy tales and script drama analysis.' *Transactional Analysis Bulletin 7*, 26, 39–43.

Larner, G. (1999) 'Derrida and the Deconstruction of Power as Context and Topic in Therapy.' In I. Parker (ed.) *Deconstructing Psychotherapy.* London: Sage.

Maguire, N.J., Johnson, R., Vostanis, P., Keats, H. and Remington, R.E. (2009) 'Homelessness and complex trauma: a review of the literature.' University of Southampton.

Maroda, K. (2004) *The Power of the Countertransference: Innovations in Analytic Technique.* Hillsdale, NJ: Analytic Press.

Ogden, T.H. (1982) *Projective Identification and Psychotherapeutic Technique.* London: Karnac.

Prochaska, J.O. and DiClemente, C.C. (1982) 'Transtheoretical therapy: toward a more integrative model of change.' *Psychotherapy: Theory, Research and Practice 192*, 76–288.

Public Health England (2014) *Harrogate District: Health Profile 2014.* Accessed October 2017 at www.harrogateandruraldistrictccg.nhs.uk/data/uploads/publications/health-profiles-for-harrogate-2014.pdf

Read, S. (2014) 'The Therapeutic Relationship in the Helping Professions.' In D. Charura and S. Paul (eds) *The Therapeutic Relationship Handbook: Theory and Practice.* Maidenhead: Open University Press.

Ritchie, C. (2016) *Creating a Psychologically Informed Environment.* Accessed October 2017 at www.homeless.org.uk/sites/default/files/site-attachments/Creating%20a%20Psychologically%20Informed%20Environment%20-%202015.pdf

Stern, D.N. (2004) *The Present Moment in Psychotherapy and Everyday Life.* New York: Norton.

St Mungo's (2016) Stop the Scandal. Accessed December 2017 at https://www.england.nhs.uk/wp-content/uploads/2016/07/stop-the-scandal.pdf

11

I HELD THE TICKET IN MY HAND

TERRY HUTTON

I held the train ticket to Brighton in my hand with a death grip, and I was painfully aware I couldn't afford it. 'Blast,' I said to myself, I shouldn't have bought it, but breathed a deep sigh of relief none the less.

Poverty, homelessness, destitution comes in many speeds…for me it was slow. My first blurry vision of it was when I met an old friend called Will, who was also English, living in Los Angeles, California like myself. I knew Will as we had worked together as artists on a commercial project in Pasadena, California. Will told me he was homeless, sleeping rough in shop doorways, in Santa Monica. I didn't believe him at first. I honestly felt he was pulling my chain, on a bit of a wind up, but when I questioned him seriously, he casually talked about how he beds down in one of the most expensive cities in the world, Santa Monica. This was a hard swallow for me, as I knew Will as a high earner, picturing him on rolling scaffold making brush strokes that transformed a brand-new home into what would look like a 200-year-old monument when we had all finished. How did this happen to you, Will? In a nutshell, work dried up for him, he lost everything and poverty…this news scared me as the doors were beginning to close on me too. Interior designers and architects who I had worked for in the past were asking me to work at a loss. I at the time was bidding on projects that other companies shredded in half. How? Simply put, seven men in my trade were willing to sleep in a one-bedroom flat and also cut corners on the project. I was a fully licensed, bonded and insured contractor with lots of funny looking artist tools; I couldn't afford to cut corners, besides the fact it's against the law to do so. How do you compete against companies who have nothing to lose? They have no licence to lose, no insurance to be cancelled, no bond to be suspended, let alone a reputation to keep. As I drove away from Will, I had an overwhelming, daunting feeling.

During 2008, commonly known as the Great Recession, when banks were being 'bailed out' to the tune of untold billions, and the term 'too big to fail' was coined, work did dry up for me in LA like it had for Will. The only calls I was getting were designers and architects asking me to fix the work done by other cheaper companies, the same companies that had shredded my bid in half. For the first few times I showed up to look at the project, but the story was always the same. 'Can you fix it?' the designers would always ask. 'What do you want me to do?' I would reply. 'Well, do that thing you do, you know, that thing that makes walls look good.' They were talking about finessing, using what you have and adding a little extra something that makes it look cohesive and as it should look. However, what they were asking me to work with was unfixable. It was wall finishes, like no other wall finishes I was familiar with. For example, venetian plaster – or polished plaster as it is known in the UK – is meant to be super smooth with many layers creating a beautiful, almost marble-like wall finish. Instead what was in front of me to fix was layered on like gypsum mud or concrete, with thick trowel marks and no cohesion. I would deliver the bad news and tell the designers they had two solutions – one, start all over again with a company that knew what they were doing, or two, learn to live with it. During these times came that familiar overwhelming, daunting feeling again.

I really felt I was in the corner getting rope burns; I had to make a bold decision and a change. I moved to a place that rich and famous people love, and where an artist like myself would surely thrive, Palm Springs, California. My cost of living was almost halved, and for a while it was OK. Then, even the rich felt the first pangs of economic fear, and Greenspan's 'trickledown effect' soon became the rare, occasional drip. Just like Will's experience, my well was beginning to run dry.

It was outside an Alcoholics Anonymous meeting in Palm Springs where I got my second blurry vision of poverty. Another commercial artist like Will and me, an American man this time, who told me he was also homeless. The penny dropped. Would I be next? Surely not me. I had several medium-sized projects on the go, I had been self-employed for over 25 years in good times and bad, so of course I would weather this storm. Ah, the lies I tell myself.

It's hard to describe the feeling you have when you arrive for work, only to see you are locked out. On one of those three projects I just spoke of earlier, I stood and looked at the heavy chain and padlock as an affront. I kept rattling the lock as though it would sympathetically open for me. I discovered from the interior designer during a phone call that the project was closed down the day before. The developers had pulled the money. And then over the course of the next few weeks, I had two more phone calls just like that...money pulled, work shut down. In politically correct circles they called it *work suspended*, though it was a long suspension, some for several years, some never to be reopened. Unless you have untold funds or are very rich, no amount of personal savings in the bank can cross lengths of time, to weather such economic storms. Suddenly the old idea that working hard and being honest in life would always hold you in good stead crumbled...a lie appeared like a hairline crack, and reality set in. Were my ethics and principles of being honest and hardworking now a liability? I have to admit as I write this, my conclusion to this question has not changed. Yes, they most definitely were! It seemed we had entered into a dog-eat-dog world, where common decency and fair play were replaced by individualism, and a 'get out of my way' attitude, and the saddest part for me was that it was applauded and encouraged by the majority of the public.

As a member of Alcoholics Anonymous I sponsored men who confided in me their struggles, their hopes, their fears. Some were already sleeping on their mum's or brother's sofa. My mum lived 6000 miles away. What was I to do? As money became even tighter, and opportunities even fewer, I drastically went deep into the desert, 29 Palms, California, and lived in what I like to describe as a shotgun shack – no water, no power, no walls, no windows – pretty much a frame with a roof on it. This was my last-ditch effort to stay afloat and not hit the streets along with Will in Los Angeles. In heat of at least 110 degrees, soaring high winds, lots of sand, scorpions and snakes I made my home, while making oil paintings to sell at a weekly street fair in Palm Springs. The only trouble was that great minds think alike, so everyone else had the same idea, and what was once a good way to make pocket money, a little extra pin money, became the sole source of income for many families. The art market was saturated.

Here in the desert, where I lived for almost a year, I frankly believe I lost my mind. I have never been the same since (at least I look at myself that way). I went from being a popular, well-liked man to a person whose phone calls went unanswered, texts ignored, emails not replied to, and a sinking feeling that I was alone. I turned into a man, who from a bird's perspective, was wandering around talking to himself, ranting at the skies and laughing hysterically, but in actuality was desperately trying to cling to any thread of my previous life. Here I would go days without food, then cry with gratitude when I got some. How did I get here? Why is this happening to me? I came to the conclusion there was something innately wrong with me, it was the only thing that made sense to me. I couldn't bear the thought that God was punishing me, that would have been a crime to imagine...God at this point was my only friend, my rock, my salvation. So, of course, it's easier to blame myself...there was surely something deeply wrong with me.

With all my stuff gone, my home, my furniture, my money, my clothes, my work, my contacts, and sadly my friends (most of them), I was desperate. I had one luxury item left, my car. It kept me in drinking water in a place where you will die within hours if you don't have it. I felt I had been placed in a position where I was left two more options: sell the car and use the money to live off in the desert for a short period of time, or use the car to make another move. Selling art at the Palm Springs Art Fair was certainly not sustaining me, so another move seemed the only option. I came to the conclusion I couldn't carry on like this. My self-worth was on the floor, I was completely alone, and there was no future. I planned my escape carefully. New York, NY, so good they named it twice. However, money was the important and missing ingredient. On my calculations I had enough for fuel and would be left with a few hundred dollars to get me by...it was thin ice, but what other option did I have...wither away in the desert?

I loaded my car up, mostly art supplies, with the idea I would get to New York, unload my car into a really cheap storage unit, thus opening the back of my car to sleep in. Great plan I thought. Sadly Duluth, Georgia, almost bang in the middle of the USA, was as far as I got. Damn that transmission! I couldn't believe my luck or lack of it. With my car gasping, but still moving, I made three stops while in Duluth, Georgia. First, to an art consignment shop that took all of my paintings and promised they would pay my commission, and thankfully did, then a charity shop that welcomed all my other stuff. And then finally a skip where I tossed everything that was of no value to anyone else but me. I stood at the skip and saw my journal writings from Asia and family photos drift to the murky bottom. When poverty strikes there is little room for sentiment. That evening I got on the Greyhound bus bound for New York, with a single ticket in my pocket, and a suitcase in each hand.

After a brief spell in New York I gratefully ended up spending a length of time (nine months) in New Jersey, living in a tent city. As the Great Recession ravaged parts of America, tent cities were popping up like hot cakes. The government in their compassion and true democracy tried to stop them, and literally stamped them out, but the demand for them was high, as hard working people like me were left without a home and destitute. I had gone from the searing heat of the desert to freezing temperatures of the East Coast. The Christian minister who ran this tent city in New Jersey welcomed me into what can only be described as a haven for those with nowhere else to go, and generously gave me a tent and bedding. In the midst of cock fights, pit bulls, and an underlying feeling of violence, I gratefully accepted my new home contained in two clear plastic bags, which I could hold in one hand. I witnessed episodes here that would make you scream with outrage and indignation. Police officers and firemen standing in a circle laughing as they watched homes (albeit tents and shanties) burn to the ground. During the demolition of Tent City I heard of men being swept up with the debris while they slept in their homes made of colourful sheets of plastic and poles. Once they came to pick up a man who had died and just threw him in the back of the truck, as though he were nothing. I wondered where all the human respect and dignity had gone. And when people protested, it was met with laughter and contempt. Having said all that, I will be eternally grateful to that pitch in the woods and the generous kindness I received from many people at Tent City, NJ.

Scrambling money together through work (cheap labour) in New Jersey, I finally brought a single airline ticket to London. It was a hard decision, and never occurred to me until a cousin I grew up with in London said, 'Come home cous' on social media. The seed was sown. I felt like a man returning to the scene of the crime, back in London, with some family members and friends telling me I wasn't English any more. Of course, my close family felt very concerned for me, and deeply wanted to help and support me. I, however, discovered quickly through government offices and local councils, I would not receive any help unless I slept rough, which I was already doing, sleeping in one of my nephew's garages, but *to be seen to be sleeping rough* by the authorities was the crucial element. I discovered that the taxes I had paid while I worked in my teens and mid-20s were not to my credit any more. They apparently had been spent a long time ago (not on me though). It was almost as though I had never been born in Stepney E1 in 1960, or even lived here in the UK the first 27 years of my life. I was treated by the authorities as though I had no history with England whatsoever. I did understand the policy on one hand, but felt slighted on the other hand, as I knew how much money I had paid in taxes during those 11 years before I took off to the USA, during Maggie Thatcher's government. Even a boy like me from the wrong side of Stepney could see where she was heading, quite happy to crush and demoralise the working classes of the UK. In my youthful arrogance, I despised everything she stood for and couldn't wait to leave.

I suppose it makes sense that sleeping rough my first night in Brighton had more appeal than London. I admit that thought terrified me. That's why I clutched onto that train ticket I mentioned in the first paragraph for dear life and breathed a sigh of relief. They say London is the loneliest city in the world. I would agree, especially when you have no front door to close and lock. With a backpack and my sleeping bag I looked for a place to sleep, and in sheer exhaustion I found a bench along the beach front and settled down for my first night as a *rough sleeper*. I slept like a log, thank God, like I always do. The next day I read about a public demonstration in the newspaper against austerity taking place in London, and ran to Brighton station to get the first train back to Victoria. I had to be part of that cry to the 'powers that be'. Why has this happened to me...I did all you asked me to do, I played by the rules...why?

I finally got my second night under my belt, sleeping rough just around the corner from Victoria station. The fear of making my claim under a building's overhang to sleep was intense. I had remembered a spot earlier that afternoon, and it took all I had to sit down, and then finally hunker down for the night. I spent nine months sleeping rough in that spot. During that time I was introduced by one of the staff at a homeless day centre in Victoria to a specialist medical centre. It's an exclusive club in Soho with only one requirement: you have to be homeless to use their facilities. Here I received warmth, kindness and an understanding that was like a breath of fresh air. I must admit I got choked up as the psychiatric nurse left the room and gave me a moment to myself, after we had talked about my past in brief. She and I talked about my faith, and how I was struggling with my circumstances, staying sober on the streets, and feeling so isolated and disconnected. We also talked about my attempts to bring life to an end when I was in my 20s...and the shame, guilt and endless torment I always seem to feel, even when things look rosy in my life. Today we in the UK call it mental illness. I call it my natural state, which over the years I have painfully learnt to cope with...simply because it never leaves and never ends.

Words cannot describe the amount of support and help I received from that medical centre, from the GPs, to counsellors like Mike who are on the frontline of real tragic circumstances, I marvelled at their dedication and compassion. Here were these doctors, highly educated, attractive people working with people who have nothing to offer in terms of the material world. And yet all I ever witnessed was their deep concern and care for the next patient.

Thankfully, through the help of the psychiatric nurse, Jean, I met with Mike weekly to talk frankly about what was going on with me while sleeping on the streets. I needed the help, guidance and support he offered during those sessions. I hate to admit this, but I think both Mike and Jean could clearly see that I was in a fragile state, close to the edge. I even felt alienated from the rooms of Alcoholics Anonymous, which was hard to cope with, as I love the fellowship. But something was missing, a new city maybe (London), new rooms and new fellow travellers. Where were my peers from California, who I had formed friendships with over the course of my 25 years' sobriety? Oh, that's right, they weren't answering my phone calls any more. On reflection and with a more sober mind, I can see now how it must have been hard for them to stay in touch with me...what can you do or say with a relationship that is fractured by poverty? Sadly, to this day I still struggle with trusting members in the fellowship who talk so gallantly about loving one another unconditionally...it sounds nice and rolls off the tongue so easily, and to a greater degree is true for many, but that wasn't my experience during my homelessness. A good example of this was a friend who offered me money while I was living in Tent City. I, in turn said a choked up thank you, and suggested maybe we could do a trade with some artwork. I wanted to repay his kind and generous gesture. To this day I have never heard from him again.

Working with Mike was a God shot: his honest desire to help and nonjudgemental approach was just what I needed. I would talk, rant and metaphorically climb the walls of his office, while he calmly listened and grasped, and fully understood everything I said. We started at the beginning and why I always felt awkward and uncomfortable with myself...even as a little boy I felt different with lots of awkward, peculiar ways. We talked about my school days that were anything but normal, how I ended up in a comprehensive school in Clapham, South London that was nothing more than a borstal for violent teenage boys. There I witnessed animals being tortured, teachers being assaulted by bricks and fibreglass fishing rods. I personally experienced acid in my face, frequent beatings and kickings with steel toe capped boots, which at the time were the fashion accessory of that generation. The greater injustice was my attempt to defend myself, only to be met outside school with the boy I had fought with earlier and several of his mates. Everyone including the teachers turned a blind eye, as it was rampant and out of control. I personally believe I was robbed of my education, as I clearly remember being top of the class on the subjects I took. Sadly, I left school at the age of 13 simply because the physical and mental abuse were intolerable. I did have a welfare officer who threatened to take me away from my family for truancy, but he confessed the school couldn't keep me safe as it was so large...my dad sent him away with a flea in his ear, to put it mildly.

On these weekly visits with Mike, I would tell him and other members of staff at the medical centre that my body could cope with the hardness of concrete, or the frost making its way through the fibres of my sleeping bag. It could almost cope with people thinking it is fun to abuse and punch me while I slept, but I struggled with and couldn't comprehend the looks of disgust and contempt I felt. It was beyond me to understand how people behaved, as though I were a leper with something contagious, and something to be feared. With a hint of humour, and tongue in cheek, I am sure I wasn't the freshest of daisies, but I showered daily and had my laundry cleaned regularly at the homeless day centre, so why were there always empty seats either side of me, when all other seats were packed. I wasn't drunk, I've been sober for over 25 years, I wasn't noisy or disruptive, I certainly wasn't begging or asking for change, so why the wide berth? I remember a woman fell down right in front of me, and as I tried to help her I was shuffled off by members of the general public. I felt without a shadow of doubt, had I have been wearing a suit and tie my experience would have been completely different, but because I was around Victoria station with a sleeping bag under my arm, I was someone to be protected from, someone to treat with suspicion.

I truly believe that unlike during World War II when many people suffered critical food shortage, shelter and daily needs, and also the Great Depression during the 1930s, we have been slowly taught over time to regard the homeless and less fortunate as bringing it upon themselves, as though they asked for it, or somehow deserve their individual plights. I believe we have lost all compassion, all empathy and all humanity that was the cornerstone of the UK, and made us different from most of the world. And regrettably these virtues have been replaced by disdain, apathy and arrogance. We have been taught to turn against one another, and the hand of brotherly love that I witnessed in the past has been withdrawn with cries of 'Why should I help her/him, it's none of my business', or 'they brought it upon themselves, they deserve it'.

With fear of sounding like I jumped up on my soap box, I think we all have to ask ourselves who is it giving the disgusted contemptuous looks to those less fortunate than us? What I mean is, before I became destitute and poverty stricken, my income for over 20 years was good and at times high. And during that time of prosperity I would help homeless and the elderly in my 12-step work in AA. I would bundle food and provisions together and feed the homeless living under tarps in downtown San Diego and Los Angeles. I would see whole families living under 10ft x 10ft sheets with no hope of any future. But strangely, in polite conversation, sitting around a dining room table, for example with friends, everyone else would claim they too were helping, and full of compassion. I certainly never witnessed anyone go off on a rant that the homeless and poor deserve it or brought it upon themselves. So again, if the vast majority of people I witnessed looked with disdain upon me, who is giving the looks? Apparently, no one I know.

The idea that people choose this way of life, more commonly known as a lifestyle choice, is a great 'Get out of jail free' card for those that want to wash their hands of a plight right in front of them. Like Pontius Pilate, they see the problem and what is happening all around them, but don't want to do anything about it, or stop it. If I can say one last thing before I get down off my soap box…no one in their right mind would choose destitution, poverty and homelessness…no one.

At the very least something extraordinary has happened to these people who are daily rejected, ostracised, mocked, abused, and at the very least, pitied. Like Maggie Thatcher putting on a coal miner's helmet, and going to the coal face, we have famous people and politicians hitting the streets for one night to sleep rough. The undeniable truth is they will never have a full experience of homelessness. Yes, they may feel the cold discomfort of sleeping on a hard surface, and may even feel the pangs of hunger, but like Maggie going to the coal face, all things will be scrubbed clean and sterile, and the true ugliness of looks of contempt and disgust will not be experienced.

With the help of Mike I was able to see that most people will thankfully not experience being without a home, stripped of all possessions by virtue of a declining economy. They'll not completely understand what it feels like to be marginalised and ostracised, unheard or silenced. Poverty is like no other condition, that if we are all honest with ourselves, we all fear. But unlike bad health or death, there is no sympathy, no empathy, no compassion or heartfelt comfort. Poverty is met with coldness, apathy and a strong desire to condemn those that suffer it, as though the sufferer deliberately sets out to upset the status quo, cause trouble and ultimately needs to be put down, put in their place, punished.

I truly believe I suffer from a stigma now. Like many former homeless people, this mark will never leave me, and like a brand it will remain. I am now known as Terry, the guy who was homeless, who slept rough on the streets of London. All my former successes, albeit small, will now always come second place to this mark, which is sad when you think I moved to the USA with a small chunk of change in my pocket, and built two successful businesses over the course of 25 years from nothing, travelled Asia for two years teaching English and volunteering in orphanages, while studying in ashrams and monasteries. Helped a lot of people by virtue of my 12-step work in AA, or simply being a good Christian Samaritan.

The hardest struggle today on the other side of all that I have described is my self-esteem. Mike and the medical centre helped me tremendously with that, but I still have a long way to go. I admit I fear people might find this this story *too something*: too self-indulgent, too revealing, too righteous, too critical, or such. But I beg you to indulge me right now…close your eyes, imagine a friend you know walking up to you…they calmly and quietly ask you to hand over your house keys, then your credit and debit cards, they also ask for your car keys, and all your savings and money, and then they whisper you have no job or career to go to from now on. As your friend leaves the room, they tell you not to bother calling other friends, as they will not answer (the unkindest cut of all). They finally tell you to pack as many clothes as you can fit into a back-pack and generously leave you a ten pound note...you are now homeless. If you did that little exercise sincerely, even in part, you may have caught a small glimpse of many people's daily reality, people you are likely to pass on the way home from work this evening. You may, on the other hand, hold fast to the idea after that exercise, that that would never happen to you, simply because you are too smart, with a wealth of degrees, too savvy and connected, too beautiful. If that's true you are more than likely right, but it has nothing to do with you as a person, it is just different circumstances, ultimately *different classes*, yes that word that sums up so much even today, as much as many would deny its existence – class.

My hope for the future is difficult for me to put into words, as I have an internal fear I need to put a smiley face on it, as I truly believe we have all been conditioned to do in this social media world we all seem to feel comfortable in, but frankly I don't truly feel that way, well, not entirely. Yes, I am grateful I am no longer wandering the desert frothing from the mouth, or waking with a sheet of ice on me that shattered as I got out of bed in New Jersey, and then finally sleeping on the concrete pavement around the corner from Victoria station. Yes, I am eternally grateful I have a well-fed stomach, fresh water and now another small group of friends I stay in touch with. But the challenges of being a 57-year-old man desperately trying to shed the shame of the benefits system is uphill and fraught with hurdles and dead ends that I believe are deliberately placed in the centre of a long and narrow path. Unquestionably I cannot do what I used to do with such ease and confidence like climb scaffold, then plaster for ten hours a day, and crawl into spaces on my hands and knees for hours on end. I cannot climb a ladder with heavy buckets of plaster or paint on my shoulder, or leap from one scaffold floor to another to help a colleague who is in trouble with a wall finish. With tongue in cheek there was a time I moved so quickly that the sponge I was using to faux finish a wall, literally went up in flames while I worked...true. As a direct result of these so-called occupation hazards in my chosen career I have been left with lower back problems that are chronic and often paralysing. I wake daily to my hands feeling the size of bananas, with numbness and tingling fingertips, and water that balloons in my injured knee, if I bend any longer than five minutes. I cannot tell you of the frustration I have felt as I follow one more dead-end after another to be retrained. On first appearances I had hope, when I saw what appeared to be lots of help and assistance for a change of career, but as I drew closer and on further inspection, I discovered sadly that many of these programmes are closed down due to lack of funding. Apprenticeship programmes that are quite rightly for the young are no longer available to people over a certain age. The oldest age limit programme I came across was for 35-year-olds and younger. Even with the most optimistic outlook, it's not hard to succumb to disillusionment and begin to feel very pessimistic, and excluded.

While drawing benefits and the stigma that goes along with that, I have made an impression with volunteering my time. I have devoted time with the homeless day centre, the Salvation Army and also a charity run by homeless people for homeless people. With them I would take vulnerable men and women to their respective NHS appointments, whether that be to their dentist, local GP or even hospital visits. This was good for me and also for the clients too, as I could relate, where someone who was being paid a wage might struggle to form a relationship. Often these partnerships of cooperation I was trying to form would change immediately once the client discovered I too was once homeless and wasn't being paid – an immediate connection would develop, where there may have been some tension before.

As I write, I am looking at spending my own money (which I am happy and feel fortunate enough to do), in some form of retraining. I have my eye on several courses from bike mechanic, to white goods installation (engineer), or becoming qualified as a Gas Safe engineer. All of them have pros and cons, and are expensive. However, on the plus side I try to convince and sell myself on the idea that with the education and training, I will be better than the other guys, simply by virtue of some great idea, or niche I have up my sleeve, some business model no-one else has yet thought of. Of course, I suffer from no illusion there is any reality in this notion, with 25 years of self-employment under my belt, no amount of positive thinking will override my own past personal experiences. As a man who is closer to 60 then 55 years old, I know it takes hard work and diligence to succeed and start a business from scratch; it's certainly not magical thinking. I know when

I first got sober, I started a cleaning business with a roll of kitchen towels and a spray bottle of Windex. I can also comically remember turning up to a minor flood with nothing more than a black bag of beach towels…the audacity of it all…the home owner said, 'no way', but I pleaded to her to let me have a go at mopping up the water damage…she kindly conceded, and with the same speed of a burning sponge, I had her washing machine area shipshape and Bristol fashion. With an emotional lump in my throat as I write, I don't have that vigour and enthusiasm any more. Actually, I often feel pretty tired of my circumstances of deeply wanting to do the right thing, to being once again independent, but as time passes that light of optimism loses its brightness, and becomes cloudy.

Gratefully my confidence is not in what is out there, whether that is successive governments promising all sorts of changes and delivering nothing, but the same ol' status quo, from affordable housing, blind justice, equality for all, workers' rights, healthcare, education for the young and the not so young, and looking after the elderly…the list goes on ad infinitum. Because most of us know that is like going down a rabbit hole, coming out the other end even more confused. I also don't believe in all honesty that getting the next perfect job is the answer too, or the next wonderful relationship with her, or my bank accounts looking really, really healthy. Thankfully, I pull from within, on my inner resources, knowing that no matter what comes down the pike, I will manage to navigate it, and be reasonably happy doing so. And in the final analysis, trusting that no matter what happens, you cannot take my faith away from me, and my loving God, who has never abandoned me, even when all else seemed lost and barren. Yes, I will still go to public demonstrations and protest marches to do my public duty that is now sadly, commonly ridiculed and scoffed at, because I only have to look at history to see that this is the only tool the working man and woman has. History shows time after time this is where the poor, marginalised and hated have ever made progress in a world that seems to take delight in stacking the cards against them…the Establishment. The very same group of people who give themselves accolades and awards for leading such privileged, luxurious lives. I suppose the natural response to this comment in many circles is to claim I am just jealous, that I envy the rich. And if you hold this position strongly, I suspect there is little I can do or say to convince you otherwise. I know without a shadow of doubt what I have within myself is worth much more than any gold mine, but it came at an extremely high cost...for a length of time I had to be stripped of all that I held dear. And while I went through this assault I was alone, with no silver lining except God. You see on that day, in that moment, in Brighton, when I was about to spend my first night on the streets, I intuitively knew my limitations; I knew the streets of London were too big for me, they were terrifying, but a bench on the coast of Brighton was do-able.

Fundamentally, I am blessed with many people doing their best to help and support me. Left to my own devices, I would more than likely have self-destructed, but thankfully even in the midst of such circumstances, when one dead-end was followed by another, there was always a complete stranger telling me where to get my next slice of metaphoric bread. These people and institutions still amaze me as they seem to devote their lives to help others. These institutions fully get behind men and women who try to better themselves, and climb out of deep ditches of poverty and destitution. Of course, it goes without saying that the medical centre holds the prize spot in my heart. From that initial chat with Jean, to the doctors, and finally to Mike, I owe these men and women a debt of gratitude I can never repay. I am not smug enough (I have thankfully had that knocked out of me) to believe I had anything to do with any of these events and my small recovery I have described in these few pages...my part was simply to show up. It was the kind, generous men and women who pointed me in the right direction, to get me on the other side of what seemed like a never-ending personal crisis. And because of that, I am convinced of my state of grace, or more commonly known as *unmerited favour*. I have in the past always found it difficult to find the right few words for the last sentence, and have cheated a little, using my trump card more than several times because it is as true now, as it was then...that I am truly blessed to *remain to pray*.

4

CONCLUSION
CONTEXTUALISING THE PROBLEM IN THE CULTURE AND SYSTEM OF CARE

12

THE PROBLEM AND POTENTIAL OF COMPLEXITY

DR PETER COCKERSELL

Where does the problem of complexity lie?

That homeless people and rough sleepers have a complex range of health conditions and social problems, usually called 'complex needs' in homelessness circles, or multiple deprivation in the research and policy fields, or multi- or poly-morbidity in clinical conversations, has been well documented. Many homeless people and rough sleepers experience having no housing, poor education, diagnosed and/or undiagnosed mental health problems, substance dependencies and physical health problems: many have several mental health and several physical health conditions (Brighter Futures, 2011; Homeless Link, 2014; Bramley *et al.*, 2015; this book, Chapter 1).

The problem that then arises, when people have so-called complex needs, is that they are seen as too complex by most of the social and healthcare agencies that are purportedly there to help them. Unfortunately, data is not kept by statutory healthcare or social services on who and how many are refused a service, so there is no exact information on the level of exclusion that homeless people with complex needs encounter. St Mungo's produced peer research on mental health and homelessness that found that while 70 per cent of rough sleepers had sought help for their mental health, only 11 per cent had received any treatment (St Mungo's, 2009). Research by Brighter Futures (2011) in Sheffield found that rough sleepers reported being turned away from hospitals, and Pathway (2017) has documented ongoing problems for homeless people in registering with GPs. Some of this is, no doubt, the result of prejudicial negative attitudes towards homeless people, but far more usually people with complex needs are excluded on the grounds that they do not meet the criteria that the service is built around, or because the services cannot deal with complexity.

In a process that is ongoing, healthcare provision, and to a lesser extent social care and support, has increasingly been organised along single diagnosis and treatment 'pathways': social care and support services are also often (though less so than healthcare) organised to deal with one problem, one issue. This is done in the name of service efficiency, and the distribution of expertise: these are currently highly valued management concepts, and are seen as the best way to organise the provision of services: all the cancer patients should go to the cancer specialist unit, and all the heart patients should go to the heart unit, and all the people with psychosis should go to the psychosis pathway, and those with personality disorder (if they're offered treatment at all, because it remains a diagnosis of exclusion) are supposed to follow the personality disorder pathway. And in social care and support, the elderly with dementia go down one route, and those who are younger go down another, and those who do not meet the criteria of being in 'critical' need are usually offered only support, if anything.

This funnelling of people into pre-set pathways enables managers to limit the number of staff they need to employ with specialist skills, limit the number of places offering particular treatments, and enables them to reduce demand (by making services less accessible) and increase throughput, so reducing cost per person. So-called frontline services increasingly become assessment and referral centres, channelling the patients or people with social care and support needs down the most relevant pathway, or excluding them from the service altogether because they do not meet the criteria. These assessment and referral staff are often not the best trained or highly skilled: indeed, they are often entry-level staff with limited training focused on the delivery of the specific manualised, tick-box assessment process that that service uses.

When people with complex needs come to these efficient services, they usually do not fit the assessment criteria; even if they do fit the criteria, the treatment, care and support options they are offered are all on different pathways, and it is often quite difficult to follow even one pathway at a time because of complex referral and appointment systems and time-consuming and costly travel, let alone to follow several pathways at once. Often they are passed from one service to another, so that it is still the case in most areas that people with mental health problems and substance dependencies are told they must follow the substance dependency treatment pathway before their mental health will be treated. Many substance dependency treatment centres won't work with people with mental health problems, and many people with mental health problems take the drugs and alcohol as a way of coping with their mental distress, so no way are they going to give them up before they get the mental health treatment. Even when the homeless person with complex needs does succeed in getting through the first stage assessment and referral process, and does accept the particular pathway or set of pathways that they have been told to follow, then all too easily they fall foul of rigid appointment systems, complex travel arrangements, hostile receptions from staff or fellow patients, and easy exclusion for non-compliance or failing to get to an appointment on time. It is extremely difficult for people with complex needs to use these efficient, highly focused, single diagnosis (whether a healthcare or social need 'diagnosis') services effectively, and they do not. The people with the complex needs are then blamed for their inability to use these efficient, highly focused, single diagnosis services, and this inability is put down to their lack of engagement, their 'chaotic' nature, their challenging behaviours and their non-compliance.

I am suggesting that actually the problem of complexity is not because of the complexity of the person with so-called complex needs: it is the problem with the way that services are organised. It is the services and their management that have created a system of complexity that works against people with multiple presenting problems and conditions. Complex services are a problem for people with complex, or rather multiple, needs.

Obviously, this matters for homeless people and rough sleepers who so often have multiple health conditions that would benefit from treatment, and multiple psychological and emotional problems and social situations that would benefit from therapeutic interventions too. Homeless people and rough sleepers make up a very small percentage of the population and in many cases are not taken into account at all when planning large-scale healthcare provision, mental healthcare provision, or even the provision of social care and support. In areas where there are relatively large homeless populations, they are taken into account, but at a specific local level, with specialised services directed to them as a specific population – I will talk more about these later. According to the *Hard Edges* report there are 165,000 people in England who meet two or more of their criteria for severe, multiple deprivation (Bramley *et al.*, 2015); and there were just over 4000 rough sleepers in England on one night in the 2016 rough sleeper count, up 134 per cent since 2010 (Homeless Link, 2017a); the numbers of single homeless in England are not known exactly, but are estimated at between 30 and 40,000 (Homeless Link, 2017b) (note that this population overlaps with the *Hard Edges* population). It could be argued then that the creation of complex healthcare provision through splitting it into multiple ever more narrowly defined, specialist single-diagnosis services only disfavours this relatively small population of the multiply deprived, and single homeless people and rough sleepers with complex needs, and so 'doesn't matter' in the grand scheme of things if it achieves greater effectiveness for the rest of the population.

However, that is questionable. I am not going to argue that the centres of excellence do not deliver the very best care in their fields of expertise: that is the argument put forward by those who wish to create more single-diagnosis, highly specialised pathways and services, and it is a good argument. It is certainly a good argument from a management perspective and on paper, and is good for people who have just that one condition that the unit specialises in (assuming they can get there). However, what it doesn't take into consideration is the prevalence or otherwise of single-diagnosis health conditions. If having multiple health conditions, and some social needs, is actually a more common occurrence than single diagnoses, then the single-diagnosis, specialised pathway and service model begins to look like an ineffective response, one that introduces unnecessary complexity and reduces overall healthcare benefit, and may even be damaging, as it is to rough sleepers with complex needs.

I have long been familiar with the presence of complex healthcare and social needs in the homeless population, but it was only when I became specifically involved in discussions and provision of healthcare services that I came across the fact that among those that specialised in care for elderly people the words 'complex needs' were just as commonly used. The London Borough of Enfield, for example, estimates that 20 per cent of its over 65s now have complex needs, and that this will rise to 30 per cent by 2025: 'Older people with complex needs are: "people aged 65+ who need a lot of support in daily living due to physical frailty, chronic conditions or multiple impairments. Many are affected by factors such as poverty, disadvantage, ethnicity, lifestyle etc.'" (London Borough of Enfield, 2017). This is not a very different profile to homeless people with complex needs. This is not just a problem in Enfield, of course. In Scotland, research found that:

> Most people aged over 65 had multi-morbidities, but the onset of multi-morbidity occurred 10–15 years earlier among those living in deprived areas; people in these areas were also more likely to experience mental health problems alongside physical illness or disability. (Barnett *et al.*, 2012)

There is no reason to believe that figures for England would be significantly different, but there do not seem to be exact figures available; however, 50 per cent of over-50s and 80 per cent of over-65s have at least one long-term condition, and it seems reasonable to assume that a significant proportion of these are likely to have co-occurring conditions and social or mental health problems, especially when linked with social deprivation and poverty (King's Fund, 2013).

The numbers of children and young people with complex needs in the UK are also not available (Joseph Rowntree, 2003). However, the Council for Disabled Children estimates, by extrapolating data from children in special schooling at state schools, that the numbers of children with special needs has more than doubled since 2004 (Council for Disabled Children, 2017). Despite all these unknowns, and the fact that data is not kept on either people with complex needs who are treated or people with complex needs who are excluded, the Department of Health itself estimated in 2012 that the number of people with multiple conditions is likely to rise to 2.9 million by 2018, i.e. by the time this book is published (DH, 2012).

Dame Christine Lenehan, Director of the Council for Disabled Children, remarked about the lack of information on children with complex needs:

> You'd think that because these disabled children are known to health services, social services and education teams, we'd have a good idea of the numbers involved. That simply isn't the case. The national data on disabled children is not fit for purpose: it has gaps, anomalies and inconsistencies, and raises the question how can we plan to meet the needs of these children and their families, when we don't know what those needs are? (Council for Disabled Children, 2017)

The same could be said of all people with complex needs: how can we plan to meet these needs when we don't know the number of people experiencing complex or multiple need, and we don't have a clear picture of what all those needs are? This goes back to the problem of what the NHS and social care and support services measure: if they only measure what they do, then they can't assess unmet need or indeed their own effectiveness in anything except the task they set themselves. They cannot know from the data they currently collect whether or not they are meeting the needs of their patients and clients, only whether or not they are meeting their own criteria and targets. It is like asking KwikFit what the most common problems are for people's cars: they will say exhausts and tyres, because that's what they do, that's what people get from them and that's what they keep data on, but if you asked motorists, or garages with a full mechanics' service, you would get a much more complex picture.

Talking of KwikFit, the diagnosis-led, narrow criteria provision model currently being followed in healthcare and much social care and support is rather like a set of multiple KwikFit businesses, each specialising in a particular part or aspect of the whole car. This might work with a car, where it is often only one thing that goes wrong, but it seems a very strange and complex way to organise a system that works with human beings, for whom good health and social integration and psychological wellbeing and relative wealth/poverty – whole person in a context – are so closely interwoven. Social isolation, for example, has a bigger effect size on morbidity and mortality than do obesity, smoking or alcohol (Holt-Lundstadt *et al.*, 2010): this makes treating individual parts of a person's body in isolation from the rest of their body and from their social context in a sort of 'KwikFit model' of health and social care seem very strange, and likely to be ineffective and inefficient.

Despite the gaps in knowledge, and the lack of data on the true numbers, we can guess that the multiple conditions of all these groups of people contain the combination of physical health problems, mental health problems and social care/support problems, often accompanied by deprivation and poverty, that we are familiar with in homelessness, because this is the picture painted by all the agencies involved (see Chapter 1 in this book on homeless people; Joseph Rowntree Foundation, 2003, on children with complex needs; King's Fund, 2013, on older people). If a significant number of people – and

2.9 million is, I think, a significant number of people – have so-called complex needs ('multiple conditions' seems a better phrase), and the complex healthcare and social care and support service structures don't effectively meet the needs of those with multiple conditions, then it is the complexity of the healthcare and social care service delivery systems that is the problem, not the supposed complexity of the multiple conditions people, it seems quite commonly, experience.

At the very least, therefore, it seems pertinent to ask the question, how can we say that the provision of healthcare and social support through an increasingly single-diagnosis-focused, narrow criteria pathway and service model is the most efficient or most effective way of delivering it if we don't know how many people have multiple or complex needs?

There is suggestive evidence that models other than the single-diagnosis, narrow criteria, 'KwikFit model' work better. The splitting apart of services into multiple pathways creates an inefficient and ineffective sort of complexity that disables holistic care, which makes for poorer care for people with multiple conditions; but complexity is not the problem per se. The problem is that the *system* of health and social care and support is complex, but the *services* are not.

The potential in complexity

Complexity is often seen as problematic in itself, but it is not – we live in a complex universe, a complex world, and we are complex organisms with complex minds. Humans are complex adaptive systems, and human society and culture is a complex adaptive system comprising multiple complex adaptive systems, and the human mind is a complex adaptive system (as we have seen throughout this book) that works in interaction with other human minds equally complex. Our success as a species and our ability to adapt to every environment on earth and to exploit it (too successfully, some might say, like locusts in a wheat field) arise from the enormous capacity for creativity arising from our complex minds in association with other complex minds. If it wasn't for the creative potential of complexity, we wouldn't have healthcare and social care and support systems, and we wouldn't have psychotherapy or psychologically informed interventions with people with complex needs.

First of all, let us think a bit about complexity, using complexity theory.

> The notion of complexity has its origins in the field of natural sciences. Complexity theory absorbed elements of general systems theory, cybernetics, chaos theory and information theory. In all these fields, [there was] an evolution from reductionist Newtonian models of a well-ordered universe to paradigms that focus on non-linear dynamics. (Marchal *et al.*, 2014)

Complexity theory is designed to think about situations that are multifactorial, and where there is multiple agency or dynamism within all, most or some of the multiple factors involved (which is why linear dynamic models don't apply). Man-made global warming is an example of the sort of situation that requires complexity theory to think about – and so, I will argue, is developing effective services for homeless people and rough sleepers with complex needs.

Unsurprisingly, complexity theory is useful for thinking about problems of complexity, but first let us differentiate between simple, complicated and complex problems. Marchal *et al.*, following Glouberman and Zimmerman (2002), make it very straightforward to distinguish simple, complicated and complex:

- Simple problems have simple causes. Causality is linear and simple problems have standard solutions. These can be applied without specific expertise; technical skills are sufficient.

- Complicated problems consist of sets of simple problems, but cannot be reduced to them. They are compounded by scale and coordination problems. Solving complicated problems requires expertise and collaboration between experts. Formulae and instructions to solve complicated problems can be developed and are critical to success. If experts apply the formulae correctly, outcomes can be predicted.

- Complex problems include sets of simple and complicated problems to which they are not reducible. The interactions between determinants of the sub-problems can lead to non-linear causal relations between potential causes and outcomes. Also context-sensitivity can make a problem complex. As a consequence, outcomes are unpredictable. To solve complex problems, formulae and standardised solutions that proved

> effective in the past provide little guidance. Instead, complex problems are solved through safe-fail experiments that allow learning by doing or by making sense of events post facto.
>
> (Marchal *et al.*, 2014, p.8)

One of the major problems in the complex healthcare and social care and support system we have is that managers at the highest level have tried to apply, and continue to try to apply, solutions befitting simple or complicated problems to complex ones. In many cases linear, technical solutions are academically tested by reducing the question to a simple problem (stripping away variability and inconsistency is part of most health research methodology); this 'solution' is then considered to be evidenced, and then 'rolled out' into the complex reality of real health systems, and then (to the surprise and consternation of the senior management) it fails to deliver, or indeed makes the service worse. As Paul Plsek, an expert in complex healthcare systems puts it, 'Unfortunately, many of the instinctive actions of leaders in the health care system who are trying to meet the challenges of innovation are not well informed by what we know about complexity' (Plsek, 2003). The single-diagnosis, narrow-criteria services talked about in the preceding section are examples of treating health and social care problems as if they are simple problems.

A step beyond treating the problem of providing effective services for people with complex health and social care needs as if it were a simple problem, is to treat it as a complicated problem. This is what very often happens with integrated care and multidisciplinary teams, both of which have been strongly promoted in recent years as a response to the rising levels of (or the rising perception and acknowledgement of) complex needs in patients. There is nothing wrong with either integrated care or multidisciplinary teams. Far from it, as I shall argue below, but unfortunately in practice they are very often more like parallel systems running side by side, each trying to provide their own simple solution to one part of the complexity, rather than being truly integrated. They are structured as responses to a complicated problem, i.e. a problem that consists of multiple simple problems, rather than as a response to a complex problem. In this case it is not necessarily the fault of non-complex thinking by senior management: it is perhaps caused by the fact that the managers of the individual elements of these multidisciplinary services are still thinking in linear dynamics, within the thought constraints of the dominant model within their own discipline, and usually with the pressures of their own budget, limited resources and specific target outputs. It is these systemic restraints that in many cases militate against the multidisciplinary team becoming truly integrated, and doing what it needs to do itself to solve the complex problem – become a complex adaptive system.

Formulaic, manualised approaches beset with target throughputs and simple linear, short-term target outputs make solving complex problems impossible; when applied to each element within an 'integrated care' system or a multidisciplinary approach, they also make solving complex problems impossible. These sorts of approaches, designed for resolving simple or complicated problems but not complex ones, cannot efficiently provide effective services for people with complex needs.

However, the best specialist homeless services do provide effective health and social care and support for people with complex needs, and they do have multidisciplinary teams and they do provide integrated care. They provide complex services, with highly differentiated but highly integrated roles within their teams. Some of the specialist homeless primary care services are so good that, as well as being awarded the highest level possible by the Care Quality Commission (CQC), the UK Government inspectorate of quality in health and social care, they have been held up as examples of best practice to primary care services delivering healthcare to the general public. I see this as an interesting piece of suggestive evidence that if health and social care services were designed to meet complex needs, rather than being based on the single-diagnosis narrow-criteria model, they would actually provide better care all round. Similarly, non-healthcare services that operate as Psychologically Informed Environments (PIEs), integrating an element of clinical practice into teams of homelessness staff, also deliver effective multidisciplinary services to people with complex needs (see Chapters 5, 8 and 9 in this book; Cockersell, 2016). I would suggest that this is because both PIEs and specialist homeless healthcare services behave like a particular kind of complex adaptive system.

What is a complex adaptive system? A system can be defined as 'a unit made up by and organised through relations between elements (or agents), structures and actions (or processes)' (Marchal *et al.*, 2014), and a complex system is, fairly obviously, a system made up of multiple such systems. Note the use of words like 'agents', 'relations' and 'processes': we are talking dynamic here, because systems are dynamic – the parts are in relationship to each other and changes in one affect the others. Central heating is a simple dynamic system: a thermostat receives temperature information from the environment and then turns on or off the boiler which, via the water circulating through the radiators, in turn regulates the temperature in the environment. This is a simple feedback loop. All dynamic systems have them. A complicated system, for example a central heating system that allows different temperatures in different rooms and can also be controlled remotely from your smartphone, has a series of feedback loops, but a series of simple feedback loops operating in sequence (rather like a complicated problem). However, complex systems have multiple feedback loops which may well operate at the same time and interact with each other. This is what makes them complex rather than just complicated: they display 'emergent behaviour and unpredictability' (Marchal et al., 2014). In other words, they have complex adaptations to their environments through multiple feedback loops that are also influenced by their internal adaptations and feedback loops, their histories of adaptation (no two are the same), and which are not linear and not predictable. Complex systems have their own agency. All organisms are open complex adaptive systems (Zagier Roberts, 1994); the human mind is a complex adaptive system (Siegel, 2015); and healthcare systems are complex adaptive systems (Plsek and Greenhalgh, 2001).

I have said that much interdisciplinary working and allegedly integrated care is actually a complicated problem response, rather than a complex adaptive system response, and I have castigated the senior management of health and social care services for trying to apply simple problem solutions to delivering effective responses to people with complex needs. Yet now I am agreeing with Plsek and Greenhalgh that healthcare systems are complex adaptive systems… and at the same time I am saying that specialist homelessness care services and PIE services are effective because they are a particular kind of complex adaptive system. So, what am I saying? Just because a system is complex and adaptive doesn't mean that it is *well* adapted. If it were otherwise, we wouldn't have any people with complex physical health needs or with the psychological and emotional difficulties and mental health problems that we see. Humans wouldn't, as a species, risk changing their planet dangerously and irreversibly through global warming if complex adaptive systems were always well adapted.

What, then, makes the difference between a well-adapted system and a poorly adapted one? Essentially, it can be seen in its effectiveness: the best-adapted system is the one that is most effective at what it does, whatever that is. That was what Darwin was talking about when he spoke of the 'survival of the fittest' — he meant those most fitted (adapted, with the best fit) to the environment in which they operated. This goes back to the acknowledgement of and negotiation with external reality that we considered in Chapter 4: the best adapted complex system uses its differentiated internal processes to come up with the best adaptation it can to meet whatever the changing circumstance is in its reality-tested environment. It changes to enable it to meet its own needs within the environment in which it finds itself, as far as it can without losing its own integrity.

The attitudes in this approach are not dissimilar to what the King's Fund, in the context of older people's complex needs, called for in mainstream healthcare and social care and support, using what they called their 'house of care' model:

> Implementing the model requires health care professionals to abandon traditional ways of thinking and behaving, where they see themselves as the primary decision-makers, and instead shifting to a partnership model in which patients play an active part in determining their own care and support needs. In personalised care planning, clinicians and patients work together using a collaborative process of shared decision-making to agree goals, identify support needs, develop and implement action plans, and monitor progress. This is a continuous process, not a one-off event. An important feature of the approach is the link between care planning for individuals and commissioning for local populations; it aims to make best use of local authority services (including social care and public health) and community resources, alongside more traditional health services. The house of care metaphor is used to illustrate the whole-system approach, emphasising the interdependency of each part and the various components that need to be in place to hold it together. (King's Fund, 2013)

This is different to the way that much of the health and social care and support system works: it tries to be an open adaptive system, but it operates within a rigid framework of a pre-determined 'evidence-based' reality, not a practice-tested (i.e. feedback loop tested) local environmental reality, and often within a rigid separation of the units of the system so that their interactive dynamism is constrained by their own internal feedback loops based on realities and environmental pressures other than their own skills and the needs of the people who present to their services. In this situation, they are constrained by their histories – as so many of our clients are constrained by their histories of compound trauma – to activate maladaptive, self-conflictual, and ultimately ineffective and inefficient strategies. These internal tensions and contradictions lead them to be ineffective: they end up not serving well any people with complex needs, let alone homeless people and rough sleepers.

When we look at services that are effective for people with complex needs, like those described in this book or like many of the specialised homeless health services, we see that the most effective services operate in a thoughtful and reflective way, with a lot of dialogue between those who collectively deliver the service about what they are doing and how they are doing it, and they use these collective processes to tailor the service to meet the needs of the person who they are trying to support into, or further into, recovery. Many of these services have regular, frequent, formal, reflective practice sessions, often externally facilitated by psychologists or psychotherapists; some are run overtly on PIE principles. The emergent process is organised through internal reflection, relation to the internal reality of the person they are trying to help, and the environmental context s/he, and they themsleves, find themselves in. The services' own internal processes, from which their response emerges, are organised around thinking about the best they can do for the person they are trying to help, utilising the most appropriate of their differentiated skills and resources. The PIE guidance (Keats *et al.*, 2012) is essentially a system for organising such a reflective, collective, tailored response in services, just as psychotherapy is a system for enabling individuals to become more 'open adaptive systems' in this reflective and reality-testing way.

From this perspective, PIE offers a way for services for people with multiple conditions to structure themselves so that they are able to coherently manage dynamic responses to complex problems: PIE provides a framework for designing 'frontline' services that can react as a benign, reflective, complex adaptive system and therefore deal creatively and effectively with complex problems and the complex people experiencing them.

PIE, however, is an operational framework (see Chapters 5, 8 and 9 of this book): it is designed as a framework for services to deliver care and support of whatever kind directly to people with histories of compound trauma. It is, as such, less well fitted to being a framework for those who commission such services, or for the senior managers who lead the organisations that deliver such services. Commissioners and senior managers are dealing, on the whole, with a different environmental reality and a different set of problems to those that are encountered by direct services. Commissioners and senior managers also tend to be more committed than frontline staff to seeing the problems as 'complicated' rather than 'complex': management studies are awash with talk of prioritisation, reducing variation, streamlining processes and enabling higher throughputs as a mark of efficiency. These concepts are all fairly inappropriate responses to the problem of multi-morbidity and multiple deprivation that people experiencing homelessness and rough sleeping, and the services that try to serve them, face. They are the solutions to 'complicated' situations where there can be a string of linear solutions to simple, specific, and often recurrent, problems. They cannot be a response to uniqueness, or to high variability, or to situations where the agency of the recipient of care has to be taken into account as an integral and crucial part of the design of the care provision. As someone once remarked to me, linear management solutions are fine for car production, but delivering healthcare to real patients is like trying to do car production with the driver of the car and their family in it, all of them having different opinions which need to be taken into account as the car moves along the assembly line.

So if PIE, designed as it is as a framework for direct service delivery, has limitations as guidance for commissioners and senior managers in designing benign, reflective complex adaptive systems that can respond appropriately to complex problems, is there another framework that could help? I think there is, in the Enabling Environments (EE) approach which influenced the origin and direction of the PIE guidance in the first place (Johnson and Haigh, 2011). The EE initiative has two different aspects: it is a quality assurance system validated by the Royal College of Psychiatrists, and it is a conceptual framework designed to support and organise high-level reflection on the qualities that go to make up a humane and humanly responsive system – in other words, a benign, reflective adaptive system – and to use those qualities as a benchmark for service design and implementation.

The key components of EE are:

- the nature and the quality of relationships between participants or members are recognised and highly valued
- the participants share some measure of responsibility for the environment as a whole, and especially for their own part in it
- all participants – staff, volunteers and service users alike – are equally valued and supported in their particular contribution
- engagement and purposeful activity is encouraged
- there are opportunities for creativity and initiative, whether spontaneous or shared and planned
- decision-making is transparent, and both formal and informal leadership roles are acknowledged
- power or authority is clearly accountable and open to discussion
- any formal rules or informal expectations of behaviour are clear; or if unclear, there is good reason for it
- behaviour, even when potentially disruptive, is seen as meaningful, as a communication to be understood.

(Johnson and Haigh, 2011, pp.19–20)

The principles of EE could be used by commissioners and senior managers to inform the design of proposed *systems* of healthcare or social care and support so that they are more likely to deliver effective solutions to complex problems; they could then use the complementary PIE principles to design the actual *service delivery* to people with multi-morbidity, multiple deprivation, and histories of compound trauma and social exclusion.

EE is not a rigid prescription, more an ethical framework, and so has the plasticity to be adapted to multiple environments and respond to multiple needs. Assuming the commissioners and senior managers themselves are in an open, dialogical and benign relationship – following the EE principles and forming a benign, reflective complex adaptive system – then EE can form a high-level holding framework within which PIE, as an operational framework, can really flourish.

Conclusion

The problem of providing effective services for people with complex needs can be seen as a problem of complexity, but not of the complexity of the clients; rather it is a problem of the complexity of service delivery systems.

Many of the current service delivery systems do not meet the needs of people with complex needs; the services do not even measure the number of people who access them who have complex needs, and generally undervalue the level of people who have complex needs, or better, who have multiple conditions.

We can see that many of the services supposed to be able to cater for people's health and social conditions are structured to respond to simple problems, or sometimes complicated ones (which are essentially strings of simple ones), but that actually such responses are inadequate for complex – i.e. multiple and interactive, and so unpredictable – problems of the sort that many people have in the real world.

Multidisciplinary teams and integrated care are a useful and positive response, but not an answer in themselves because all too often they are organised in a way that means they are actually offering responses within their own discipline in a series of parallel simple problem-type solutions: this is related to their own internal systems and histories as separate disciplines with separate budgets, resources, targets, cultures, etc. They are also constrained by a series of pre-determined adaptations that each discipline has accepted as evidence based from external systems rather than tested against their own specific realities, and which are not therefore amenable to reflective adaptation and environmental feedback.

For multidisciplinary teams and integrated care to work then, there has to be an internal reflective process which enables dialogue and task-focused feedback loops internally that are related to the real environmental reality of what the service and its practitioners can offer and the relationship they have with the person with complex needs who is in contact with them. By collectively reflecting on what is the most appropriate and therapeutic response, without the constraints of rigid pre-determined adaptations, the adaptive capacity of the service can be directed to delivering the most efficient and effective healthcare and social care and support to that person within the reality context within which they find themselves.

Further, I have suggested that there already exist frameworks for both the commissioner/senior manager level and the direct service delivery level that can be implemented to support the development of effective services for people with complex needs: these are EE and PIE respectively. Delivered together in a series of 'communities of practice' (Cornes *et al.*, 2014) at different hierarchical levels these would be powerful influences for positive change that would enable healthcare and social support and care to provide the holistic, flexible, benign, adaptive care system that people with complex needs require to enable them to make their recovery journeys.

It seems likely, given the increase in either the prevalence or the awareness of complex needs, multiple deprivation and multi-morbidity (see Chapters 13 and 14 in this book) that developing these frameworks in practice and enabling a system that really is effective in providing services for people with multiple needs will benefit not just homeless people and rough sleepers, but a significant proportion of the wider population as well.

What is needed is an area with the courage to pilot this embryonic system…

References

Barnett, K., Mercer, S.W., Norbury, M., Watt, G., Wyke, S. and Guthrie, B. (2012) 'Epidemiology of multimorbidity and implications for health care, research, and medical education: a cross-sectional study.' *The Lancet 380*: 9836, 37–43.

Bramley, G., Fitzpatrick, S., Edwards, J., Ford, D. *et al.* (2015) *Hard Edges: Mapping Severe and Multiple Disadvantage.* London: Lankelly Chase.

Brighter Futures (2011) *Brighter Futures Academy, Research paper No. 6/11, Rough Treatment for Rough Sleepers.* Sheffield: Brighter Futures.

Cockersell, P. (2016) 'PIEs five years on.' *Mental Health and Social Inclusion 20*, 4, 221–230.

Cornes, M., Manthorpe, J., Hennessy, C., Anderson, S., Clark, M. and Scanlon, C. (2014) 'Not just a talking shop: practitioner perspectives on how communities of practice work to improve outcomes for people experiencing multiple exclusion homelessness.' *Journal of Interprofessional Care 28*, 6, 541–546.

Council for Disabled Children (2017) *Numbers of Children With Complex Needs Up By 50% Since 2004.* Accessed July 2017 at https://councilfordisabledchildren.org.uk/news-opinion/news/numbers-children-complex-needs-50-2004

DH (2012) *Long Term Conditions Compendium of Information*, 3rd edition. London: Department of Health.

Glouberman, S. and Zimmerman, B. (2002) *Complicated and Complex Systems: What Would Successful Reform of Medicare Look Like?* Accessed December 2017 at https://qspace.library.queensu.ca/bitstream/handle/1974/6884/discussion_paper_8_e.pdf?sequence=33

Holt-Lunstad, J., Smith, T.B. and Layton, J.B. (2010) 'Social relationships and mortality risk: a meta-analytic review.' *PLoS Med 7*, 7, e1000316. doi:10.1371/journal.pmed.1000316

Homeless Link (2014) *The Unhealthy State of Homelessness: Health Audit 2014.* London: Homeless Link.

Homeless Link (2017a) *Rough Sleeping – Our Analysis.* Accessed July 2017 at www.homeless.org.uk/facts/homelessness-in-numbers/rough-sleeping/rough-sleeping-our-analysis

Homeless Link (2017b) *Support for Single Homeless People in England: Annual Review 2016.* Accessed July 2017 at www.homeless.org.uk/facts/our-research/annual-review-of-single-homelessness-support-in-england

Johnson, R. and Haigh, R. (2011) 'Social psychiatry and social policy for the 21st century: new concepts for new needs – the 'Enabling Environments' initiative.' *Mental Health and Social Inclusion 15*, 1, 17–23.

Joseph Rowntree Foundation (2003) *Children with Complex Support Needs in Healthcare Settings for Long Periods of Time.* Accessed July 2017 at www.jrf.org.uk/report/children-complex-support-needs-healthcare-settings-long-periods

Keats, H., Cockersell, P., Maguire, N.J., and Johnson, R. (2012) *Psychologically Informed Services for Homeless People: Good Practice Guide.* London: Department of Communities and Local Government. Accessed October 2017 at https://eprints.soton.ac.uk/340022

King's Fund (2013) *Delivering Better Services for People with Long-Term Conditions.* Accessed July 2017 at www.kingsfund.org.uk/sites/files/kf/field/field_publication_file/delivering-better-services-for-people-with-long-term-conditions.pdf

London Borough of Enfield (2017) *Older People with Complex Needs.* Accessed July 2017 at www.enfield.gov.uk/healthandwellbeing/info/18/the_health_and_wellbeing_of_older_people/57/older_people_with_complex_needs

Marchal, B., Van Belle, S., De Brouwere, V., Witter, S. and Kegels, G. (2014) *Complexity in Health: Consequences for Research and Evaluation.* Accessed July 2017 at www.abdn.ac.uk/femhealth/documents/Deliverables/Complexity_Working_paper.pdf

Pathway (2017) *Helping People Who Are Homeless into GP Practices.* Accessed July 2017 at https://frontlinenetwork.org.uk/media/1123/pathway-blog.pdf

Plsek, P (2003) *Complexity and the Adoption of Innovation in Health Care.* Accessed July 2017 at www.nihcm.org/pdf/Plsek.pdf

Plsek, P. and Greenhalgh, T. (2001) 'The challenge of complexity in healthcare.' *British Medical Journal 323*, 625–628.

Siegel, D. (2015) *The Developing Mind,* 2nd edition. London: Norton.

St Mungo's (2009) *Homeless People's Views about Breaking the Link between Homelessness and Mental Ill Health.* Accessed October 2017 at: www.mungos.org/happiness_matters

Zagier Roberts, V. (1994) 'The organization of work: contributions from open systems theory.' In A. Obholzer and V. Zagier Roberts (eds) *The Unconscious at Work.* London: Routledge.

13

THE TREATMENT OF MULTI-MORBIDITY

DR PETER COCKERSELL

We looked in the preceding chapter at complexity, and suggested that the *problematic* complexity lies in two places other than the client/patient. The problematic complexity lies in the disjointed systems of healthcare, with their single-diagnosis-led pathways, and the disjointed systems of social care and support, with their criteria for inclusion being in reality justifications for exclusion. We also looked at the design of these systems as being based in a misunderstanding of multiple conditions and seeing treating them as being amenable to 'simple' or 'complicated' solutions – i.e. linear solutions individually or serially applied – rather than requiring a 'complex' solution, which is one that is dynamic, multifaceted and responsive. We suggested further that to be dynamic, multifaceted and responsive required a reflective and self-aware 'complex adaptive system approach' applied to the multidisciplinary team and integrated care framework. Finally, I suggested that Psychologically Informed Environments (PIE) and Enabling Environments (EE) might provide the frameworks, at service delivery and commissioning/senior management levels respectively, to implement such an approach (this book, Chapter 13).

This is not to deny that there is also complexity within the client/patient: human beings are complex adaptive systems themselves, and the range of negative mental and physical health conditions experienced by many homeless people and rough sleepers, exacerbated each and every one of them by the processes of social exclusion, form a complex system themselves. That is, each health condition interacts with each other health condition, as well as each interacting with the environment, and all of this interacts with the client/patient's sense of themselves and sense of themselves in relation to the other: all this leads to a significant level of presenting complexity for the clinician faced with treating them.

The clinician, who is also human and who only has expertise in certain areas of human experience, psychology and/or physiology, tends to try to tackle these presenting problems as if they were 'complicated', not 'complex' – that is, as a series of individual problems that are amenable to (relatively) 'simple' solutions either offered by that clinician, or by a colleague, or by a team of different clinicians/professionals. The clinician, or group of clinicians, starts off by drawing up a list of conditions they see the person as having, a list of different sets of criteria they see the person as meeting, or, in more clinical terms, a set of diagnoses. Having lots of these diagnoses is what multi-morbidity, complex needs, multiple conditions, etc. mean in healthcare terms.

The following data illustrating multi-morbidity in a rough sleeper population are taken from the evaluation of an Intermediate Care service set up in a rough sleepers' hostel in Lambeth, London, and look at the morbidity of 35 individuals who were cared for in a period of one year (see Table 14.1).

Table 14.1 Cohort morbidity[1]

Condition	%
Infections	
HIV	23.5%
Hep A current	-
Hep A past	37.5%
Hep B active	-
Hep B past	34.4%
Hep C active	53.3%
Hep C past	29.7%
Hep C total	84.4%
Syphilis active	10.7%
Syphilis past	10.3%

1 Expressed as percentages of cohort; cohort = 35; the percentages in the table add up to more than 100% because all of the cohorts had multiple conditions.

Syphilis total	13.5%
TB past	15.2%
TB current	12.1%
MRSA past	13.5%
MRSA current	3%
MRSA total	20.6%
Head lice	32.4%
Addictions	
IVDU current	82.9%
IVDU past	-
Alcoholism	74.3%
Alcoholism past	-
Tobacco smoker	100%
Mental health	
Mental health problem (SEMI and depression/anxiety) current	87.5%
Mental health problem (SEMI and depression/anxiety) past	88.2%
Documented past suicide attempt(s)	71.4%
Chronic conditions	
Asthma/COPD	44.1%
Cardiac condition (including endocarditis)/hypertension)	25%
Fits (epilepsy, and/or other, ever had)	30.3%
Liver cirrhosis (ever had diagnosis)	45.5%
Memory problems (presumed neurological in cause)	25%
Anaemia (current)	58.8%
Skin	
Skin (all persons with a skin problem)	41.2%
Leg ulcer	11.8%
Abscess	33.3%
Other wound	23.5%
Other	
Nutritional problem (including malnutrition)	51.5%
Chronic pain issues	37.5%
Mobility issues	27.3%
Foot problems	21.2%

Condition	%
Other	
Eyesight problems	18.2%
Acute dental problems	66.7%

Source: Hendry and Dorney-Smith, 2009, pp.10–11

'The number of current and past condition problems logged for each client varied between 3 and 19. The average number of current and past condition problems logged for each client was 10.5 per client' (Hendry and Dorney-Smith, 2009, p.11).

Three diagnosed health problems constitute multi-morbidity: here we see a population where three is the minimum, just over ten the average and 19 the top score. There is a tendency for the clinician, within the culture of the medical approach, to take these patients as presenting a series of individual problems.

The medical approach, which is also applied in some mental health treatment systems and by some mental health clinicians, demands this serialised approach of taking complexity as 'complicated' rather than 'complex' (see Chapter 12) precisely *because* the fundamental premise of its approach and process is diagnosis and treatment. The 'art' of medical interventions is to diagnose a condition correctly, and then to apply the correct or most highly recommended treatment for that condition.

There are two logics to this process of diagnosis and treatment. One is ancient: if you don't identify the condition, then you are treating blindly and randomly, and that is likely to impact negatively on the effectiveness of your treatment. This approach has been applied for centuries, though the identification of the condition has changed over time: what was once attributed to 'bad humours' is more likely now to be attributed to 'bad hygiene' for example. Treating without identifying the condition you are treating, or after misidentifying the condition, also runs the risk of contravening the 'Hippocratic Law' of 'First, do no harm.' It is so fundamental to the medical approach because it lies behind the whole idea of the 'expert physician': the reason we seek out a physician (and pay them well) is because of their expertise in identifying the health problem we have and then proposing an effective treatment for that problem. It is fundamental to a physician's sense of professional self, and core to their clinical training (and to that of some mental health professionals). However, not to treat without identifying accurately the condition is a general rule, not an absolute one, and the desire to be seen as expert and able to treat is stronger than the adherence to the diagnosis–treatment model itself: medical clinicians have a catch-all diagnosis that actually means very little or nothing at all in explanatory or descriptive terms – 'medically unexplained symptoms' – and they are still willing to treat people with this 'diagnosis', which by definition means that they are treating people without understanding the condition that they are treating.

The second logic of the diagnosis–treatment process is that if you identify the condition accurately, then you have a far better chance of being able to also identify its cause and the course it will run as a disease, in other words its aetiology. This means the clinician can then do something more sophisticated than merely try to eradicate or diminish the impact of the symptoms of the disease: they can actually tackle the root cause of the illness and eradicate it. This is at the basis of much modern medicine and medical treatment, even if the treatment model is sometimes relatively unsophisticated (i.e. cut out the problematic part. Fortunately, this treatment model is no longer applied in mental health, though it was less than fifty years ago; see Le Doux, 1999).

This twin or dual-aspect logic is based on the two types of diagnostic criteria – the descriptive and the explanatory. Some diagnoses, and especially those used in mental health categorisations like the DSM's, are largely descriptive, and broadly speaking list a set of criteria (in the case of mental health often comprising a range of social behaviours) by which a diagnosis can be made; other diagnoses, like septicaemia or measles, are based on observed criteria, as in the first case, and also a particular understanding of the aetiology of the criteria, which provide an explanation of the condition and a guide to treatment – now we know that septicaemia is caused by a bacterial infection, for example, we can treat it with penicillin rather than cut off the infected part (as was standard treatment up until the middle of the last century).

When we have multi-morbidity, and we are presented with the range of conditions we saw in the example cited from the Lambeth intermediate care service above, then the tendency of clinicians is to think of them serially because they want to treat them, and because treating them means invoking the diagnosis–treatment model at the base of their expert skill sets. They then treat the multi-morbidity as a 'complicated' problem – one of sequencing a series of solutions to individual 'simple' problems, often beginning with a question along the lines of 'What do you treat first?'. The answer to this is usually seen in terms of medical urgency, for obvious reasons – the clinician wants to treat the most serious, i.e. life-threatening, conditions first. This does not always coincide with the perspective of the client/patient, however, who may have different medical priorities – treating the most painful first, for example, or treating the condition that limits mobility, or the ability to walk or stand, rather than the condition that may kill them next year, or even next month. There can be other problems to the clinician's treatment priorities being implemented: for example, the client/patient may see being in hospital as more of a problem than being ill – perhaps because they can't take drugs of their choice or drink alcohol, perhaps because they are scared of hospitals or have bad experiences of hospitals – especially once their immediate problem (whatever it was that got them to seek clinical help in the first place) is dealt with; or the treatment requires a series of appointments and attendances, whereas the client/patient has a mobile and immediate-needs-led life situation that makes following a complex pathway a challenge too far because it is difficult for them to keep the health treatment priority prioritised over time (especially once any life-impeding symptoms decline). The clinician, often acting under throughput imperatives from their management, who in turn are often acting under imperatives downloaded from industrial management, then discharges the patient because they are 'non-compliant', 'not engaging', 'self-destructive' or just too 'chaotic'.

In these situations, both clinician and patient are seeing multi-morbidity as a set of discrete problems, and are both acting on priorities based on their perceptions of what is important. Almost inevitably, if multi-morbidity is seen as a complicated set of simple problems, the answer to which is to follow several healthcare pathways, then the idea of prioritisation has to follow; everyone can recognise that it is difficult or impossible to follow multiple pathways simultaneously, even for someone who is not homeless or living on the streets. Many homeless people die of multiple treatable conditions (Marie Curie and St Mungo's, 2013), and in part this is because they and the clinical staff cannot agree on prioritisation – either in terms of what should be treated, or in terms of whether following treatment is more important than, for example, finding safe shelter, or food, or money for drugs, or doing what the voices tell you – and so the multiple treatable conditions go untreated.

Clinicians also, of course, see that at least some of the conditions in multi-morbidity are interactive and related. Typical of this is a focus on, for example, alcohol-related conditions such as liver and other organ damage and failure (multiple organ failure was the biggest cause of death in homeless people in a survey by St Mungo's; Marie Curie and St Mungo's, 2013) and continued drinking; or drug and alcohol use and mental health problems, so-called 'dual diagnosis', or drug- or alcohol-induced psychosis. However, very often this is again seen as a 'complicated' problem made up of a series of 'simple' problems: if the client/patient would just stop drinking, then we could treat the organ degeneration; if the client would just give up drugs, we could assess their mental health problems. NICE guidance enshrines this by suggesting that drug treatment should take precedence over treatment for mental health problems in dual diagnosis (NICE, 2011). In many cases, this simply leads to curtailment of the clinical process: the clinician proposes a course of treatment that the client/patient is unwilling to embark on. The clinician classifies the client as 'unmotivated' or 'unwilling to engage'; and the client classifies the clinician as 'unwilling to listen', 'not understanding', or 'unhelpful' at best, or as prejudiced or hostile at worst. This is not just true in cases where clinicians propose drug or alcohol treatment as the first step: it often applies to other conditions too where 'lifestyle' or behavioural changes are proposed as the first line of treatment, before other more directly clinical interventions will be agreed to.

Most homelessness specialist medical services treat on an opportunistic basis: while still acknowledging desirable priorities for treatment, and advising their patients of them, where possible they provide the treatments that the clients seek in the order they seek them, and also take the opportunity to provide a few treatments the clients will accept at the same time. These clinics also typically spend more time with their patients, and listen more to the whole story of their lives: they form relationships, and then move on to diagnoses. This is a more engaged and interactive process with multi-morbidity, and seems to recognise the reality that multi-morbidity is a complex problem, not just a complicated one: it requires an interactive response that incorporates a dialogue with the patient. Opportunistic treatments over a period of time, with continuity of care by the same team of multidisciplinary clinicians in the specialist homelessness services, enables more and more of the multi-morbid conditions to be treated or at least engaged with. The Pathway approach (Pathway, 2017) in hospitals could be said to apply this same opportunistic and dialogical principle to hospitalisations, seeking to take advantage of the homeless person's admission to hospital to persuade the hospital teams to treat as many conditions as possible while they are there (rather than just the one condition that got them admitted in the first place), and to persuade the homeless person to accept staying there for these treatments, and then to try to ensure they have an ongoing healthcare plan when they leave: they do this, partly at least, by providing continuity of support for homeless people from the moment they enter hospital to the time they leave, and by providing peer support to facilitate greater engagement between the homeless patient and the clinicians (Pathway, 2017).

This idea of engagement, of relationship, between the homeless person and the clinicians as being important in the treatment of multi-morbidity offers us a clue that brings us back to the question of diagnosis and treatment again. If we take a longer look at what is going on, I think we begin to see a different, or perhaps another, diagnosis which has an explanatory value both in terms of multi-morbidity itself, and in terms of why it requires a 'complex' solution, not a 'complicated' one. If we can identify the causes of multi-morbidity, we can begin to try to treat them, rather than just either eliminating or reducing the symptoms of multi-morbidity: looking at the aetiology of multi-morbidity offers a perspective that can inform more effective treatment systems.

I said above that the idea that the relationship between the client and clinician being especially important in the treatment of multi-morbidity offers us a clue to the aetiology of multi-morbidity. In talking about the processes of recovery, I suggested that 'trauma arises from bad experiences and damaging relationships, and that healing trauma arises from good experiences and healing relationships' (this book, Chapter 12). There is a resonance here. As well as multi-morbidity being highly prevalent among homeless people and rough sleepers, we know that compound trauma is too (this book, Chapter 1). Are they by any chance related?

We looked in Chapters 1–3 at the levels of mental health conditions in homeless people and rough sleepers and their correlation with the processes of social exclusion and compound trauma. There are many, many more studies that have found a positive correlation between adverse childhood events, compound trauma and multiple mental health problems in adulthood. There have been approximately:

- seven hundred studies linking affect dysregulation and impulse control disorders with adverse childhood events and compound trauma
- four hundred studies linking disturbances of attention and cognition with adverse childhood events and compound trauma
- fifty studies linking distortions in self-perception and meaning with adverse childhood events and compound trauma
- a hundrd studies linking somatisation with adverse childhood events and compound trauma
- and 1800 studies linking co- and poly-morbidity with adverse childhood events and compound trauma.

(Van der Kolk, 2010)

The evidence for the link between adverse childhood events, compound trauma and co-morbid mental health problems is overwhelming, I think, and the link between the high levels of mental health problems and the high levels of compound trauma among homeless people is further evidence for this association.

There is also a very strong link between so-called 'dual diagnosis' and adverse childhood events/compound trauma. In the Adverse Childhood Experiences Study of 17,000 adults in the USA, Felitti (2004) found a direct, proportional 'dose-response' between adverse childhood events/compound trauma and addictions. In other words, the higher the level of adverse events – the more compound the trauma is – the higher the likelihood of addiction. I use adverse childhood events/compound trauma as a joint noun because Felitti enumerated different types of adverse event – emotional, physical and sexual abuse, exposure to domestic violence, bereavement, divorce, etc. – and gave the participants in the study an 'ACE score' depending on the number of adverse experiences (2004, p.4). Someone with an ACE score of, say, more than three or four therefore can be thought of as having experienced compound trauma. If we look at people with an ACE score of six, there is:

- A 250% increase in the likelihood of tobacco addiction

- A 500% increase in likelihood of alcoholism
- A 4600% increase in likelihood of injecting drug use

(Felitti, 2004, pp.5–7)

The whole concept of 'dual diagnosis' is challenged by these findings. It seems much more likely that we are dealing with a single diagnosis for people with mental health problems and substance dependencies: both are reactive responses to the psychological, emotional and physiological impacts of compound trauma. This also has profound implications for the treatment of so-called dual diagnosis. The absurdity of trying to treat the substance dependence as a separate, individual 'simple' problem with a simple solution becomes apparent (as does the misguidedness of NICE guidance on this subject). In this case, we could argue that the single-diagnosis pathway approach of trying to tackle substance dependency and then mental health problems is often likely to be harmful – because it ignores the aetiology of the condition, and then projects treatment failure on to the patient, thereby adding to their trauma – as well as being deeply ineffective and inefficient. If dual diagnosis is actually just dual symptomatology but a style aetiology, then to create effective treatments we have to effectively deal with the impacts of compound trauma which at their root are psychological and emotional, as well as physiological.

Let us consider next physical health conditions in multi-morbidity: is there a correlation there as well?

The ACE Study found that there was also a 'dose-response' correlation between adverse childhood events/compound trauma and ischaemic heart disease, cancer, chronic bronchitis/emphysema, hepatitis and skeletal fractures (Felitti *et al.*, 1998); people with ACE scores of four or more are 300 per cent more likely to experience chronic obstructory pulmonary disease (COPD), for example, than people with no histories of adverse childhood events (Felitti, 2004). Felitti concluded that 'adverse childhood experiences are the main determinant of the health and well-being of the nation' (Felitti, 2004, p.4).

The ACE Study produced a diagram which the authors said explained the impact of adverse childhood events/compound trauma on later health outcomes, attributing the impact to high or higher risk health behaviours (see Figure 14.1).

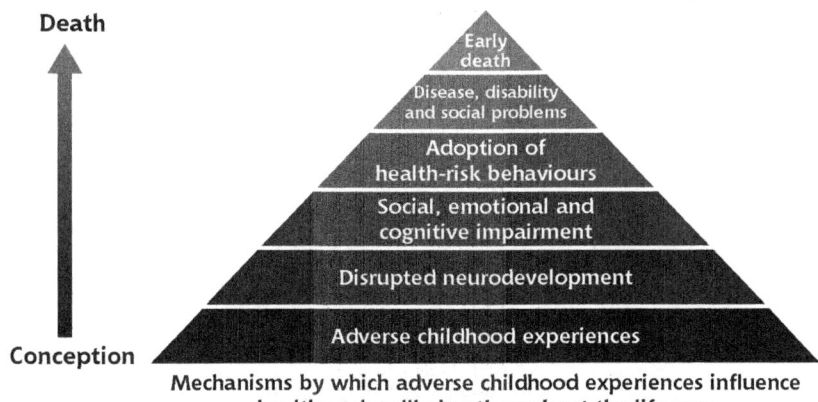

Figure 14.1
Source: Felitti et al. (1998)

Although high-risk behaviours such as smoking, heavy alcohol consumption and sleeping rough undoubtedly have a part to play in the trajectory from compound trauma to physical illness, multi-morbidity and premature death, more recent studies have suggested that the negative impact of compound trauma on physical health is actually detectable even when screening for high-risk health behaviours. D'Andrea *et al.* (2011) found a positive correlation between compound trauma and increased levels of disease in cardiovascular, immune functioning, respiratory, gastro-intestinal, genitourinary and musculoskeletal conditions remained after screening for high-risk behaviours. They go on to suggest that the mechanism by which compound trauma leads to high levels of physical illness and multi-morbidity is through chronic hyper-stress reactions (D'Andrea *et al.*, 2011). The reality seems likely to be that both chronically over-aroused stress responses and high-risk behaviours go together, and that in tandem they are significant causes of the correlation between compound trauma and multi-morbidity.

However, for homeless people and rough sleepers the situation doesn't stop there. Homelessness, and particularly rough sleeping, are situations of the most direct and 'in your face' social exclusion, and are the culmination of a profound process of social exclusion (this book, Chapter 2). And social exclusion is of itself traumatic: it activates the same neurological processes as physical pain, and arouses the same stress, fear and shame responses as physical trauma (Eisenberger *et al*, 2003; Kross *et al.* 2011). Social isolation has a greater effect size on mortality rates than either smoking or high alcohol consumption

(>6 units per day) (Holt-Lunstad *et al.*, 2010). If we take these factors into account as well as the 'dose-response' correlation between compound trauma and multi-morbidity, then it is not surprising that we see the figures of an average age at death of 47 for men and 43 for women who die on the streets or in hostels in the UK (Crisis, 2011).

What are the implications of all this for our diagnosis–treatment model and our response to the problem of multi-morbidity?

The evidence points fairly and squarely to the fact that if we encounter multi-morbidity, there is very likely to be a history of compound trauma behind it. The origin of much, probably most, possibly all, of the multi-morbidity which we encounter when working with homeless people and rough sleepers, and other highly socially excluded groups, lies in histories of compound trauma. This is the meaning of multi-morbidity.

We should therefore take the next step and consider multi-morbidity as a diagnosis in itself. Multi-morbidity as a diagnosis is both descriptive – it is a condition defined by multiple symptoms in multiple physical, psychoneurological and behavioural systems – and explanatory, with compound trauma as the driving force behind the development of the multiplicity of conditions and symptoms. This has significant implications for the effective treatment of multi-morbidity.

If multi-morbidity is characterised as being a complex set of interactive conditions triggered or arising from experiences of compound trauma, then responses, to be effective, have to respond to the complex set of interactive conditions and to the experience of compound trauma that underlies them. It is ultimately ineffective to do one without the other because the psychoneurological processes of trauma will undermine the physical healthcare, and the effects of poor physical health will undermine psychoneurological recovery. We have to throw the Cartesian dialectic out of the window: mind and body are irrevocably and inextricably a single complex adaptive (or in this case, maladaptive) system.

This means that we need to have trauma-informed responses to multi-morbidity. PIE is one model designed specifically to enable services to work effectively with people with experiences of compound trauma. It is notable that many of the effective specialised health services for homeless people are organised either specifically or in practice in ways that are aligned with the principles of PIE: social and enabling spaces, managing relationships, reflective practice, access to psychotherapy and a psychological framework (again, sometimes on an informal rather than specific level: a shared awareness of the impact of experience and context on the health conditions of their patients). Services that work with multi-morbidity need to be able to form relationships with their patients that are understanding of, and have the time and capacity to work with, their physical and mental conditions within the reality of the patients' contexts, and their past and current experiences of life. Recovery from trauma requires good experiences and positive relationships. Patients need to feel emotionally safe, experientially contained and to have a good experience of their relationship with the clinician as the starting point of their treatment because traumatising experiences and relationships are at the starting point of their multi-morbidity.

Once the patient feels relatively safe and engaged in a relationship with the health service (in the broadest sense – by 'health service' I mean the team of people who are working with the client to enable and support recovery; they may be located within a day centre, a therapy service, a formal clinic or hospital, or a combination of these), then treatment of the symptomatology of multi-morbidity begins to become more possible. To be effective, though, it still requires one thing more, and that is for the clinical team (again, in the broadest sense) to act as a benign, reflective, complex adaptive system itself. The client/patient has an experience based on non-benign, reactive adaptations: to recover, they need to move their own internal world to one of more benign, reflective and positively interacting adaptive systems. They learn this, as we all do, through interacting with positive examples: in this case, the team in the service they are working with. This is why managing relationships is so central to the PIE concept, and indeed to everything in every chapter of this book.

Working together as a benign, reflective complex adaptive system (an enabling environment in practice; a multidisciplinary team truly integrated through shared thought and purpose), the clinicians can then negotiate with the client about treatment options for the multiple conditions the client presents with, what can and cannot be done, how they interact, and what the likely outcomes of various actions and inactions are likely to be. The clinicians and patient can then come to an agreed position – what I call a 'negotiated reality' – about the course of treatments that the client/patient will engage with, and what support the client/patient needs to do so effectively. I'd just like to highlight two points here – first, there is no point in a non-negotiated reality:

then we're back to the 'You must give up drinking and drugs'/'No I won't' stand-off described earlier; non-negotiated reality is a way of excluding while pretending we're not. Second, note that this interactive relationship between clinicians and client/patient enables the client/patient to form a mature dependency on the clinicians: one in which they are neither treated like babies and 'done to', nor are they considered completely separate (alienated, excluded?) and expected to do it all by themselves; instead, their experience is acknowledged and their participation in the process is valid and really matters.

We then have a complex response to multi-morbidity – complex in the sense of multifaceted, negotiated, involving multiple entities with agency, and with immanent and unpredictable trajectories and outcomes – that is appropriate to multi-morbidity because it is a complex condition. We also have a response that is far more likely to be effective than the 'complicated' response of serial simple solutions that have kept the revolving door revolving for so long.

In summary, it is important that multi-morbidity is recognised (or regarded as) a diagnosable condition in itself, and that it has its root cause in compound trauma, despite the fact that it has an individual experience-related trajectory and so variable and multiple manifestations (no two people with have exactly the same combination of multi-morbidity expressed in the same way). It is important that anyone who presents with multi-morbidity is treated as if there is a history of compound trauma, because it is very likely that there is.

The treatment of multi-morbidity requires a trauma-informed response based on positive relationships and emotional safety, and then a dynamic, interactive dialogue between the patient and the reflective, benign multidisciplinary team about the take-up (or otherwise) of treatment options that collectively constitutes the 'service response'. For this to happen, the team must share reflective processes so that its own thinking and behaviours remain benign, and it can process vicarious trauma as well as its own pathologies, and so enable positive benign change in the patient's internal world, thereby enabling them to become a more effectively adapted person, a less-trauma-impacted person, and so ultimately less prone to multiple-cause negative health outcomes – or early death, as they're commonly known.

References

Crisis (2011) *Homelessness: A Silent Killer.* Accessed July 2017 at www.crisis.org.uk/ending-homelessness/homelessness-knowledge-hub/health-and-wellbeing/homelessness-a-silent-killer-2011

D'Andrea, W., Sharma, R., Zelechoski, A.D. and Spinazzola, J. (2011) 'Physical Health Problems After Single Trauma Exposure: When Stress Takes Root in the Body.' *Journal of the American Psychiatric Nurses Association, 17,* 6, 378–392.

Eisenberger, N.I., Lieberman, M.D. and Williams, K.D. (2003) 'Does Rejection Hurt? An fmri Study of Social Exclusion.' *In Science 302,* 290–292.

Felitti, V.J. (2004) 'The origins of addiction: evidence from the Adverse Childhood Experiences Study.' English version of the article published in Germany as: Felitti VJ. Ursprünge des Suchtverhaltens – Evidenzen aus einer Studie zu belastenden Kindheitserfahrungen. *Praxis der Kinderpsychologie und Kinderpsychiatrie, 2003, 52,* 547–559.

Felitti, V.J., Anda, R.F., Nordenberg, D., Williamson, D.F., *et al.* (1998) 'The relationship of adult health status to childhood abuse and household dysfunction.' *American Journal of Preventive Medicine 14,* 245–258.

Hendry, C. and Dorney-Smith, S. (2009) *Economic Evaluation of the Homeless Intermediate Care Project, NHS Lambeth and St Mungo's: Service Evaluation Document.*

Holt-Lunstad, J., Smith, T.B., Layton, J.B. (2010) 'Social relationships and mortality risk: a meta-analytic review.' *PLoS Med 7,* 7, e1000316. doi:10.1371/journal.pmed.1000316

Kross, E., Bermana, M.G., Mischel, W., Smith, E.E., and Wagerd, T.D. (2011) 'Social rejection shares somatosensory representations with physical pain.' *PNAS, 108,* 15, 6270–6275.

Le Doux, J. (1999) *The Emotional Brain.* London: Phoenix.

Marie Curie Cancer Care and St Mungo's (2013) *Homelessness and End of Life Care.* Accessed October 2017 at www.mariecurie.org.uk/globalassets/media/documents/commissioning-our-services/current-partnerships/homeless_report.pdf

NICE (2011) *Psychosis with Co-existing Substance Misuse.* Accessed July 2017 at www.dualdiagnosis.co.uk/uploads/documents/originals/NICE%20Substance%20Use%20and%20psychosis.pdf

Pathway (2017) *Pathway: A Model of Integrated Healthcare for Single Homeless People and Rough Sleepers.* Accessed July 2017 at www.pathway.org.uk/services

Van der Kolk, B. (2010) 'Towards a Developmental Trauma Disorder Diagnosis.' In R.A. Lanius, E. Vermetten and C. Pain (eds) *The Impact of Early Life Trauma on Pain and Disease.* Cambridge: Cambridge University Press.

14

THE DEPENDENCY PARADOX

DR EMMA WILLIAMSON

'It is not dependency that is the problem, but fear and hatred of dependency, which destroys the link to the source of support that may be the ground of our well-being – our welfare.'

(Cooper and Lousada, 2005, p.195)

Contrary to the widely held societal belief that dependence is of concern and the enemy of healthy self-sufficiency, this closing chapter takes up the position that being able to 'depend' on others and trust in reliable sources of support *is* the path to growth, psychological health and true independence. Many homeless people have had a lack of reliable close relationships upon which they can depend at times of need. As a result, we often see that they have not been able to internalise the capacity for self-care and establish an independent competent sense of self. We therefore feel it is particularly important to understand dependence and hatred or fear of dependence within this sector. We will look at the political, economic and societal factors which sustain discourses promoting fear and disgust of dependence, discourses that, even if well intentioned at times, can perpetuate social exclusion and unhelpful patterns of service provision. We will explore the concept of dependence at an individual and interpersonal level, elucidating some of the underlying psychological and developmental processes mapped out by attachment theory. By looking at how these dynamics can be set up between caregivers and those seeking care, and within organisations, teams and systems, we hope to take a fresh look at how services are designed and delivered. Whilst acknowledging the challenge and pain of staying in touch with the levels of trauma and deprivation found in homelessness, we want to think about the systems of care that might inadvertently hold back an individual from taking up residence in their life and recognise the need for 'interdependence' across the lifespan.

Putting the relational back at the heart of services

Human beings are fundamentally relational and driven by the need to attach (Bowlby, 1973, 1980, 1982). Unlike many species, the human infant is born fully dependent on its primary caregiver for survival and development. This dependence is clear to see at the beginning of life, but optimal functioning relies on the availability of a healthy dependable attachment figure across the lifespan (Bowlby, 1988). Attachment relationships support growth by acting both as a *secure base* from which to explore, that scaffolds psychological, social and intellectual development, and a *safe haven* to which one can retreat at times of stress for comfort, reassurance and assistance (Feeney and Thrush, 2010). Through this process, people flesh out their representational models of themselves, other people and their environment and internalise the functions the dependability. This allows excursions away from the secure base to become longer in time and space, along with the threshold for situations that activate the attachment system and proximity-seeking behaviours to increase. Nevertheless, there will always be situations where direct contact with an attachment figure is needed. In order to sustain confident autonomous exploration, people need to feel secure and be able to rely upon the continued availability of dependable responsive attachment figure(s). As Feeney (2007) challenges us – this should not be seen as unhealthy or childish but as an 'intrinsic part of human nature' and the root to independence and self-sufficiency (p.269).

When a secure available attachment figure has not been available in early life we see that individuals can be less confident at receiving care at times of need. They can become anxiously insecure and struggle to be autonomous, avoidant and fail to take up support when appropriate, or disorganised with no coherent reliable way of eliciting care. For people who have developed an insecure attachment pattern as a result of unpredictable, absent or abusive caregiving – as many homeless people have – there is an opportunity to develop learned security through subsequent dependable relationships. Beyond the primary caregiving relationship, people go on to form attachment relationships across the lifespan with a network of individuals who can offer a *secure base–safe haven* (including extended family, partners, friends, health professionals, therapists, employers and supervisors). However, the opportunities for safe reliable personal relationships can be restricted for homeless people when their peers have equally complex interpersonal needs, leaving them at risk of replicating earlier destructive patterns of relating. As a result, services have a noted role to play in the provision of dependable support if there is to be an opportunity to scaffold growth and development.

It can be anxiety provoking for organisations and teams to begin to recognise that rather than dependence being a harmful, infantilising process it paradoxically holds the key to greater independence. Feeney (2007) found that adults who had romantic partners who accepted their dependency needs were more self-efficacious and less needy than those that didn't. As she explains – 'it is easy for people to take risks, accept challenges, and try new things when they know that someone is available to comfort and assist them if things go wrong' (p.284). This is also supported by infant, child and adolescent research. Multiple studies have found that babies who had a mother who promptly responded when they cried, cried significantly less by the age of one than babies whose mother let them cry to develop self-soothing (Bowlby, 1988). It has also been found that children raised in environments that were supportive of their dependency needs exhibited more independent exploratory behaviour (Ainsworth, 1982; Bowlby, 1988) and that secure parental attachment relationships were crucial for adolescents to be most autonomous (Noom, Dekovic and Meeus, 1999).

There is a need nonetheless for a balance of available, reliable support that leaves room for growth, exploration and self-discovery. It is acknowledged that if the match is 'too perfect' it can become stifling and lead to an enmeshed relationship that interferes with development because the child is not able to develop a sense of separateness (Winnicott, 1960). This is also something observed with 'compulsive caregiving' tendencies and the danger that in order to satisfy their own needs, the anxiously attached caregiver delivers care that is out of sync with or overwhelming for the recipient (Feeney and Thrush, 2010). A secure base therefore needs to be available and encouraging but not unnecessarily interfering or intrusive as this can inhibit exploration and lower confidence and self-esteem.

It is clear we need relationships, but it can be complicated and terrifying to take up an offer of care and intimacy. Despite the need to attach we can all have varying degrees of challenge and anxiety with recognition of our own dependency needs and others' dependency upon us. Bateman describes '[the] patient who begins a relationship with someone only to find that contact arouses such powerful feelings of dependency and need that retreat becomes necessary to ensure feelings of survival' (1991, pp.342–343). The irony is that the moment someone is consciously able to recognise and stay in touch with their own dependency needs is the moment they can become freer and able to move towards greater autonomy. For homeless people this can, unsurprisingly, often be amplified by a background of childhood adversity, complex trauma and frightening, frightened or absent caregivers (Roos *et al.*, 2013). Here, as Glasser (1996) noted, an intense 'longing for' and 'profound fear' of attachment can develop, impacting on the individual's ability to trust in and take up care in a straightforward way when it is offered. This can often be seen in people with complex needs and unavoidable dependencies who reject the care they urgently need and want as it painfully reminds them of their need for it. Being in need and dependent on others can trigger primitive feelings of anger, injustice, grievance, blame and envy directed towards those attempting to help. As Cooper and Lousada (2005) understand, this can be distressing for staff who feel unable to confront such self-defeating behaviour and become 'tyrannised or enslaved by the dependent person, who in turn experiences themselves as imprisoned by their own limitations' (p.193). Staff can be surprised to find those they offer support to are not grateful but instead can despise and thwart their attempts at support. Hatred of dependence lies at the very core of envy and the pain of being reliant on another – 'to bite the hand that feeds' (cited in Stein, 1999, p.454).

Dependence is so provocative because it touches on our own struggles with vulnerability and neediness. Indeed, 'it is never only the identified clients who find themselves struggling to articulate their dependency needs and their feelings: it is all of us' (Scanlon and Adlam, 2012, p.76). As a result, these needs can be evacuated and projected into more vulnerable parts of society and then disavowed. Despite the discomfort, we must resist the idea that dependence can somehow be eliminated within ourselves, others and our systems of care and support.

Organisations of dependency

Rejection of support is seen all too often in those who are in the most need of support and can set up a defensive reaction in those trying so hard to help:

> Just as people may turn on their own internal sense of weakness or vulnerability and repudiate it, it may be possible for professionals to deny their clients' needs, and to turn upon their own associated sense of pain and fear, when they have experienced their own efforts to help being severely attacked and repudiate it. (Cooper and Lousada, 2005, pp.51–52)

The needs of the homeless and other complex needs populations are not decreasing and, if anything, are becoming more complex and entrenched, whilst resources are ever more constrained. As Scanlon and Adlam (2012) warn, in the current socio-economic climate all accommodation, care and support services will become 'increasingly (dis)stressed as they find themselves stuck in the middle between… the "rock" of increasing demand and dependent need and the "hard place" of apparently decreasing resources' (pp.74–75). Alongside this, there is growing scrutiny and emphasis on auditing, outcomes and proving your worth. This has an undeniable impact on organisations and staff and has been linked to burnout and high staff turnover (Maslach, 1981). This can make the provision of dependable services a challenge to produce if those who are asked to provide them do not feel secure in their own position and provision. Thus, despite recognition of the importance of supportive relationships to foster growth and development, it can be difficult to deliver in systems where there is rapid staff turnover or where staff burn out and become emotionally cut off to cope with the distress of the work. The resulting combination of these pressures, the work itself and the service user's relationship to help, as described above, is complex. One way to tackle this is to focus on the levels of staff support, structures and processes required to help teams function (e.g. reflective practice, supervision, training, staff–client ratios, incident debrief). These forums can provide teams with a space to recognise and work with the dynamics and primitive anxieties stirred up by their roles.

Through powerful parallel process, systems of care can also avoid contact with service users who are refused access or passed from one service or setting to another and labelled as 'not ready', 'stuck' or even 'too attached'. Scanlon and Adlam (2008) caution about the dangers of systems of care that if we are not careful can 'thoughtlessly mirror wider social prejudices in establishing ever more elaborate ways of excluding such people from our services and from our minds' (p.541). Traditional institutions, asylums and long-stay psychiatric hospitals were there to 'contain' the distressed, risky, needy or dispossessed for society – taking them 'out of sight, out of mind' (Cooper and Lousada, 2005, p.113). These institutions, when working well, were able to meet the individual's dependency needs, when they were not able to find this within family or community contexts, but have also been critiqued for promoting segregation and marginalisation. 'Care in the community' policy and closure of many long-stay institutions attempted to address this, but did little sustainable work to address the dependence and attachment needs of those individuals.

Welfare dependence, political fear and the economy

We all need support and care at different times in our life. However, making caretaking central to the role of the state has concerningly been positioned as the 'nemesis' of political and economic autonomy rather than, as we propose here, the path to a higher-functioning interdependent society. In their book *Borderline Welfare*, Cooper and Lousada (2005) observe the political and economic threat posed by true acknowledgement and a deeper engagement with the population's social and personal ills:

> [T]here is a terrible irony in the current fashion for promoting British health and welfare services as dependable. For it is far from clear whether we actually want people to depend upon them, and where they do, whether we believe and communicate to them that this is acceptable, rather than evidence of someone's failure – theirs, ours, or some undefined other's. (p.200)

In order to recognise and meet unavoidable dependent care needs, Kittay and Feder (2003) suggest that we must rethink the three basic institutions – the state, the market and the family. In the current political climate, autonomy is seen as the key to both a free state and a free market, and dependency is disavowed or relegated to the job of the family. But what happens when the 'family' provision reaches its limit, breaks down or is unavailable for whatever reason? Fineman amongst others, challenges the myth of autonomy altogether, and strongly argues that 'dependency is a universal and inevitable part of the human condition' and part of all of our experiences rather than something to be shunned, avoided or projected into the more fragile parts of society, such as children, the elderly or those who are infirm of mind or body (cited in Kittay and Feder, 2003, p.115). Here the relationship between the state and the market need to be restructured to recognise the importance and centrality of dependency needs and dependent care to a well-functioning state, market and society. However, political and economic changes are presently taking us in the opposite direction. Reduced investment in health, social care and public infrastructure and an increase in individualism has led to greater emphasis on individuals fending for themselves, and less emphasis on a society that takes a more interdependent moral stance.

Throughout history there have been periods of increased pejorative societal discourses regarding the prevalence and impact 'scroungers and malingerers' have on the wider society (Cooper and Lousada, 2005). Before the industrial revolution, society was an interwoven net of dependencies and social hierarchies, supported by a moral economy where certain members were subordinate to others but their contribution was visible, understood and valued. Discussions of the caste system in India, for example, illustrate how all members of society, whether celebrated or reviled, were acknowledged as having a role to play in the functioning of society (Ghurye, 1969). With the growth of science and industry, the post-industrial social science discourses' pathologising of 'dependency' began to take root and brought into question the legitimacy and centrality of our needs for lifelong interdependence which had been understood and valued at earlier periods in history. The Victorian Poor Law sent destitute individuals to the workhouse where they were shunned as the lowest in society. This fell into disfavour in the postwar heyday of the welfare state, when the community shared the cost of individual misfortune. In the 1980s, however, the economic downturn and increased unemployment placed a strain on social spending. Intertwined with this, political rhetoric fuelled fears of a 'dependency culture' where some members of society were taking more than their fair share (Hartley and Taylor-Gooby, 1992). In the

1980s in the USA this 'cultural panic' led to escalating fears around the concept of dependency and the emergence of disorders such as 'Dependent Personality Disorder' (American Psychiatric Association, 1987), the stigma of welfare dependence and its connotations to drug dependency (Kittay and Feder, 2003). These shifts not only had a negative impact on those seeking support, but also in contempt for those delivering the caring; with reduced investment and social status for stay-at-home mums and the female-dominated helping professions (Shapiro, 1990).

Currently there is widespread concern that the welfare state can no longer be supported. An anxiety that providing more will open the floodgates to an unquenchable need that will drain resources and damage and enslave society and the economy. When thinking about the cost of welfare and the marketised health care system in the USA, Bollas and Sundelson (1995) believe there is an intrinsic incompatibility between the primary task of companies to make money and unbiased delivery of the most appropriate clinical interventions. As the 'business' of UK health and social care becomes increasingly commercialised we need to be mindful of the impact this can have on service provision and the opportunity for primitive fears to be mobilised socially and politically. With a growing focus in recent years on the need to evaluate and make health–economic arguments to defend service provision, there is a call for us to be 'talking the business talk', demonstrating how health interventions can act as a labour driver or make savings elsewhere in the system. With increasingly tighter social care and welfare budgets, there is a valid and prominent place for considering service costs and effectiveness but when we do so, we also need to keep an eye on what is lost, denied or can't be attended to of human need and the pain of staying in contact with severe deprivation that can't quickly or cheaply be resolved. With austerity, housing shortages and the call for us to do more for less by offering briefer treatments or shorter accommodation stays, we are in danger of losing sight of the mutative components to wellbeing upon which growth and independent functioning is built. We know everyone's psychological health depends on the availability of personal and social systems of relational care and nourishment and yet in our avoidance of dependence we are in danger of overlooking this.

Solutions – the call for interdependence

When looking for what works to support people to have full and functioning lives, we need to take up the mantel of dependence and recognise its centrality rather than continuing to shun and pathologise it. We are therefore calling for a recognition of our lifelong need for 'interdependence':

> Between the fear of absolute dependence and the illusion of complete independence, there does indeed lie a third way. It seeks development and growth as its goal, not cure; it embraces inter-dependence and acknowledges degrees of relative dependence as facts of psychological and social life; and it understands that work is a relationship neither of total estrangement nor harmonious merger. (Cooper and Lousada, 2005, p.201)

Rather than looking at development and growth from the traditional point of view of separation and individuation, Irene Stiver's work (in Jordan *et al.*, 1991), amongst others, highlights the need for connection in order to achieve growth and that by relying on others one will find themselves enhanced. Interdependence is consequently understood by Stiver as a blend of dependency and self-sufficiency – 'a process of counting on other people to provide help in coping physically and emotionally with experiences and tasks encountered in the world when one has not sufficient skill, confidence, energy, and/or time' (p.160). They recognise the impact that being raised in foster care, or coming from a background of multiple, unstable placements can have on the ability to form connections and the need for tailored programmes to help address this (Propp, Ortega and NewHeart, 2003).

Research into the transition of youths from social care (Kerman, Wildfire and Barth, 2002) and adolescents leaving home (Bowlby, 1988) provides useful information about the need for continuity of relationships with significant others. We more comfortably accept the need for child services to be constructed around the principles of attachment and replication of a family-like setting. But as soon as young people transition through adolescence this is forgotten and the focus becomes self-sufficiency (Propp *et al.*, 2003). As discussed earlier, attachment research shows us the importance of available *secure* base–safe *haven* attachment provision 'from the cradle to the grave' (Bowlby, 1979, p.129), and we therefore feel this should not be forgotten in the design and delivery of adult services. Indeed, it is surely more than coincidental that the phrase 'cradle to grave' appears not only in Bowlby's argument for the universal need for lifelong attachment but in The Beveridge Report, the blueprint for the modern welfare state (Beveridge, 1942).

The reality of the constraints on housing and employment opportunities can be prohibitive and trap workers in a system where service users are moved on or resettled from one short- or medium-term place to another, struggling to find a home of their own where they can settle with reliable support when needed. By moving away from a philosophy of self-sufficiency towards a framework of interdependence, there will however, be fundamental challenges to the way systems of support, care and accommodation are provided (Propp *et al.*, 2003). In one such service redesigned long-term housing and support is being provided in recognition that stable environmental and relational attachments create less rather than more dependency. The Permanent Supportive Housing (PSH) model is an evidence-based housing intervention from the USA combining non-time-limited affordable housing assistance with wrap-around supportive services for those who are homeless, as well as other at risks groups. It has been shown to be cost effective, particularly for entrenched homeless people, and results in housing stability, improved physical and mental health and reduced use of crisis services (including shelters, hospitals, and psychiatric and criminal justice services) (US Interagency Council on Homelessness, 2017). Here we could argue that rather than denying or fearing dependency needs, by accepting them and offering sustained accommodation and support structures, independence has been achieved and maintained. Similarly, these needs can be address in smaller ways by existing services understanding the need for consistent dependable relationships. In the Lambeth Psychology in Hostels Psychologically Informed Environments Project they understand the need for 'transitional support' when moving to new accommodation. The project and individual workers holding that *secure base* function is invaluable. This can be supported by former residents making visits, coming for lunch or dinner, returning for activities such as therapeutic groups or graduating onto volunteering or peer mentor services where they can return in a different capacity. Continuity of relationships with workers who have become attachment figures has been found to be of great benefit.

Conclusion

Despite the current cultural allure of independence and demonisation of dependence, we must recognise the complex relationship between the two, that autonomy can only grow from a *secure base*, and that we all require the ability to return to a *safe haven* from time to time. Although it may appear paradoxical that the acceptance of dependency needs promotes development and independence, this is consistent with theories of 'mature dependence' or 'healthy dependence' and the need for human connection throughout life for healthy functioning (Solomon, 1994; Bornstein, 2005). The tragedy of those individuals who never had the opportunity to develop their *secure base–safe haven*, who we encounter on the streets, in hostels and clinical settings, is that they are so often denied opportunities, at both an institutional and personal level, to develop the attachments that are necessary for wellbeing. Indeed, when such attachments do develop they are often pathologised and disrupted by the system rather than acknowledged and fostered. Rather than pushing such individuals towards a mythical 'independence', we need to look to interdependence and the need we all have to form dependable and healthy attachments. Doing so, however, requires questioning the powerful political and cultural rhetoric that pathologises dependency as unhealthy and childish. To challenge this discourse, we must appreciate that it is a product of a particular cultural and political moment rather than an absolute truth. Then we may be able to see dependency not as a crutch to be rapidly abandoned to 'self-sufficiency', but as a necessary life-long skill and psychological mechanism: to be able to appropriately give and safely seek and receive comfort and assistance at times of stress (Feeney and Thrush, 2010).

References

Ainsworth, M.D. (1982) 'Attachment: Retrospect and Prospect.' In C.M. Parkes and J. Stevenson-Hinde (eds) *The Place of Attachment in Human Behavior.* New York: Basic Books.

American Psychiatric Association (1987) *Diagnostical and Statistical Manual of Mental Disorders,* 3rd edition. Revised. Washington, DC: American Psychiatric Association.

Bateman, A. (1991) 'Borderline Personality Disorder.' In J. Holmes (ed.) *Textbook of Psychotherapy in Psychiatric Practice.* London: Churchill Livingstone.

Beveridge, W. (1942) *Report on Social Insurance and Allied Services,* Cmd 6404. London: HMSO.

Bollas, C. and Sundelson, D. (1995) *The New Informants.* London: Karnac.

Bornstein, R.F. (2005) 'Dependency across the Life Span.' In R.F. Bornstein (ed.) *The Dependent Patient: A Practitioner's Guide.* Washington, DC: American Psychological Association.

Bowlby, J. (1973) *Attachment and Loss: Separation, Anxiety and Anger.* New York: Basic Books.

Bowlby, J. (1979) *The Making and Breaking of Affectional Bonds.* London: Tavistock.

Bowlby, J. (1980) *Attachment and Loss: Sadness and Depression.* New York: Basic Books.

Bowlby, J. (1982 [1969]) *Attachment and Loss: Vol. 1. Attachment.* New York: Basic Books.
Bowlby, J. (1988) *A Secure Base.* New York: Basic Books.
Cooper, A. and Lousada, J. (2005) *Borderline Welfare: Feeling and Fear of Feeling in Modern Welfare* (The Tavistock Clinic Series). London: Karnac.
Feeney, B.C. (2007) 'The dependency paradox in close relationships: accepting dependence promotes independence.' *Journal of Personality and Social Psychology 92,* 268–285.
Feeney, B.C. and Thrush, R.L. (2010) 'Relationship influences on exploration in adulthood: the characteristics and function of a secure base.' *Journal of Personality and Social Psychology 98,* 2, 57–76.
Ghurye, S.G. (1969) *Caste and Race in India,* 5th edition. Bombay: Popular Prakashan.
Glasser, M. (1996) 'Aggression and Sadism in the Perversions.' In I. Rose (ed.) *Sexual Deviation,* 3rd edition. Oxford: Oxford University Press.
Hartley, D. and Taylor-Gooby, P. (1992) *Dependency Culture: The Explosion of a Myth.* London: Taylor and Francis.
Jordan, J.V., Kaplan, A.G., Miller, J.B., Stiver, I.P. and Surrey, J.L. (1991) *Women's Growth in Connection: Writings from the Stone Centre.* New York: The Guilford Press.
Kerman, B., Wildfire, J. and Barth, R. (2002) 'Outcomes for young adults who experienced foster care.' *Children and Youth Services Review 24,* 319–344.
Kittay, E.F. and Feder, E.K. (2003) *The Subject of Care: Feminist Perspectives on Dependency.* New York: Rowman and Littlefield.
Maslach, C. (1981) *Burnout: The Cost of Caring.* Englewood Cliffs, NJ: Prentice-Hall.
Noom, M.M., Dekovic, M. and Meeus, W.H.J. (1999) 'Autonomy, attachment and psychosocial adjustment during adolescence: a double-edged sword?' *Journal of Adolescence 22,* 771–783.
Propp, J., Ortega, D.M. and NewHeart, F. (2003) 'Independence or interdependence: rethinking the transition from "ward of the court" to adulthood.' *Families in Society: The Journal of Contemporary Human Services 84,* 2, 259–266.
Roos, L.E., Mota, N., Afifi, O., Katz, L.Y., Distasio, J. and Sareen, J. (2013) 'Relationship between adverse childhood experiences and homelessness and the impact of axis I and II disorders.' *American Journal of Public Health, 103,* 2, 275–281.
Scanlon, C. and Adlam, J. (2008) 'Refusal, social exclusion and the cycle of rejection: a cynical analysis?' *Critical Social Policy 28,* 4, 529–549.
Scanlon, C. and Adlam, J. (2012) 'The (dis)stressing effects of working in (dis)stressed homeless organisations.' *Housing, Care and Support 15,* 2, 74–82.
Shapiro, V. (1990) 'The Gender Bias of American Social Policy.' In L. Gordon (ed.) *Women, the State and Welfare.* Madison, WI: University of Wisconsin Press.
Solomon, M. (1994) *Lean on Me: The Power of Positive Dependency in Intimate Relationships.* New York: Simon and Schuster.
Stein, M. (1999) 'Envy and leadership.' *European Journal of Work and Organizational Psychology 6,* 4, 453–465.
US Interagency Council on Homelessness (2017) *Supportive Housing.* Accessed October 2017 at www.usich.gov/solutions/housing/supportive-housing
Winnicott, D.W. (1960) 'The Theory of the Parent–Infant Relationship.' In *The Maturational Process and the Facilitating Environment.* London and New York: Karnac.

Authors' Biographies

In alphabetical order:

Dr Catriona Reid trained as a Clinical Psychologist at University College London, and did her doctoral research on the impact of Psychologically Informed Environments on homeless people. She previously worked as an Outreach Worker for several organisations in London including St Mungo's, and was also a Link Worker at Hackney Winter Night Shelter. She now works as a Clinical Psychologist for the veterans' mental health charity Combat Stress.

Dr Emma Williamson is a Principal Clinical Psychologist and Clinical Lead at South London and Maudsley NHS Foundation Trust; she has for the past six years been working in partnership with third sector organisations, notably Thamesreach, to develop innovative mental health and support services for homeless people in the London Borough of Lambeth using a Psychologically Informed Environments framework. Emma formerly worked at the Tavistock and Portman NHS Foundation Trust and has a personal interest in contributing to the evidence base for applied psychoanalytic ways of working with socially excluded and complex needs populations. Emma also works in private practice and teaches on the Clinical Psychology Doctorate at the Institute of Psychiatry.

John Conolly is a UKCP-registered Psychoanalytic Psychotherapist and Lacanian Analyst, and a Member of the Centre for Freudian Analysis and Research. Homelessness and social exclusion have always been major themes of his professional life. As an Organisational Psychologist he conducted a GLC-funded action research project on the service usage patterns of homeless people in East London. He joined the NHS in 2002 as a bilingual counsellor in a trauma stress clinic for refugees and asylum seekers, and specialised in trauma. He has been leading the Westminster Homeless Health Counselling Service at the Central London Community Healthcare NHS Trust since 2009 with a special interest in personality disorder and compound trauma. He is an accredited trainer for the Knowledge and Understanding Framework (KUF) on personality disorder. He is Co-founder of the Westminster Complex Needs Network and sits on the conference and education and training committees of the Faculty of Homeless and Inclusion Health for whom he wrote the counselling section in their *Health Service Standards for Commissioners and Service Providers*. He has recently accepted an invitation to teach on the PhD programmes on the psychotraumatology of homelessness at Trinity College, Dublin, and to be a contributing member to its advisory panel.

Nicola Saunders trained as a Psychoanalytic Psychotherapist at the Bowlby Centre, and as a Group Clinical Supervisor at the Institute of Group Analysis. Prior to working in LifeWorks, St Mungo's psychotherapy service for homeless people, Nicola's psychotherapy work included substance use and mental health services and primary care. From 2002–2007 Nicola was a member of the first Stella Project Steering Group which was set up by the Greater London Domestic Violence Project and Greater London Alcohol and Drug Alliance to develop practice and research for domestic violence and drug and alcohol services for women who were substance users and victims of domestic violence. Within LifeWorks, alongside individual psychotherapy, Nicola has been running women's groups as well as developing psychosocial and trauma-informed training in psychologically informed women's and mixed homeless hostels in St Mungo's.

Dr Peter Cockersell trained as a Psychoanalytic Psychotherapist with Nafsiyat Intercultural Therapy Centre and UCL Department of Psychiatry and Behavioural Studies, and became UKCP registered in 2001. He has worked as a psychotherapist in the NHS, third sector and private practice. Peter also worked for over 20 years in homelessness services, latterly as Director of Health and Recovery for St Mungo's. He was a pioneer in developing PIE services, and was one of the authors of the National Guidance on PIEs. He was also a founder member of the Faculty of Homeless and Inclusion Health and he is a member of the Health Committee of Feantsa, the European umbrella organisation for homelessness agencies. Peter currently works as Chief Executive of Community Housing and Therapy, a charity providing psychologically informed therapeutic communities for people with diagnoses of psychosis and/or personality disorders. He is also an Associate Lecturer in Psychodynamic Theory and Practice on the Counselling Psychology training at University of Surrey, a consultant in PIEs to various European homelessness organisations and maintains a small private psychotherapy practice. Peter has written various articles and book chapters, and is available on petercockersell@intapsych.org

Dr Sally Read's interest in complex trauma, addiction and social exclusion began when she was a GP at what is now York Street Health Centre in Leeds. She has worked with people who are homeless since 1999, and is now a UKCP-registered integrative psychotherapist. Together with the team at Harrogate Homeless Project, she set up Streetlight Psychotherapy, a service for people living on the margins.

Terry Hutton was born 1960 in Stepney, London, and experienced his childhood as happy until about 11 when his family moved to Streatham, so happy, he says, that he didn't even know he had a lazy eye (cross eyed) until that move. After that move everything changed. He remembers being marked for extra bullying for being top of the class, and he left school at 13 to work with his dad. Started work at 16 legally, and had many jobs working in pubs and hotels, working behind the bar, or silver service waiting, and became an alcoholic. In 1987 he left for America, and there had a variety of jobs from working in the swamps, car valet parking, roofing, window cleaning, house cleaning, scaffolding, building bowling alleys, hotel management, bartending, gardening, to finally building two businesses from scratch, a cleaning company and then finally going onto a painting company. Terry now lives in London thankfully, training to be a Gas Safe Engineer, while still painting his art at his home: www.terryhuttonart.com

Subject Index

acceptance
  as psychotherapeutic principle 90–1
accessibility
  as psychotherapeutic principle 90
adolescence
  and women 141–6
Adults Facing Chronic Exclusion (ACE) programme 89
Adverse Childhood Experiences (ACE) Study 234–7
alcohol usage
  and access to psychotherapy 91
  and women 144–5
anger
  support groups 124–9
  and women 146–7
appointments-based counselling sessions
  as health counselling sessions 129–30
aspiration
  and recovery 74–7
attachment theory
  ambivalent styles 116–17, 118
  avoidant styles 116
  and dependency 243–5
  and development of babies 42
  disorganised styles 117, 118
  at Harrogate Homeless Project 181–2
  and interaction styles 115–18
  and PIEs 166–7
  secure styles 116
  and women 138–9

babies
  and attachment theory 42
  and development of self 38–41
  homelessness journey to 46–52
  motivational systems in 39–41
  and object relations 41–6
  social exclusion journey 46–52
  thinking capacity of 44–6

Borderline Welfare (Cooper and Lousada) 247
boundaries
  crossing 122–3
  as psychotherapeutic principle 91–2
childhood
  and complex needs 33–4, 212–13, 234–7
  and compound trauma 19–20, 30–2, 46–52
  motivational systems in 39–41
chronic homelessness
  description of 15
co-construction
  and pre-treatment therapy 114–15
cognitive dissonance
  in therapy 120–1
complex needs
  and childhood 33–4, 212–13, 234–7
  description of 22
  and Enabling Environments principles 221–2
  and homelessness 22–4, 210–12

complex needs *cont.*
  and maladaptive behaviours 30–1
  and mind-body-body system 32–3
  multifacted expression of 34–5
  older people with 211–2
  and PIEs 220–1
  potential in 214–22
  prevalence of 213–14
  problems of 208–14
  and self-actualisation 32–3
  services for 208–10
complex trauma *see* compound trauma
complexity theory
  potential in 214–22
compound trauma
  association with homelessness 17–22
  and childhood 19–20, 30–2, 46–52
  and clinical practice 27–8
  complexity of 28–9
  cumulative nature of 26–7
  description of 17
  impact of 33–4, 53–7
  and maladaptive behaviours 19
  and multi-morbidity 237–8
  prevalence of 17–18
  psychological impact of 53–7
  research into 21–2
  as term 26–30
Cycle of Change model 64

dependency
  and attachment theory 243–5
  organisations of 246–7
  solutions for 250–1
  and welfare dependency 247–9
domestic violence 145–6
drop-in support and counselling
  as health counselling service 123–4
drug usage
  and access to psychotherapy 91
  and women 144–5

eclectic practice
  as psychotherapeutic principle 92–3
Enabling Environments principles 95–6, 221–2
epigenetics 33
exclusions
  and access to psychotherapy 90–1

false self 118
fear
  and women 146–7

Grass Arena, The (Healy) 166

Haigh, Rex 95
Hard Edges (Lankelly Chase) 21–3, 211
Harrogate Homeless Project (HHP) 175–90
health counselling services
  anger support groups 124–9
  appointments-based 129–30
  drop-in support and counselling 123–4
home
  aspects of 164–6
homelessness
  and aspects of home 164–6
  baby's journey to 46–52
  chronic homelessness 15
  and complex needs 22–4, 210–12
  compound trauma association 17–22
  counselling challenges 110–12
  experiences of 192–205
  growth in 16
  as housing issue 16–17
  as most 'visible' form of social exclusion 14–15, 23–4
  prevalence of mental health problems 20–1
  psychological understanding of 150–1
  psychotherapeutic principles 90–4
  transient homelessness 15–16
  types of mental health problems 110–11
  views of 161
housing
  and homelessness 16–17
'housing first' movement 16

Improving Access to Psychological Therapies (IAPT) programme 89

Johnson, Robin 95–6

Keats, Helen 21

LifeWorks psychotherapy model
  acknowledgement for 93
  clients for 84, 85
  engagement rates 88
  funding for 93
  length of intervention 87–8
  location of 86
  management of 93
  models of therapy in 87–9
  outcomes 89–90
  staffing for 85, 92, 93
  and women's services 134, 136, 147

Maguire, Nick 95
Meeting the Psychological and Emotional Needs of People Who Are Homeless (Maguire) 18, 162
mentalisation 119–20
mentalisation-based treatment (MBT) 155–6
Miliband, David 14, 24
motivational systems
  in child development 39–41
multi-morbidity
  and compound trauma 237–8
  data on homeless 227–9
  dual-aspect approach to 229–38
  and PIEs 238–40

object relations
  in development of babies 41–6
Outcome Star 89–90, 187–8

Pathway approach 233
personality disorders (PD) 110, 111
  and anger management 129
  and attachment styles 118
  and mentalisation 119–20
  recovery from 121–2
PIEs
  aspects of home 164–6
  attachments in 166–7
  case study for 153–6
  components 163
  and complex needs 220–1
  description of 151–3
  guidance for 21, 95, 96–8
  at Harrogate Homeless Project 176–90
  in homeless service 94–6
  implementation of 98–103, 162–3
  and multi-morbidity 238–40
  other service providers 102
  outcomes of 103–4, 157–8
  principles of 96
  psychological support 100
  and recovery 71–2
  reflective practice in 99–100, 168–9
  research background 163–4
  staff impact of 167–9
  staffing for 100–1, 102–3
  support for 99
  theory and practice of 169–71
  thinking space in 103
  training for 100–1
  uniqueness of 171
post-traumatic stress disorder (PTSD) 110–11
pre-treatment therapy
  building blocks of 113–14
  and co-construction 114–15
  description of 112–3
Psychologically Informed Environments *see* PIEs
Psychologically Informed Planned Environments (PIPEs) 96
psychology
  branches of 82
  challenge of therapy 109
  in homelessness setting 94–6
  reasons for application of 80–3
  understanding of homelessness 150–1
Psychology in Hostels Project (PiH) 152, 153–6, 157
psychotherapy
  in homelessness setting 94–6
  LifeWorks psychotherapy model 84–94
  in multidisciplinary team 182–3, 187–8
  principles of with homelessness 90–4
  and social interventions 104–5

recovery
  case study for 65–7
  as enacted aspiration 74–7
  meanings of 62–4
  from personality disorder 121–2
  and PIEs 71–2
  processes of 67–77

recovery *cont.*
   'recovery from' 69–72
   'recovery from starting point' 72–3
   'recovery of' 67–9
   and resilience 73–4
   and therapeutic approach 77–8
   user-defined process 121–3
resilience
   and recovery 73–4

St Mungo's
   annual review on homelessness 16–17
   LifeWorks psychotherapy model at 84–94
   women's support at 134, 136–7, 147
Seven-Stage Crisis Intervention Model 123
severe and multiple disadvantages (SMDs)
   levels of 21–2, 30, 211
   and childhood trauma 19–20
self-actualisation
   and complex needs 32–3
self-harm
   and women 142
sexual relationships
   and women 142–3
sexualisation
   of women 143–4
shame
   management of 118–20
Shattered Lives (St Mungo's) 20, 134
social exclusion
   baby's journey to 46–52
   definition of 14
   homelessness as most 'visible' form 14–15, 23–4
   physical impact of 34
   psychological impact of 53–7

Social Exclusion Unit
   definitions of social exclusion 14
social interventions
   and psychotherapy 104–5
Standards for Commissioners and Service Providers (Faculty for Homeless Health) 178

therapy
   cognitive dissonance 120–1
   description of therapeutic 64–5
   and recovery 77–8
transient homelessness
   description of 15–16
   reasons for 16
trauma
   definition of 26
   and women's services 137–9

welfare dependency 247–9
women
   and adolescence 141–6
   anger 146–7
   and attachment theory 138–9
   demographics of 136–7
   domestic violence 145–6
   drug and alcohol usage 144–5
   fear 146–7
   and gender development 140–1
   need for women-only 14
   at St Mungo's 134, 136–7, 147
   self-blame 139
   self-harm 142
   sexual relationships 142–3
   sexualisation of 143–4
   and trauma 137–9

Author Index

Adlam, J. 17, 69, 118, 149, 154, 180, 181–2, 183, 245, 247
Adshead, G. 168
Agenda 146
Ainsworth, M. 167, 244
Allen, J.G. 115
Alwin, N. 110
American Psychiatric Association 249
Anthony, W.A. 121
Asay, T.I. 169
Ashton, P. 112
Attenborough, J. 161
Awad, M. 150

Baguley, T. 162
Baradon, T. 29
Bargh, J.A. 41
Barker, C. 169
Barker, P. 176
Barnett, K. 168, 212
Barth, R. 250
Bateman, A. 46, 70, 115, 118, 120, 155, 245
BBC 161, 175
Berry, K. 116
Beveridge, W. 251
Bion, W. 44
Biven, L. 32, 38, 39, 44, 70
Blackwell, R. 183, 184
Bleiberg, E. 111
Bollas, C. 249
Borghol, N. 33
Bornstein, R.E. 252
Bowlby, J. 42, 43, 68, 71, 74, 115, 138, 166, 181, 243, 244, 250
Boyle, D. 114
Bramley, G. 161, 162, 208, 211

Brighter Futures 23, 208
Brown, G. 187
Brown, R. 163
Brown, V.B. 92
Brown, V.B. 145
Buber, M. 180
Buchanan-Barker, P. 176

Caligor, E. 41–2
Campbell, J. 158
Cartwright, N. 19
Casey, R. 135
Castaldo, M. 94
Castillo, H. 121, 122, 129
Charura, D. 182
Clarkin, M. 42
Clarkson, P. 182
Cloitre, M. 162, 165
Cockersell, P. 15, 19, 20, 72, 90, 103, 104, 157, 164, 183, 187, 217
Cohen, L. 162
Connolly, T. 171
Conolly, J.M.P. 112
Cooper, A. 151, 242, 245, 246, 247, 248, 250
Cornes, M. 224
Council for Disabled Children 212
Covington, S.S. 144
Crisis 14, 16, 236
Cue, K. 168

Daniel, S.I.F. 116, 118, 119
Danquah, A.N. 116
Davis, S. 165
Dekovic, M. 244
Department for Communities and Local Government (DCLG) 160, 177

Department of Health 110, 212
DiClemente, C.C. 64, 176
Dorney-Smith, S. 229
Dowds, B. 181
Dozier, M. 168
Dykeman, B. 157

Ebrahim, S. 33
Eduqna 31
Eichenbaum, L. 140
Eisenberger, N.I. 34, 63
Ellen, Sister 29
Erikson, E.H. 141
Essali, A. 150
Esch, T. 34

Faculty for Homeless Health 178
Fairbairn, W.R.D. 43, 68, 139
Fallot, R. 145
Faulkner, A. 121
Fazel, S. 149, 162
Feantsa 16
Feder, E.K. 247, 248, 249
Feeney, B.C. 243, 244
Felitti, V.J. 162, 234–2, 236
Filoni, A. 94
Fiske, S.T. 32
Fitzpatrick, S. 161
Focus Ireland 81
Fonagy, P. 46, 70, 111, 115, 118, 119, 120, 155
Foster, A. 150–1
Frawley, M.G. 139
Freud, S. 32, 41, 74, 75

Geddes, J.R. 162
Ghurye, S.G. 248
Glasgow Homeless Network 18
Glasser, M. 245
Glouberman, S. 215
Goffman, E. 112
Gomez, L. 184
Goodwin, I. 166
Goudie, R. 135
Greenberg, J.R. 31
Greenhalgh, T. 218
Griffiths, S. 89
Groundswell 17, 71, 72, 74, 76

Guardian 14
Guntrip, H. 41, 45
Gutheil, T.C. 122

Haigh, R. 95, 111, 151, 162, 163, 171, 221, 222
Harris, M. 114, 145
Hartley, D. 248
Healy, J. 166
Heard, D. 38, 39, 70, 138
Hendry, C. 229
Herman, J.L. 115, 119, 124, 165, 166–7
Holmes, J. 70, 114, 115, 116, 117
Holt-Lunstad, J. 34, 236
Homeless Link 15, 21, 23, 89, 164, 208, 211
Hooper, C-A. 29
Hutson, S. 160, 170

Johnsen, S. 161, 162
Johnson, R. 95, 145, 151, 162, 163, 171, 221, 222
Jordan, J.V. 250
Joseph Rowntree Foundation 212, 213

Kane, E. 110
Karpman, S. 184
Keats, H. 21, 71, 95, 96, 97, 110, 120, 151, 162, 163, 220
Kerman, B. 250
Kernberg, O. 42
King's Fund 212, 213, 219
Kittay, E.F. 247, 248, 249
Klein, M. 31
Koenen, K. 162
Kross, E. 34, 236
Kushel, M. 162

Lake, B. 38, 39, 70, 138
Lambert, M.J. 169
Lanius, R. 30, 31, 32, 70
Lankelly Chase 21–2, 30, 57
Larner, G. 187
Lawrence, M. 142
Layton, J.B. 34
Le Doux, J. 44, 230
Levitas, R. 14, 23, 24

Levy, J.S. 112, 113, 165
Lieberman, M.D. 34, 63
Liotti, G. 30
London Borough of Enfield 212
Lousada, J. 151, 242, 245, 246, 247, 248, 250

Maguire, N. 18, 19, 110, 149, 151, 162, 163
Marchal, B. 215, 216, 217
Marie Curie 231, 232
Martijn, C. 18
Maroda, K. 182
Maruna, S. 124
Maslach, C. 246
Masten, A.S. 73
Masters 150
McCann, I. 168
McCluskey, U. 29, 70, 138
McDonagh, T. 112, 120
McGilchrist, I. 32, 39, 44
McGrath, L. 169
Meeus, W.H.J. 244
Merriam-Webster 64, 73
Messler Davis, J. 139
Mitchell, S.A. 31, 146
Morsella, E. 41
Motz, A. 142, 145

NewHeart, F. 250
NHS Hammersmith 90
NICE 110, 123, 232
NIMHE 111, 121
Noom, M.M. 244
Norcross, J.C. 113, 125
North, C.S. 18

Ogden, T.H. 176
Orbach, S. 140, 142
Ortega, D.M. 250
Orwell, G. 160
Osborne-Davies, I. 171
O'Shaughnessy, E. 156
OUP 26
Oxford Dictionary 14
Oxford University 75

Pain, C. 30, 70
Panksepp, J. 32, 38, 39, 44, 70
Parsell, C. 161
Parsons, M. 155
Pathway 208, 233
Paul, S. 182
Pearlman, L. 168
Phipps, C. 164
PIElink 103
Pines, D. 142, 143
Pistrang, N. 169
Plesk, P. 216, 218
Porges, S.W. 70, 71
Portner, M. 112
Power, C. 161
Prochaska, J.O. 64, 113, 125, 176
Propp, J. 250, 251
Prouty, G. 112
Public Health England 177
Punzi, I. 94

Ramsden, D. 124
Read, A. 91
Read, S. 177
Reeve, K. 135
Rey, J.H. 150
Ritchie, C. 188
Roberts, A.R. 123
Roberts, G. 70
Roos, L.E. 30, 149, 245
Rossouw, T. 111
Rothschild, B. 115
Royal College of Psychiatry 95

St Mungo's 20, 23, 134, 135, 150, 179, 208, 231, 232
Sanderson, C. 131
Saunders, R. 166, 167, 170
Scanlon, C. 17, 69, 118, 149, 154, 164, 180, 181–2, 183, 245, 247
Schön, D. 99
Schore, A. 29, 32, 38, 40, 44, 46, 63, 68, 70, 74
Seager, M. 164, 170, 171, 172
Segen's Medical Dictionary 22
Shapiro, V. 249
Sharpe, L. 18
Siegel, D. 29, 32, 38, 40, 46, 68, 71, 218

Smith, E.M. 18
Smith, T.B. 34
Solomon, M. 29, 71, 252
Stahl, S.M. 70
Stamm, B.H. 168
Steen, S. 89
Stefano, G.B. 34
Stefano, J.M. 34
Stein, M. 245
Stern, D.N. 180
Stoppard, J.M. 143
Sundelson, D. 249
Sundin, E.C. 162

Tarboush, M. 150
Target, M.T. 115, 118, 119
Taylor, H. 18
Taylor, K. 158, 164
Taylor, S.E. 32
Taylor-Gooby, P. 248
Teixeira, L. 161
Thrush, R.L. 243, 244
Timms, P. 164

UKCP 89
US Interagency Council on Homelessness 251

Van der Kolk, B. 29, 30, 32, 34, 70, 74, 136, 139, 164, 166, 234
Van Werde, D. 112
Vermetten, E. 30, 70
Vostanis, P. 162

Wallin, D.J. 115, 117
Welldon, E.V. 142
Wildfire, J. 250
Williams, C. 171
Williams, K.D. 34, 63
Williamson, E. 158
Winnicott, D.W. 38–9, 74–5, 115, 118, 244
Winston, A.P. 155
Wolford, C. 34
Wordsworth, W. 31

Yalom, I.D. 109
Yeager, K.R. 123
Young, G. 15
Young, J.E. 117, 122

Zagier-Roberts, V. 32, 33–4, 218
Zerger, S. 150
Zimmerman, B. 215